TOURISM *in* EUROPE

Rob Davidson

PITMAN PUBLISHING
128 Long Acre, London WC2E 9AN

A Division of Longman Group UK Limited

© Longman Group UK Limited

First published in Great Britain 1992

British Library Cataloguing in Publication Data
A catalogue record for this book is available
from the British Library

ISBN 0-273-03829 X

Typeset by Avocet Typesetters, Bicester, Oxon
Printed and bound in France

© TECHNIPLUS 1992
6, rue Pierre-Sarrazin – 75006 PARIS

CONTENTS

INTRODUCTION

With its enormous diversity, its rich supply of natural resources, and its wealth of cultural heritage, the continent of Europe is the world's principal destination for international tourism. Western Europe alone currently accounts for well over half of all international tourist arrivals. The majority of these international flows comprise visits made by Europeans themselves to other European countries, but an economically significant element is composed of tourists from other continents, many of whom regard Europe as a single and unified destination.

By the early 1990s, some 250 million international tourist trips were being made to, or within, Europe every year, compared to only 25 million in 1950. This phenomenal growth has been accompanied by the increasingly important impact of tourism on the economic, social and cultural aspects of life in individual European countries. Not all of tourism's effects are positive, however, and as the industry in Europe has matured from the boom years of the 1960s and 1970s, there has been a corresponding growth in awareness as to its capacity for damaging the environment and the quality of life of those living in tourist destinations.

Moreover, despite the rapid growth in tourist arrivals which it has enjoyed during the past 40 years, Europe is now facing fierce competition from a vast number of new destinations in other parts of the world. Many of these offer relatively unspoilt environments and fresh, new images, as well as obvious novelty value. Consequently, Europe's traditional markets for tourism, as well as its own inhabitants, are increasingly turning to these new long-haul destinations, to the point where Europe's actual share of total world tourist arrivals is now actually in decline. Reversing this decline will be the major challenge for Europe's tourism industry during the years ahead.

There exists a compelling case for the treatment of Europe as a coherent unit of analysis, in matters of tourism. First of all, a fast-growing proportion of tourism employment in Europe is to be found in companies operating in a continent-wide business environment. The anticipated removal of trade barriers within the European Community has resulted in the acceleration of the trend towards international-isation of ownership in every sector of this industry, from airlines and tour operators to hotels and theme parks. Increasingly, therefore, managers require a degree of familiarity with Europe-wide tourism trends and issues, not only to enable them to work more effectively with colleagues in other European countries, but also to make progress in their own careers in those countries.

The foremost justification for the study of tourism in a Europe-wide context, however, arises from the fact that many current trends and developments in tourism are common to all Western European nations. The growing communality of tourism interests of European nations and their advancing economic cooperation are leading to the extension of major tourism developments throughout the continent: the construction of high-speed rail networks, the budget hotel phenomenon, the spread of business tourism, the promotion of rural tourism, etc. Within this context, the purpose of this book is to provide those destined for careers in tourism with a solid body of background knowledge of the major tourism trends and developments operating in Europe as a whole, and how these will shape Europe's tourism industry during the second half of the 1990s.

In Britain, *Tourism in Europe* will appeal particularly to students following the BTEC National Diploma in Travel and Tourism, as well as to those following other BTEC business and finance programmes with options in travel and tourism at both National and Higher National level. Those following college diploma courses in tourism, or taking tourism options on BTEC Leisure Studies or Hotel and Catering programmes will also find it a valuable source of background information. It will also make useful background reading for students on degree-level courses in tourism, as well as for those already employed in tourism who wish to broaden their knowledge of how their industry operates throughout Europe.

For the rest of Europe, this book answers the need for a textbook in English, on the subject of Europe-wide tourism trends. English is the international langue of tourism, and this book will help its readers acquire the technical vocabulary of tourism in that language. For tourism students in other European countries, therefore, this book fulfils a double requirement.

For all readers, *Tourism in Europe* will provide a sound appreciation of the trends and issues influencing tourism throughout the continent, complementing textbooks which examine tourism in their own country only, and providing the wider context necessary for a fuller understanding of the subject.

The book is structured in such a way as to prepare the reader for the new tourism patterns which will emerge in Europe during the late 1990s. Chapter 1 reviews current tourism patterns in Europe, and Chapter 2 introduces the impact of EC legislation on the tourism industry. These are followed by three sectoral chapters dealing with innovations in transport, accommodation and tourist attractions in Europe. Next, four contrasting markets for tourism are examined: business tourism, social tourism, responsible tourism and rural tourism. The final chapter looks at Eastern Europe as a tourist market and tourist destination.

Apart from this final chapter, however, the perspective of this book is essentially that of Western Europe. Indeed, the proliferation of information on the tourism industry of the EC countries, produced by and on behalf of the European Commission, means that examples and evidence used in certain chapters derive principally from the Member States themselves. By way of balance, I have included examples and case studies from non-EC European countries, wherever possible. Each chapter provides an in-depth analysis of its theme, drawing on up-to-date reports, statistical data and media coverage from different countries. In each case, the role of the relevant pan-European organisation is examined. The main body of information in each chapter is followed by detailed case studies on the theme, drawn from a range of countries. Assignments to develop understanding are included at the end of each chapter.

Rob Davidson
January 1992

EUROPE AND TOURISM

Europe's diversity, its wealth of natural resources, history and culture have made it the world's principal tourist destination. Tourism is now a major activity throughout Europe, crucial to the economies of many countries, and by the end of the century, it will be the continent's most important industry. However, the 1990s have brought new challenges for the tourism industry, and Europe now has a declining total market share as a world tourism destination, as new products in new destinations come on to the market. Furthermore, momentous events worldwide and within Europe itself have changed, and will continue to change, the face of European tourism in the 1990s.

This chapter examines:
- The structure of Europe
- Europe's assets as a tourist destination
- Europe's incoming and domestic markets
- The economic impact of tourism in Europe

THE STRUCTURE OF EUROPE

The European Community and EFTA

These two major trading blocks dominate economic activity in Western Europe.

Events in Europe during the 1990s will be greatly influenced by the increasingly closer cooperation of the European Community countries: Belgium, Luxembourg, Denmark, France, Germany, Greece, Ireland, Italy, the Netherlands, Portugal, Spain, and the United Kingdom – the 'Europe of 12'. The economic and political destinies of these 12 countries are already firmly interlinked, and this process can only continue as internal frontiers are removed, with the advent of the single internal market (*see* Chapter 2).

The European Free Trade Association (EFTA), the EC's major external trading partner comprises Austria, Norway, Iceland, Finland, Switzerland, and Sweden. In October 1991, the EFTA countries formally joined together with the EC in creating the European Economic Area, a common market of 380 million people. This was the sudden culmination of over a decade's discussions between the two trading blocks, aimed at enlarging the European Common Market. The events which jolted the EC's timetabled progress towards unity took place on the other side of what had been the 'Iron Curtain'.

East and West

For the greater part of the period since the Second World War, the 'Iron Curtain' divided Europe into two ideologically-contrasting blocks, East and West, as shown in Fig 1.1.

The rigid distinction between the socialist, planned economies of Eastern Europe and the democratic 'free world' of capitalist Western Europe became obsolete with the fall of the Berlin Wall in 1989. As new nations with new freedoms emerge in the East and the mighty USSR evolves into the Commonwealth of Independent States during the 1990s, the impact on tourism in Europe will be tremendous. This phenomenon is examined in Chapter 10.

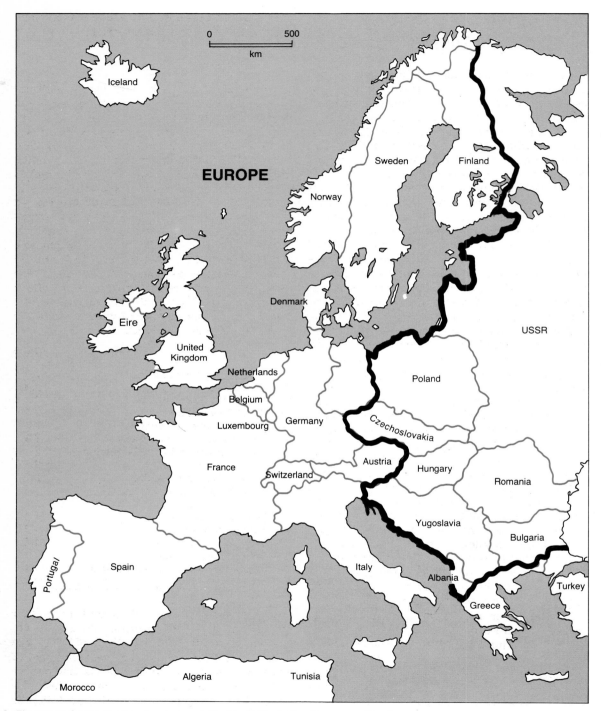

Fig 1.1 Europe's dividing line between East and West after German unification

EUROPE'S ASSETS AS A TOURIST DESTINATION

In terms of international tourism, Europe is not only the *origin* of most tourists, but also the *destination* for most international travellers. Two out of every three international tourists are Europeans – approximately 200 million every year, according to the Organisation for Economic Cooperation and Development (OECD), which represents the industrialised countries of the world. OECD figures show that in 1989, total spending on international tourism by all its members was US$165 billion, of which US$96 billion was spent by Europeans.

Similarly, despite being the second smallest of the seven continents, Europe attracts far more international tourists and more spending on international tourism than any other continent. According to the World Tourism Organisation, Europe registered about 250 million international arrivals in 1989 – some 67 per cent of the world total. In the same year, about US$100 billion was spent on international tourism in Europe – about 60 per cent of the world total.

The above figures are, of course, influenced by the political geography of Europe which tends to inflate the statistics for international tourism: the proliferation in Europe of (in world terms) relatively small countries makes international travel a more effortless and commonplace feature of life than it could be in a large country, such as the USA or Australia, for example. This 'intra-European' tourism leads to some distortion in the statistics, since, for example, a Belgian travelling a few kilometres to spend a weekend in the Netherlands is counted as an international tourist, whereas a New Yorker flying to Miami for a two-week holiday does not appear in the figures for international tourism.

On the other hand, the principal tourism market for all European countries is composed of their own inhabitants. Individual countries' domestic tourism activity earns their tourist industries much more than their individual incoming markets, through holidays, short breaks and all forms of business tourism.

The conclusion, therefore, is that Europe is as successful in attracting visitors from other continents as it is in satisfying the tourism needs of its own population. The following section of this chapter outlines the assets which make Europe the world's main tourism region.

Cultural heritage

Undoubtedly, the rich and varied cultural heritage of Europe is instrumental in attracting visitors from other parts of the world, as well as motivating Europeans themselves to travel around their own, and neighbouring, countries. Many of the continent's museums, monuments, art galleries, palaces, and cathedrals enjoy a worldwide reputation, and attract visitors in their millions every year. 'Cultural tourism' of this kind is the motivation behind the vast majority of visits to Europe from the less ancient continents of the 'New World', and also plays a major part in the growing trend towards the taking of short breaks and second holidays. The most visited monuments and museums within the European Community are shown below, together with the number of visitors (domestic and international) for 1988:

	million
The Pompidou Centre, Paris	7.9
The Louvre, Paris	4.0
The British Museum, London	3.8
The Eiffel Tower, Paris	3.6
The National Gallery, London	2.8
The Château of Versailles, Paris	2.6
Madame Tussauds and the Planetarium, London	2.6
The Science Museum, London	2.4
Charlottenburg Museum, Berlin	2.2
The Tower of London	2.2
Les Invalides, Paris	1.4
The Uffizi, Florence	1.2
The Prado, Madrid	1.2
The Tate Gallery, London	1.1
The Rembrandt Museum, Amsterdam	1.1

Source: *Le Tourisme dans la Communauté Européenne*

Festivals and special events constitute another important aspect of cultural tourism. Large annual arts festivals, such as those of Edinburgh and Aix-en-Provence attract vast numbers of international as well as domestic visitors to these cities; while commemorative anniversaries – the 1989 bicentenary of the French Revolution or the 1991 bicentenary of the death of Mozart, for example – are used as the themes of a great many cultural events, which serve in their turn to attract tourists. Similarly, the annual

Fig 1.2 The Pompidou Centre, the most visited tourist attraction in the EC, with 7.9 million visitors in 1988

designation of a European town as the 'Cultural Capital of Europe' by the EC also stimulates artistic and tourist activity in the chosen city.

One great advantage of cultural tourism to Europe is that it is much less subject to seasonal variation than many other forms of tourism. For this reason, the image of Europe as a cultural destination is likely to be emphasised even more in the future, as countries aim for a better seasonal spread for their tourism.

Historical cities

Urban tourism offers the same opportunity for extending the tourist season, as second holidays and short breaks frequently focus on the attractions of Europe's historical cities. While some of these attractions are undoubtedly cultural, the assets of Europe's cities also include: shopping facilities, from department stores to speciality boutiques and designer clothes shops; entertainment, such as London's West End theatres or Paris' *Moulin Rouge*; and

sightseeing – Rome by night and canal tours of Amsterdam, for example.

According to a recent survey prepared at the request of the European Commission, only 19 per cent of Europeans' main holidays are spent in cities, well behind those spent by the sea, or in mountain or rural areas. (However, 25 per cent of their 'second' holidays were spent in cities, demonstrating the greater importance of urban tourism for off-peak travel.) Regarding visitors from other continents, there is no doubt that Europe's historical cities with their cultural and other attractions are the single most important factor in persuading them to travel to Europe.

Conference facilities

The world's top cities for business tourism – conferences, congresses, seminars and trade fairs – are all European. Paris, London, Madrid, Geneva and Brussels alone are the venues for over 1000 international congresses each year, attracting not only the delegates but those accompanying them, from all over the world. While Europe's cities offer a wide range of modern, purpose-built conference facilities, as well as many which have been converted from historic properties such as palaces and civic buildings, their cultural, shopping and entertainment resources are also instrumental in persuading conference-planners to choose Europe.

Throughout Europe as a whole, the importance of business tourism relative to leisure tourism varies enormously from country to country, with the north of Europe clearly deriving the most benefit from this activity as a proportion of all tourism. According to the Organisation for Economic Cooperation and Development (OECD), in 1989, business tourism represented the purpose of about one quarter of all visits to Britain, and 17.5 per cent of all visits to Ireland, for example, but only 9 per cent for Greece, 7 per cent for Spain, and 2.5 per cent for Portugal.

However, Europe's position as the world' top region for business tourism is under attack as other countries, often in more exotic locations, seek to attract the high-spending, all-year-round clientele which conferences bring with them. Chapter 6 examines business tourism in Europe in more detail.

Family 'roots'

People of European descent are to be found living in most countries of the world, in many cases outnumbering the original inhabitants. Ever since the 17th century, when 500 000 people from Britain sailed to settle in New England, Virginia and Maryland, Europeans have emigrated throughout the world. The Irish and the Scots led the way to North America and were followed by Germans, Austro-Hungarians and Italians. During the 18th century, the Quebec province of Canada was settled by the French, but later the majority of the immigrants to Canada came from Britain. South America has always attracted mainly the Spanish, Portuguese and Italians, with Argentina and Brazil being their principal destinations. During the 19th and 20th centuries, emigration to Australia and New Zealand has been mostly from Britain, but also includes a significant proportion from other European countries. The Dutch and the British have long been established in South Africa.

Returning to Europe in search of their family roots or to visit friends and relations is the motivation behind a substantial proportion of visits to Europe from these other continents. European cultural traditions have often been maintained in emigrant communities overseas, together with, of course, European languages, preserving links between the Old World and the New. A visit to Europe, therefore, is for many an expression of the connection they feel with their own past.

Similarly, this century, Europe itself has been the destination for immigrants who have arrived principally from the colonies and former colonies of the latter-day imperialist powers: Britain's Commonwealth, the French colonies in North Africa, and the Dutch empire, for example. Those immigrants who have settled in Europe are themselves visited by the friends and families they left behind them, creating further incoming tourism to Europe. The purpose of the trips of one in five visitors to Britain from India, for example, is to visit friends and relatives there.

Seaside resorts

In 1988, Europe had a total of 2.2 million bedspaces in resorts by the sea, 45 per cent of the coastal accommodation capacity of the entire world – predominantly concentrated in Spain, Portugal, France, Italy and Greece. Although much less important for visitors to Europe from other continents, Europe's generous supply of beaches and seaside holiday resorts plays a vital role in generating domestic and intra-European tourism. The Mediterranean beaches, in particular, are responsible for stimulating the mass tourism movements from the north of Europe to the south, which have been a constant feature of European tourism since the boom in package travel of the 1960s.

Fifty-two per cent of the proportion of EC residents spend their main holiday by the sea, with 29 per cent going there for second or additional holidays. Nevertheless, during the 1980s, Europe's seaside resorts have faced growing challenges from other kinds of destinations, many of which have escaped the environmental problems increasingly associated with coastal areas.

Rural and mountain areas

With the rise in popularity of winter sports in the 20th century, Europe's mountainous regions, in particular the Alps, were opened up for winter tourism, both mass tourism and independent. While this kind of tourist activity continues, there are growing indications that mountains, together with lower-lying rural areas, are set for a new wave of popularity as tourist destinations.

As Europe's population becomes more and more urbanised, and seaside resorts experience even greater problems of congestion, those seeking a change of surroundings while on holiday are turning towards the relatively unspoilt spaces of Europe's countryside. There, they experience the immense variety of the natural and man-made environment, from the crofting farms of the Scottish Highlands to the hilltop villages of Greece's interior. They also have the opportunity of witnessing the traces of Europe's emerging civilisation, since the European countryside constitutes the collective memory of that civilisation's evolution, through the Roman empire, the feudal system, the spread of Christianity, chivalry, and the founding of the nation states.

Still predominantly undertaken by domestic and intra-European visitors, rural tourism is widely regarded as having enormous potential. At a time when authenticity and the quality of the environment are becoming crucial factors in the choice of destination, the patchwork of natural regions with their distinctive landscapes, cultures, architecture and customs which make up the European countryside is set to become one of the continent's most important tourism assets.

The above assets of Europe as a tourist destination lead to the existence of a great variety of different clienteles practising a wide range of tourist activities throughout the continent. However, two quite distinct major client groups emerge:

The first type comprises Europeans taking holidays in their own countries or in other European countries. These 'domestic' (in the pan-European sense in which the term will be used hereafter) tourists constitute the vast majority of tourists in Europe – between three and four times the numbers of tourists coming from outside the continent. Their motivation, as regards their main holidays, is principally the search for the sun, a search which leads many of them towards the beaches of the Mediterranean, although a growing number are choosing a rural or mountain setting. Cities are popular too, although more often as short-break or other holiday destinations.

The second clientele is composed of visitors to Europe from other parts of the world. These tourists are motivated by the opportunity of directly experiencing European culture for themselves, often because their family origins may be traced back to a European country. They favour the major cities, and show a tendency towards touring around several countries in the course of a single visit to Europe. Although far fewer in number than those tourists drawn from the indigenous populations of Europe, their spending per head is higher.

The two categories are not rigidly fixed or exclusive, and there are exceptions in each case: American and Australian accents can be heard on the beaches of the Greek islands, for example; and coach holidays based on a tour of northern European capital cities are almost as popular with Spanish tourists as they are with the Japanese. However, the two clienteles are sufficiently differentiated to justify the examination of two separate markets for tourism in Europe – a '**domestic**' market, meaning that composed of those Europeans taking holidays within their own countries *and* other countries

within Europe; and an **incoming** market, composed of visitors to Europe from other continents.

EUROPE'S DOMESTIC TOURIST MARKET

The vast majority of tourism activity within Europe is undertaken by Europeans themselves, either in their own countries or in others within the continent.

A valuable snapshot of the holidaymaking habits of the majority of Europeans was provided in 1987 with the publication of a Community report entitled *Europeans and their Holidays*. This report, based on a survey carried out on a representative sample of the adult population of the 12 EC countries, provides a Community-wide overview of holidaymaking patterns and permits some interesting comparisons between Member States.

The report showed that, of the 250 million adult Europeans, some *140 million* took at least one holiday away from home lasting four days or longer, making an average of 56 per cent for the 12 EC countries. Of this 56 per cent, one in three went away on holiday more than once a year. The proportion of the population who go away on holiday varied considerably from country to country: from 65 per cent in the Netherlands to only 31 per cent in Portugal. Some of the reasons for the low rate of holiday-taking of some countries are examined in Chapter 7 on Social Tourism.

The survey provides a profile of the type of holidays taken by Europeans. It divides holidays into 'main' holidays and 'other' holiday (trips made by those who went away more than once). The responses to some of the questions are shown in Fig 1.3.

From these data, a general pattern emerges, showing strong similarities between the two types of holiday: they were taken by family groups (three or more people together in the most common case); they were taken in the respondents' own country (in two-thirds of cases); and the car was used to reach the destination (in two-thirds of cases).

The responses to further questions in the survey, however, reveal some interesting differences between the Member States. For example, although on the whole about one-third of all Europeans spend their main holidays

Fig 1.3 The general pattern of European holidaymaking

| | All 12 countries | |
	Main holiday %	Other holiday %
How many days away from home?		
four to nine days	24	62
ten to nineteen days	42	27
twenty to twenty-nine days	19	4
thirty days or more	14	3
not stated	1	4
	100	100
How many people were with you on this holiday (including children)?		
one person only	11	16
two	33	32
three	16	13
four	21	18
five or more	18	18
not stated	1	3
	100	100
Where did you go?		
in your country	67	72
in another country in the EC	20	13
somewhere else in Europe	10	9
outside Europe	3	3
not stated	—	3
	100	100
What method of transport did you use?		
car	68	67
train	14	14
plane	23	8
boat	5	4
bicycle/motorbike	1	1
other (e.g. coach)	10	11
	*	*

(*Multiple answers bring the total to more than 100)

Source: *Europeans and their Holidays*

abroad, the proportion varies considerably from one country to another. The proportion going abroad for their main holiday ranges from 94 per cent, 64 per cent and 60 per cent for the people of Luxembourg, the Netherlands and Belgium respectively, to only 7 per cent, 8 per cent and 8 per cent for the Greeks, Spanish and Portuguese.

Northern Europeans clearly emerge from this survey as the continent's main market for international travel. This characteristic is confirmed by **Eurostat**, the EC's official statistics organisation. The table in Fig 1.4 gives, for each EC country, the four most important generating markets. It is immediately clear that the source markets of the individual Member States are not the same in every case. Nevertheless, the dominant position of the British and German markets is obvious. Germany is the primary consumer of tourist services in four receiving States and second in another four. The United Kingdom is also the main market for four Member States and second for two others.

The final column of the table shows how the incoming tourist flows for each individual country are dominated by only a few markets: in all countries for which data is available except Germany, the four main markets shown account for over half the total guest-nights, and in some cases, over three-quarters. This concentration in relatively few markets leaves individual countries extremely vulnerable to sudden changes in tastes or fashions in their main market countries: as was seen during the late 1980s, for example, with the British disaffection with Spain as a destination.

The general picture which emerges of Europeans' foreign travel, therefore, is one showing a distinct north-south flow, for main holidays in particular. On average, the northern European countries are those whose populations are most likely to travel abroad for their main holiday, and their destinations are most likely to be in the south of Europe. OECD figures confirm this, showing that, in 1989, for international tourism in Europe, the German market predominated, with 25 per cent of all nights in accommodation. They were followed by the UK, with 13 per cent of all nights in accommodation. According to the survey *Europeans and their Holidays*, France, Italy and Spain are the three countries most visited by Europeans. In general, those living in southern Europe are more likely to holiday in their own countries for two reasons: they have a warm and sunny climate in summer; and they have on average less spending power for holidays than the populations of northern European countries, although this may be changing, as discussed later in this chapter.

For 'other' holidays, the proportion of those going abroad is much lower: about half of the

Fig 1.4 Main generating countries of EC Member States, 1989 (% of total foreign guest-nights)

Country	First market	%	Second market	%	Third market	%	Fourth market	%	Share of 1–4 markets (%)
Belgium	Netherlands	43	Germany	15	UK	10	France	8	76
Denmark	Germany	36	Sweden	21	Norway	11	Netherlands	7	75
Germany	Netherlands	18	USA	13	UK	9	France	5	45
Greece	Germany	24	UK	20	Italy	8	Netherlands	6	58
Spain	UK	32	Germany	28	France	9	Italy	6	75
France	UK	17	Germany	15	Italy	14	USA	10	56
Ireland	UK	61	USA	14	Germany	6	France	5	86
Italy	Germany	42	France	8	UK	7	Switzerland	6	63
Luxembourg	n/a		n/a		n/a		n/a		n/a
Netherlands	Germany	49	UK	11	Belg & Lux	7	Scandinavia	5	72
Portugal	UK	31	Germany	16	Spain	10	Netherlands	10	67
UK	n/a		n/a		n/a		n/a		n/a

Source: Eurostat, *Tourism in Europe, Trends 1989*

'other' holidays taken by the Dutch, Germans and Danish, and even less in all other cases. Europeans, therefore, are much more likely to take their second or additional holidays in their own countries.

The numbers travelling to their holiday destinations by air are still small overall, but the details of the survey reveal that this form of transport is used most extensively by the island nations – the British and, above all, the Irish. Destination location is the other main factor influencing the mode of transport used, and air travel predominates for destinations outside Europe.

An additional feature of Europeans' holidaymaking habits indicated by the survey is the high degree of independently arranged holidays taken, with only a minimum of Europeans having recourse to package tours, although this too changes according to the destination, as shown in the table below.

For every 100 holidaymakers whose main holiday was . . .	A package tour or organised trip was taken by: (%)
. . . in their own country	3
. . . in another Community country	32
. . . elsewhere in Europe	30
. . . outside Europe	40
Average for main holidays	13
Average for other holidays	9

Finally, the survey, *Europeans and their Holidays*, highlights the features considered most attractive in Europeans' holiday destinations, by asking the question, 'Looking at this list, what are the things which in your own opinion are the most attractive points when choosing somewhere to go on holiday?' The list shown, together with the responses given, were as follows:

Mentions (in declining order of frequency	all 12 EC countries
Seeing marvels of nature (waterfalls, mountains, caves, etc)	56%
Unspoilt countryside	37%
Cost of living not too high	34%
Monuments, museums, galleries	28%
Feeling of being in a really foreign country	26%
Comfortable hotels	26%
Entertainments (cinema, dancing, amusement parks, etc)	23%
Opportunity to take part in sports	14%
No reply	2%

The importance of the environment, in choosing a destination, emerges clearly from the above table. This theme is elaborated upon in Chapters 8 and 9.

The snapshot picture of the holidaymaking preferences of Europeans provided by this survey, does not, however, reveal some of the important changes currently taking place in that field of activity. Some of these trends are related to changing holiday preferences; others are the result of social and demographic changes affecting the people of Europe themselves. The principal trends which are having, and are likely to continue to have, an impact on European domestic tourism are listed below.

A slowdown in the Mediterranean area

Figure 1.5 provides evidence of a growing trend affecting the traditional summer holiday area for Europeans.

Comparing nights spent by tourists in accommodation establishments in 1989 with 1988, it reveals a general decrease of nights spent by non-residents in the Mediterranean destinations of Spain, Portugal, Greece and Italy. At the same time, northern European countries have seen notable rises in their levels of tourist activity. These two trends are related, and they both contribute to the beginnings of a modification to the traditional north-south movement of holidaymakers within Europe.

On the one hand, the north-south movement has been weakened by changing attitudes of the British and Germans in particular towards the traditional Mediterranean destinations, as concern mounts over the general quality of the product on offer, and more specifically over environmental considerations. On the other hand, the south-north stream, which until recently was negligible in Europe, is being

strengthened by the ever-increasing number of people from the southern European countries now taking holidays. The Spanish and the Portuguese, for example, are using the recent rises in their standards of living to travel more widely, both within their own countries and abroad. Nevertheless, on the whole, this trend is a source of growing concern to Mediterranean countries, where the increases in nights spent by resident tourists come nowhere near to making up for the fall in the number of nights spent by non-residents.

Competition from destinations outside Europe

The percentage of holidays taken by citizens of EC countries to non-Community destinations is growing at a regular pace, as a result of the rapid development of international competition directly affecting Europe. There is an ever-widening range of new tourism products on the market, in particular outside Europe, and Europeans are proving to be a ready market for these.

The search, by Europeans themselves, for new types of holiday experience is adding to the current worldwide growth in travel to long-haul destinations. Today's 'in vogue' long-haul destinations for Europeans include Florida, Thailand and the Caribbean. In Europe itself, environmental problems, better value long-haul

Fig 1.5
(*Source: Eurostat*, Tourism in Europe, Trends 1989)

Nights spent by tourists in accommodation establishments in 1989 % variation in comparison with the previous year			
Country	Resident tourists	Non-resident tourists	Total tourists
Belgium [1]	4.4	7.8	5.7
Denmark	6.7	13.8	9.5
Germany	3.1	11.3	4.2
Greece	4.8	-1.2	0.2
Spain [2]	8.4	-11.4	-4.3
France [2]	-0.6	20.2	6.3
Ireland	n.a.	19.2	n.a.
Italy	-0.8	-6.3	-2.8
Luxembourg	-0.4	12.7	11.2
Netherlands [3]	6.8	11.7	8.1
Portugal	0.6	-1.2	-0.4
United Kingdom	n.a.	7.8	n.a.
EC	2.1 [4]	3.2	1.2 [4]

air fares, overcrowding in traditional destinations and the general increases in standards of living are all factors in favour of the long-haul destinations which are Europe's competitors (not only for European tourists, but also for Europe's traditional incoming markets, such as the USA, Japan, Australia, etc).

Tourism consultants, *Tourism Planning and Research Associates* have estimated that by the year 2000, the long-haul market could be attracting 20 per cent of Europeans' holiday trips, compared with 14 per cent in 1989. Concern over this trend is shared not only by the holiday industry in Europe, but also by those operating in the field of business tourism, since long-haul destinations for conferences and congresses are also increasingly challenging Europe's hitherto strong hold on this market.

Growth of senior citizens' holidays

The report, *A Social Portrait of Europe*, compiled by Eurostat, shows that longer life, improving living standards and a spectacular dive in the birth rate are the trends which are turning Europe into a wealthier, but ageing, community. The report's projection is that if the present low birth rate continues, the population of the 12 existing Member States will be cut by four million by the year 2020 – equivalent to wiping out the entire populations of Ireland and Luxembourg. Only the Irish are producing enough babies to ensure that their current populations level remains stable. The trend towards smaller families began in northern European countries, but was followed during the 1980s by an even steeper plunge in the south. The projected average number of children per woman is currently 1.3 in Spain and 1.29 in Italy.

The European population profile, therefore, grows older with every passing year. There are already regions of Germany and northern Italy where less than a quarter of the population is aged under 20. In 30 years, that pattern could be repeated over most of Europe, with more than one in four Europeans aged 60 or over and fewer than one in five aged 20 or less. Taking into account the expected longer life expectancy over the next 30 years, the consequence will be a Europe whose population is not only smaller, but older as well.

These demographic changes will inevitably lead to greater numbers of elderly, retired citizens placing their own special demands on the tourism market. However, this group has already been identified by the travel industry as one with great potential. Depicted in marketing terminology as the 'Grey Wave' or GLAMs (Greying, Leisured, Affluent Middle-classes), this group is extremely attractive to the tourism industry. It is composed of people who are often financially comfortable and who have far greater opportunities for travel than those in employment or those with dependents. Since they are not restricted to school holiday periods, they often use the opportunity to travel off-peak. There is already a substantial flow of retired persons from the north European countries to the warmer climates of southern Europe during the winter months, and this market is set to grow rapidly. Increased ownership of second homes, apartments and timeshare properties is already a symptom of this trend, which is fully expected to continue.

The developing tourism market in southern Europe

Living standards have improved significantly during the past 20 years, but major disparities still exist between the 12 EC Member States. In terms of Gross Domestic Product per head of population of each country, the economic well-being of the British, Danes, French and Germans is roughly twice that of their Community partners in Greece, Ireland, Spain and Portugal. The Luxembourgers are even better off.

Nevertheless, between 1985 and 1988, it was the Spanish and the Portuguese who enjoyed the greatest growth in GDP per head, narrowing the gap between rich and poor states within the EC. As the economic development of the Mediterranean members of the EC catches up with that of the more wealthy members, increasing opportunities for travel will be one of the results. In the south, interest in visiting other countries in Europe runs high. For example, in the survey, *Europeans and their Holidays*, 46 per cent of Italians and 39 per cent of Portuguese mentioned Britain as among the three European countries they would most like to visit; while 30 per cent of Greeks and 32 per cent of Portuguese interviewed put Germany among their top three.

Therefore, as southern European countries gradually achieve the spending power which will bring international travel within their means, a new market will open up to the tourism industry. In the case of Spain, in particular, the impact could be considerable, as a recent survey has shown that that country has a tradition of spending freely on holiday, as shown in Fig 1.6.

Moves towards extending the tourism season

The season distribution of guest nights in EC Member States is shown in the graphs in Fig 1.7, which are derived from the DWIF study 'Analysis of actions taken or to be taken in

Fig 1.6 (*Source:* The European, *21–23 June 1991*)

WHAT EUROPEANS SPEND ON HOLIDAYS

Figures are per capita European holiday travel expenditure per year

$250 — PORTUGAL
$581 — FRANCE
$602 — ITALY
$758 — NETHERLANDS
$773 — UK
$942 — W. GERMANY *
$1,003 — SWEDEN
$1,133 — SPAIN

* pre-unification figures

Source: Visa International   Graphic by Anna Baker

Spanish spend most on a break

THE Spanish spend more money on holidays than any other Europeans, yet they are the least adventurous, preferring to holiday at home.

West Germans, on the other hand, spend 75 per cent of their holiday money travelling abroad.

These are the findings of a new report, *Holiday Travel Expenditure In Europe*, commissioned by Visa International. The research was carried out in eight European countries: Britain, France, the former West Germany, Spain, Italy, Sweden, the Netherlands and Portugal. Nearly 10,000 face-to-face interviews were conducted last year.

Portugal comes at the bottom of the league, spending only $250 per capita annually on holidays – less than half its nearest rival, France, at $582. The Spanish lead the field with $1,133 per capita, followed by the Swedes ($1,003) and the West Germans ($942). West Germany, however, has the largest holiday bill – $42.8

By Henry Sutton
LONDON

billion – spending 20 times as much as Portugal, the lowest overall spender at just $1.8 billion.

Domestic expenditure is by far the largest category, accounting for 41 per cent or $62.9 billion of the total European spend of $153 billion. Destinations in southern Europe, which hold second place, attract nearly a quarter of all holiday money, or $36.6 billion, while only $7.7 billion was spent on holidays in North America and just $1.6 billion was paid for cruises.

Southern Europeans feel more inclined to stay in their home region, while northern Europeans spend the largest proportion of their holiday

budget on trips to the south. Of the total $153 billion spent on holidays, 72 per cent or $111 billion was spent on independent holidays, the rest on package arrangements.

Southern Europeans are more inclined to make their own holiday arrangements than northerners. The Portuguese might spend the least on having a holiday, but they are the most independent, with nine out of ten making their own arrangements. The British, on the other hand, are the least inclined to make their own arrangements, buying more than a third of their holidays on a package basis.

A higher proportion of Swedes goes on holiday than any other nation, on average 68 per cent of the population. In Portugal, only 40 per cent take a break.

Europe and other regions for lengthening the tourist season and creating alternative destinations to mass tourism'.

The seasonal curves of the individual countries illustrate the problem of seasonality in all Member States, with a very high concentration of guest nights in the months of July and August. For Europeans themselves, two out of every three main holidays start in either July or August. About a tenth go away in June, and a slightly smaller proportion in September. This overconcentration of tourism in the high season, and the corresponding under-utilisation of capital and human resources in the low season

represents one of the greatest problems facing tourism in Europe. The resultant high degree of congestion of transport and accommodation services, and deterioration of the natural and man-made environment pose a major threat to tourism's continuing success in Europe.

Consequently, almost all countries' tourism promotion organisations are engaged in efforts to spread the load of tourism more evenly throughout the year. As well as targeting markets such as the 'Grey Wave' and young couples with no children, who are more flexible as to the dates of their holidays, efforts are being made to develop new 'alternative' forms of

Fig 1.7 (*Source: Eurostat*, Tourism in Europe, Trends 1989)

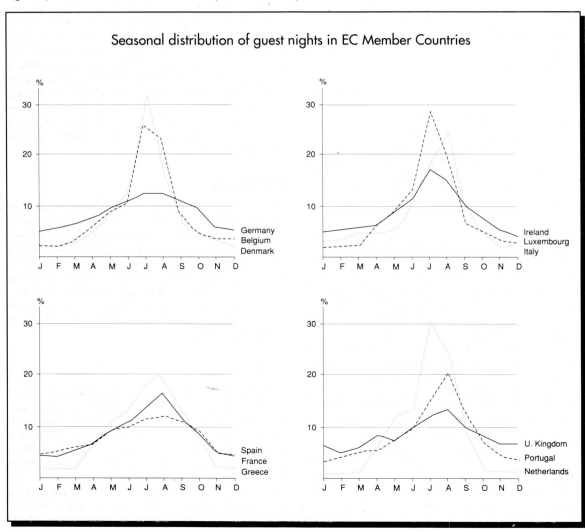

tourism which are not dependent on the summer mass-tourism market.

THE INCOMING MARKET

Although far fewer in number than domestic tourists, visitors to Europe from other continents make an important financial contribution to European tourism businesses. Total expenditure in Europe, exclusive of air fares, by visitors from outside Europe in 1990 was estimated at US$17.04 billion compared with U$15.72 billion in the previous year. Increases were recorded in both numbers of visitors and expenditure in all of Europe's main markets in other continents, as shown in Fig 1.8. Europe's main markets originating in other parts of the world – USA, Canada and Japan – show clear distinguishing characteristics.

The USA

In 1950, the number of US citizens departing for Europe by air and sea stood at 286 000. Forty years later, over seven million Americans made the journey. The increase in American visitors to Europe in 1989 capped a decade of 70 per cent overall growth from 4 047 000 visits in 1979. In 1990, Europe increased its share of the total US overseas travel market to 47 per cent, far ahead of its nearest competitor, the Caribbean region, at 24 per cent.

A significant aspect of the 1989 results was that US traffic increased at a faster rate during the off-peak months of January/April and October/December (up 8.9 per cent) than during the peak months of May/September (up 5.1 per cent). Off-peak travel from the USA now accounts for some 45 per cent of the total annual traffic from that country.

In any year, US travel to Europe is influenced by the state of the dollar, and in 1990, the US dollar reversed its downward trend and began a surge which continued well into the new year. However, a more long-term positive trend is the continuing vigorous competition among trans-Atlantic carriers which is having the effect of keeping basic advance-purchase fares down, and, therefore, increasing the variety of good-value travel packages available to Americans.

Nevertheless, Europe can never take the all-important American market for granted. Every tourist region in the world wants high-spending American visitors, and indeed the tourist economies of certain countries, including many in Europe have come to depend to a great degree on the American tourist dollar. This was well illustrated in 1986 when the Chernobyl incident, the bombing of Libya and a weak dollar caused a severe drop in the number of American visitors to Europe, sending shock waves throughout the tourism industry. The war in the Gulf led to a drop in US tourism traffic to Europe of 23, 42 and 39 per cent respectively for the months of January, February and March 1990. However, the euphoria produced by the sudden end to the fighting led to a rapid rise in transatlantic bookings.

Europe's 47 per cent share of the US foreign holiday market, is supported by a mere six per cent of the global tourism and travel advertising sponsored in the USA by both public and private sectors. While in the past, it was possible for Europe to maintain this high share with such a small proportion of the advertising impact, this is now practically impossible given the strong competition from other developed areas. More effort and more resources will be needed in future to maintain Europe's share of the American market.

Canada

1990 was a record year for Canadian traffic to Europe, with 1.513 million visitors. While there has been a steady growth in travel from Canada to Europe over the four-year period from 1987, the changing travel patterns of Canadians indicate that Europe is facing strong competition from the US and South East Asia. In addition, a new 7 per cent Goods and Service Tax has been introduced in Canada, reducing the level of disposable income.

Japan

After the 1974 relaxation by Japan of restrictions on overseas travel by its nationals, and the advent of longer holidays for the Japanese, tourism traffic out of that country grew substantially. Europe's share of the Japanese market has since grown and now stands at about 11 per cent (the majority of the Japanese still favour the USA, Korea, Taiwan and Hong Kong as destinations). In 1987, as a measure to lessen Japan's great trade surplus with the rest of the

Travel to Europe by US citizens 1984-1990.
Thousands.
Tourisme américain vers l'Europe 1984-1990.
Milliers.

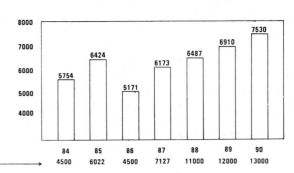

Expenditure in Europe Estimated (US $ Millions).
Dépenses en Europe. Estimation (Million de $
américains).

	84	85	86	87	88	89	90
	4500	6022	4500	7127	11000	12000	13000

Canadian residents returning from Europe
(including Eastern Europe) 1984-1990.
Thousands.
Touristes canadiens revenant d'Europe
(y compris Europe de l'Est) 1994-1990.
Milliers.

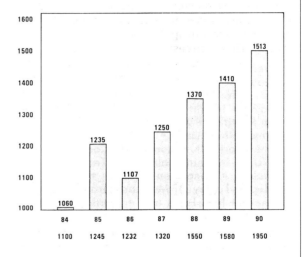

Expenditure in Europe. Estimated (Canadian $
millions).
Dépenses en Europe. Estimation (millions de $
Canadiens).

	84	85	86	87	88	89	90
	1100	1245	1232	1320	1550	1580	1950

Travel to Europe by Japanese citizens
1984-1990. (Thousands).
Tourisme japonais vers l'Europe 1984-1990.
(Milliers).

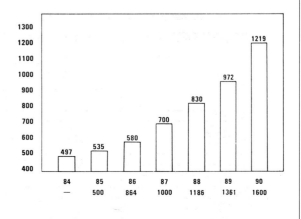

Expenditure in Europe. Estimated (US
$ Millions).
Dépenses en Europe. Estimation (millions de $
américains).

	84	85	86	87	88	89	90
	—	500	864	1000	1186	1361	1600

Fig 1.8 Travel and expenditure by US, Canadian and Japanese visitors to Europe

world, the Japanese government announced a major promotion aimed at doubling overseas travel by Japanese citizens to ten million within five years. By 1990, that figure had already been reached.

Japan's economic growth of almost five per cent in 1989 partly accounted for the 17.1 per cent increase in Japanese visits to Europe in that year. The proposed introduction of the single internal market in the Community after 1992 has helped Europe achieve a higher profile in business-minded Japan. The result was that for the first time in many years, Europe in 1989 enjoyed a larger increase in volume of Japanese visits than such regions as Oceania, North America as well as East and Southeast Asia.

Another reason contributing to this growth is the growing number of Japanese nationals taking up residence in Europe, as Japanese companies expand their investments throughout the continent and send their own managers and their families to look after the businesses. Britain hosts the greatest number of Japanese residents – some 40 000 – with Germany coming close behind. This has led to significant increases in Japanese coming to Europe to visit friends and relatives, as well as increased business travel.

THE ECONOMIC IMPACT OF TOURISM ON EUROPE

Tourism is an economic sector of major importance in Europe, and its contribution to the continent's economic welfare looks set to continue to increase in future decades. It offers opportunities for job creation and for developing the less prosperous regions of Europe. Within the EC alone, tourism accounts for more than five per cent of Gross National Product and almost five per cent of foreign trade. It employs close to eight million people, i.e., six per cent of the total number of jobs in the Community, and this figure is growing.

However, these global figures conceal some important differences between individual Member States, regarding the extent to which tourism has an impact on their own economies. Figure 1.9 shows a breakdown of tourism in each of the economies of the Member States.

This table gives three main indicators as to the position of tourism in the national economies. The first is GNP. In two countries, Spain and France, the share of tourism in their GNPs is almost twice as high as the EC average of five per cent. The second indicator is tourism employment: although most tourism jobs in absolute terms are found in the richer EC countries (due to their domestic tourism markets), the *relative* importance of tourism importance is greater in other countries, such as Greece, Portugal and Spain. The third indicator is the share of travel receipts and expenditure in exports and imports for the individual countries. Here, the vital importance of tourism to Greece, Spain and Portugal is again emphasised, with tourism receipts accounting for a relatively high proportion of their total export earnings. Similarly, the high-spending northern countries' expenditure on foreign

Fig 1.9 (*Source: Eurostat*, Tourism in Europe, Trends 1989)

Tourism in the economies of the Member States						
Country	% Share of travel receipts in exports of goods and services		% Share of travel expenditure in imports of goods and services		% GNP	% employment
	1988	1989	1988	1989	1988	1988
Belgium	3.1	2.3	4.2	3.1	3.0	3.9
Denmark	6.6	6.0	9.2	8.3	4.5	5.3
Germany	3.0	2.9	8.5	7.9	4.6	5.2
Greece	19.6	16.3	4.3	4.3	7.3	7.2
Spain	24.6	22.7	3.3	3.5	9.4	9.3
France	5.2	5.5	3.5	3.5	9.0	6.9
Ireland	6.2	6.3	6.8	7.3	6.2	6.3
Italy	8.1	7.2	3.8	3.9	4.5	6.4
Luxembourg	n.a.	n.a.	n.a.	n.a.	n.a.	5.2
Netherlands	2.9	3.1	7.4	7.2	1.3	2.3
Portugal	17.0	17.3	2.8	2.9	6.0	8.6
United Kingdom	6.0	6.0	n.a.	n.a.	4.0	6.0

travel is shown as a major element in their total imports.

Tourism's overall impact also varies between different parts of the Community, with some individual countries making a healthy profit and others a net loss from this activity: Spain, France, Greece, Italy and Portugal derive a large net surplus from their tourist trades; in Ireland, earnings slightly exceed expenditure; while in the BLEU (Belgium and Luxembourg), Denmark, Germany, the Netherlands and the United Kingdom, the balance of trade in tourism is substantially in the red. The balance of trade for tourism in each Member State is shown in Fig 1.10.

The country with the most positive tourism balance is undoubtedly Spain, with a surplus of ECU 5.6 billion. On the other hand, the country with the biggest deficit is Germany with a negative balance sheet of ECU 14.5 billion; the United Kingdom comes second (ECU −3.7 billion) before the Netherlands (ECU −3.1 billion).

TOURISM IN TURBULENT TIMES

With such great sources of national income at stake, any factor which has an inhibiting effect on travel and tourism can have a devastating impact on a country's economic situation. In recent years, international events have led to severe disruptions in the traditional patterns of tourism within Europe.

The Gulf war sent waves of instability throughout the world, leading to extensive cancellations for both business and leisure travel as the crisis deepened. For Europe's incoming market, the impact of the war may have had consequences lasting well beyond its ending in February 1991, according to the article shown in Fig 1.11.

The impact of the Gulf war on Europe's domestic tourism market was less dramatic, partly because late bookings made in March and April 1991 made up for a dearth of bookings at the beginning of the year. Nevertheless, the traditional pattern of Europeans' holidaytaking in the Mediterranean was disrupted, as tourists tended to avoid Turkey and resorts in North Africa, which continued to be perceived as trouble spots.

Civil strife in Yugoslavia in the spring and summer of 1991 provided another example of instability bringing disastrous results to a country's tourism industry. The motorists from Austria and Italy, on whom Yugoslavia relies heavily for its tourist trade were unable to enter

Fig 1.10 (*Source: Eurostat*, Tourism in Europe, Trends 1989)

Tourism balance sheet in the balance of payments (Ecu billion)			
Country	**1988**	**1989**	**Variation %** [1)] **1989/88**
BLEU [2)]	-0.9	-0.9	-2.5
Denmark	-0.5	-0.6	1.4
Germany [3)]	-14.6	-14.5	0.0
Greece	1.4	1.1	-20.5
Spain	12.2	12.0	-6.9
France	3.5	5.6	62.0
Ireland	0.3	0.4	38.6
Italy	5.4	4.7	-14.3
Netherlands	-3.3	-3.1	-4.7
Portugal [4)]	1.5	1.6	16.9
United Kingdom	-3.0	-3.7	24.3
EC [5)]	2.0	2.5	23.6

UP TO three million American and Japanese holidaymakers have turned their backs on Europe this year, plunging the tourist industry, which employs ten million people, into its worst crisis.

In cash terms alone it is costing more than $40 billion in empty hotel rooms, deserted restaurants and half-filled aircraft. More than 250,000 jobs in tourism have already been lost this year and many more are at risk, with some tour operators being forced to lay off up to 30 per cent of their employees.

The European Tour Operators Association predicts that the number of visitors from outside Europe will be down at least 35 per cent this year – worse than during the Libyan crisis of 1986. It blames the Gulf war, which was still raging during the main holiday booking period.

Peter Lloyd-Jones, the association's director, said: "The situation for the first six months of this year has been abysmal." British MEP Edward McMillan-Scott, vice chairman of the parliament's tourism committee has sent a letter to all EC tourism ministers demanding immediate action to safeguard jobs. He wants an agency set up to promote resorts and an increase in the current EC grant of $4.5 million to bolster the flagging industry.

An estimated eight million non-Europeans, most of them Americans, Canadians, Japanese and Australians, visited Europe in 1990, spending $104 billion.

Many in the industry expected business to recover after the Gulf war, but by the time the crisis was over, large numbers of potential visitors had opted instead to book their holidays in Hawaii, Mexico and Australia – destinations seen as safer, and where the dollar goes further. In Paris, among the destinations hardest hit during the war itself,

Naomi Marks and Alexandra Frean

non-European tourists are still a rare sight. Georges Terrey, manager of the Folies Bergere, said that audiences were down on last year despite the club's best efforts to fill its 1,700 seats.

He said: "If we had not saved money by closing for four weeks during the Gulf war, we might have had to lay off some of our dancers and musicians by now."

The Eiffel Tower, France's most popular tourist attraction, has reported an 11 per cent fall in the number of visitors taking the Ffr49 ($8) ride to the 276-metre high observation platform. Even a large increase in

Travel agents are writing off 1991 as 'a lost year'

visitors from eastern Europe has done little to help. Their spending power is paltry compared to the Americans and Japanese whose absence has hit the luxury end of the market. In Rome, 90 of the 377 five-star rooms at the Cavalieri Hilton were empty in June, compared with a 90 per cent occupancy rate last year. Cesar Putzo, deputy general manager, is now prepared to "negotiate" room prices.

Bookings at the 500-room five-star Hotel Palace in Madrid have suffered a "sizeable drop" and the city's famous Boatin restaurant has a dearth of Japanese and US customers.

American Express Travel Services in Athens has written off 1991 as "a lost year", estimating a 30 per cent drop in Americans arriving in Greece.

The London Tourist Board said that it expected 1.5 million fewer tourists than the ten million it welcomed last year. The number of hotels going into receivership in the UK is at its highest level since the oil crisis of 1973, says the business agency Christie.

Fig 1.11 (*Source:* The European, *19 July 1991*)

the country, as Serbian and Croatian factions blockaded roads, while mined railway tracks meant that the normal train service from Vienna to Split was cancelled. With the country's scenic Plitvice National Park turned into a base for army tanks, official figures from the Easter holiday period showed that visitors to the Istrian peninsula were down by 70 per cent on the previous year.

Natural and man-made disasters are another source of disruption to tourism movements around the world, as was seen in 1986 in the

wake of the Chernobyl accident. The frequent headlines concerning the pollution problems no doubt persuaded Europeans to change from certain destinations to others; while, more dramatically, events such as the oil slick scare along the Italian and French rivieras in 1991 threatened the tourism businesses of those regions.

Finally, events in Eastern Europe have already had a major impact on tourism in Europe, and are likely to continue to do so throughout this decade, but this is discussed further in Chapter 10.

CASE STUDY
THE EUROPEAN TRAVEL COMMISSION

Selling Europe overseas

Within Europe, the national organisations responsible for promoting tourism to and within their own countries are in strict competition with each other for tourists. London's city centre abounds with offices owned by other countries' National Tourism Organisations, such as Maison de la France, the Swiss National Tourist Office, the Greek National Tourist Organisation, etc, whose aim is to persuade British people to take holidays in France, Switzerland, Greece, and so on. This situation is repeated in capital cities throughout Europe.

However, since 1948, Europe's national tourist organisations have collaborated with each other to promote Europe as a single destination to markets outside the continent. This action is carried out under the auspices of the European Travel Commission (ETC).

Aims

In 1988, the ETC celebrated its 40th anniversary, marking four decades of working to promote the whole of Europe as a single tourist destination to the rest of the world. The ETC is a voluntary organisation, financed by, and bringing together under one umbrella the 23 national tourist organisations of the following countries: Austria, Belgium, Cyprus, Denmark, Finland, France, Germany, Greece, Iceland, Ireland, Italy, Luxembourg, Malta, Monaco, Netherlands,

Norway, Portugal, Spain, Sweden, Switzerland, Turkey, United Kingdom, Yugoslavia.

Its aims are:

● to increase the level of tourism from other parts of the world to Europe, as a result of its marketing activities, and

● to provide a forum for individual members to exchange ideas and experiences for the benefit of each member of the group.

In this way, the ETC acts as a cooperative marketing and servicing organisation for its own members and for the tourism industry in Europe as a whole. It undertakes a range of activities which can be more effectively carried out collectively by one organisation rather than individually by all the different national ones. This is clearly stated in the ETC's Strategic Market Plan:

'The European Travel Commission's marketing role is a unique one. Only the ETC can provide marketing support for Europe. It can undertake market research or launch "generic" promotional programmes on behalf of Europe. These programmes can be of invaluable support to the National Tourist Offices in their task of marketing individual countries.

The ETC has also proved that as a catalyst it can influence the marketing efforts of the industry and harness considerable funds for the promotion of Europe.'

Organisation

The ETC's organisational structure is shown in Fig 1.12.

Most of the ETC's marketing activities are carried out by its five **Market Operations Groups**, covering, and based in, the USA, Canada, Japan/Asia, Australia/New Zealand, and Latin America. These groups are composed of representatives of the ETC members which maintain tourist offices in these regions. In each case, the activities are designed to promote Europe as a whole. Each group elects its own chairman and drafts an annual marketing programme. An example of the work of one Market Operations Group, based in Canada, is given in Fig 1.13.

In general, each group works in its own region of the world to put over the same message – 'Visit Europe'. This is communicated by using

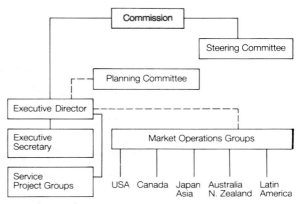

Fig 1.12 The organisational structure of the ETC

every conceivable form of promotion: advertising, public relations, print production, editorial publicity, travel shows, radio and television. An example of a typical ETC advertisement from the American press is shown in Fig 1.14.

As well as advertising directly to the public, ETC Market Operations Groups also work with the travel trade, by attending seminars for travel agents and tour operators, sponsoring workshops, and publishing tour manuals to familiarise travel agents with Europe, so that they can 'sell' it more easily to their clients.

Fig 1.13 (*Source: The European Travel Commission*)

CANADA

The attraction of a separate promotional campaign in Canada was considered in 1976. A major research of the market was carried out in conjunction with the two largest airline operators and a joint promotional activity was launched in 1978. All members are interested in Canada but a large proportion of members controlled their Canada activity from New York. Finally in 1987 it was agreed that an "autonomous" market operations group for Canada should be established as from January 1988. Since 1978 promotional activity covered consumer and trade advertising, public relations, briefing of the travel trade and, since 1984, self-financed supermarts. In 1987, advertising in the main English and French language dailies was the main item in the budget. In 1988, however, a substantially increased budget allowed also for printing a well advertised Canadian "agent guide to Europe" (at a cost of $68.000 with $43.000 contributed by the industry) and a "Travel Europe" bilingual newsletter expected to become a quarterly issue. In 1980 traffic from Canada to Europe was 787.000. By 1987 it was 1.248.000, spending Can$1,32 billion.

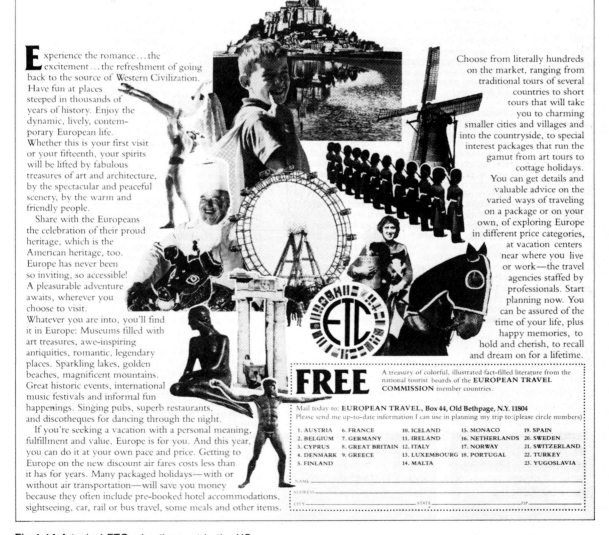

Fig 1.14 A typical ETC advertisement in the US press
(*Source: The European Travel Commission*)

Since most of the ETC's operations are undertaken by the members themselves through the Market Operations Groups, its actual permanent staff is limited to the two or three people who make up the **Executive Unit**. This office is based in Paris, where the necessary facilities (office space and equipment, secretarial assistance, etc) are provided by France's *Direction de l'Industrie Touristique*. The Executive Unit is responsible for the general coordinaton of activities, the implementation of ETC decisions, the organisation of meetings, budgetary control and the maintenance of relations with the Market Operations Groups.

The European Tourism Action Group

Close cooperation and consultation with the many different elements of the tourism industry has always been one of the principles of the ETC. It was this awareness of the need for closer technical liaison between the different sectors of the tourism industry which led to the ETC creating the European Tourism Action Group (ETAG) in 1981.

The group's terms of reference are:

'to encourage technical liaison between governments and national tourist agencies and the tourism interests in the public and private sectors, and to promote the development of Europe's tourism, and, in particular, to help eliminate restraints on the growth of tourism.'

To become a member of ETAG, an organisation has to be:

• a permanent body representative of a major tourism interest

• involved in the tourism industry at world or European level

• operating at an appropriate level to influence major developments in Europe's tourism.

At present, the members of ETAG are: Association of European Airlines; European Federation of Conference Towns; European Travel Commission; International Air Transport Association; International Automobile Federation; International Chamber of Commerce; International Hotel Association; International Road Transport Union; International Touring Alliance; International Union of Railways; Passenger Shipping Association; and Universal Federation of Travel Agents' Associations.

The group has a unique role, bringing together these representatives of the many different interests in the tourism industry and providing an opportunity for them to meet regularly and discuss the many issues which affect tourism in Europe as a whole. Matters dealt with by the group in recent years include seasonality, tourism statistics, consumer protection, and the improvement of service throughout the tourism industry.

CASE STUDY
GLASGOW – CULTURAL CAPITAL OF EUROPE 1990

Background

At the end of 1982, the International Management Consultancy, McKinsey and Company, were asked to carry out a very detailed analysis of Glasgow's position following the decline of its traditional industries of heavy engineering, shipbuilding, and manufacturing. The consultants were also asked to determine what future the city had, and how it might pursue a programme of economic regeneration.

Their recommended strategy was to adopt four main thrusts in the campaign to reposition Glasgow:

1 To put the heart back into the inner city, in order to create an environment where people would want to live and work. Glasgow's inner city core, with its magnificent Victorian architecture had to be restored, and the dust and grime deposited by the Industrial Revolution removed.

2 To expand the retail sector within the inner city, after years of stagnation.

3 To encourage company headquarters to relocate their offices to Glasgow.

4 To develop the tourism industry.

It was widely realised that the above objectives could only be achieved through the total support and commitment of the people of Glasgow, since the regeneration had to be developed from within. Thus, the '**Glasgow's Miles Better**' campaign was launched, with the express aim of creating a strong sense of civic pride within the Glasgow community. This highly successful campaign provided the city with the base on

Fig 1.15 Glasgow's highly successful campaign to boost public confidence in the city (*Reproduced by kind permission of Glasgow District Council*)

which to build the economic regeneration programme which began in 1983. It was a confidence-building exercise for the people of Glasgow themselves, not an advertising or marketing campaign to attract tourists. In that sense, its success was overwhelming, creating, in the city as a whole, a strong feeling of commitment to the 'Glasgow's Miles Better' attitude.

The campaign undoubtedly made it easier to attract investment to Glasgow by the private and public sectors, as it also changed external attitudes and perceptions of the city.

Different agencies were established to assume responsibility for the four main strands of the McKinsey strategy. The Greater Glasgow Tourist Board and Convention Bureau was established to develop and implement the tourism strategy.

Glasgow's case for being the Cultural Capital of Europe

When, towards the end of the 1980s, the opportunity presented itself for Glasgow to seek the nomination as the Cultural Capital of Europe 1990, it was the Chief Executive of the Tourist Board and Convention Bureau who was given the responsibility of putting forward the submission. Through consultation with interested parties in the cultural organisations, the Scottish Development Agency, the accommodation industry and local authorities, the submission became a collective effort on behalf of all of those determined to secure the designation for Glasgow.

The case made by these organisations for Glasgow being nominated Cultural Capital of Europe was based on four points:

1 Glasgow was already a city of culture.

2 Glasgow was fully equipped to market the concept.

3 Glasgow was able to fund its own proposals, without having to seek assistance from central government.

4 Glasgow had a unique selling proposition which no other city could match.

With regards to the first point, Glasgow, as the home of all the national performing arts organisations in Scotland – the Scottish Opera, the Scottish Ballet, the Scottish National Orchestra, Scottish Television, as well as the Citizens' Theatre and over 200 cultural organisations – has by far the greatest cultural infrastructure in the United Kingdom outside London. In the visual arts, Charles Rennie Mackintosh and the Burrell Collection have established the city's reputation internationally. In addition, the performing arts organisations have toured many cities in Europe establishing a reputation for themselves and for Glasgow, in terms of their performing standards.

With regards to marketing the concept, Glasgow was able to demonstrate that with the creation of the Tourist Board and Convention Bureau, the city had already moved from receiving 700 000 visitors in 1982 to over two million in 1987.

To prove the third point concerning the funding of the proposals, Glasgow was able to use the example of the Glasgow Garden Festival to illustrate that two years in advance of the Festival, the city had secured £6 million of private sector sponsorship. Furthermore, by projecting the budgets of its arts organisations to 1990, the city was able to show that £25 million would be spent on artistic activities that year, whether or not Glasgow was designated the Cultural Capital of Europe.

As to their unique selling proposition, Glasgow presented itself as the first *post-industrial* city in Europe, since over £2 billion had been reinvested in a unique private and public sector partnership in the creation of a new infrastructure geared towards the service sector.

On the basis of this, it was the unanimous decision of the Cultural Ministers of Europe to designate Glasgow the Cultural Capital of Europe 1990.

Impact on Glasgow's tourism industry

1990 was for Glasgow a year-long arts festival, which led to a major influx of visitors, curious to see for themselves the renaissance of this former industrial city. A budget of £55 million was spent on providing the year's cultural activities for residents and visitors. An indication of the growth in visitor numbers is given in Fig 1.16, which shows the numbers of enquiries recorded at Glasgow's Tourist Information Centre for 1989 and 1990.

CONCLUSION

Europe's natural and cultural assets have made it the world's principal destination for international tourism. Nevertheless, this position cannot be taken for granted, as new destinations around the world become available at a growing pace, tempting not only Europe's traditional markets, such as the Americans and Japanese, but also Europeans themselves.

The people of Europe have long grown used to indulging in tourist activity, and most now regard this as a normal component of their lives. Increasing leisure time and spending power for many Europeans has led to the growth in the taking of second holidays and short-breaks, to the benefit of the domestic tourism industry in

Fig 1.16 Tourist enquiries received by the Tourist Information Centre, Glasgow

	No of visitors				Telephone		
	1989	1990	%		1989	1990	%
January	18605	27696	+ 49	January	3468	4147	+ 20
February	19111	25481	+ 33	February	2917	5390	+ 85
March	28876	35724	+ 24	March	3787	6080	+ 61
April	30648	49868	+ 63	April	3684	6804	+ 85
May	35635	51276	+ 44	May	5546	8416	+ 52
June	37175	62866	+ 69	June	4215	7916	+ 88
July	55604	83658	+ 50	July	4076	10043	+146
August	69476	104389	+ 50	August	4899	9045	+ 85
September	40639	59089	+ 45	September	4990	7159	+ 43
October	31622	41770	+ 32	October	2767	5774	+109
November	24833	29857	+ 20	November	2853	4522	+ 58
December	28157	33391	+ 19	December	2340	2497	+ 7
	420381	605065	+ 44		45542	77793	+ 71

	Written				General total		
	1989	1990	%		1989	1990	%
January	767	1845	+141	January	22840	33688	+ 47
February	1307	1403	+ 7	February	23335	32274	+ 38
March	503	1447	+188	March	33166	43251	+ 30
April	792	1251	+ 58	April	35124	57923	+ 65
May	822	1361	+ 66	May	42003	61053	+ 45
June	897	1130	+ 26	June	42287	71912	+ 70
July	866	1247	+ 44	July	60546	94948	+ 57
August	1214	885	− 27	August	75589	114319	+ 51
September	910	866	− 5	September	46539	67114	+ 44
October	1562	773	− 51	October	35951	59472	+ 65
November	670	649	− 3	November	28356	35028	+ 24
December	424	324	− 24	December	30921	36212	+ 17
	10734	13181	+ 23		476657	707194	+ 48

Europe. Meanwhile, as the gap between the wealthy countries of the EC and the poorer Member States closes, new markets are opening up, creating new opportunities for the European tourism industry.

ASSIGNMENTS

1 New markets for Europe? According to the European Travel Commission, significant potential for travel to Europe exists in markets in East and South East Asia, such as Taiwan, Hong Kong, South Korea, Singapore and Malaysia.

It has, therefore, been decided to conduct some research into this potential market. The research will take the form of a detailed questionnaire used in these countries to determine the size of the market and its main characteristics. However, the ETC wishes to collaborate with a partner from the tourism industry on this project, in order to share the cost of the research.

(*a*) Suggest a suitable partner from the tourism industry. *N.B.* it must be someone with an interest in developing this new market.

(*b*) Draft the questionnaire to be used. It should reflect the 'main characteristics' which the research project is trying to determine.

(*c*) Decide how, when, where and with whom the questionnaire should be used, for maximum relevance and reliability.

2 A tourism profile of your own region. Look back at the list of tourism assets for Europe. By researching the characteristics of your own region, draw up a tourism profile for it. List its assets, regarding culture, cities, natural resources, etc. Do these assets attract predominantly visitors from your own country, visitors from other European countries, or non-European visitors? Are there any features of your region which you think could be turned into assets for attracting tourists but which have not yet been used for this purpose?

CHAPTER 2

EUROPEAN COMMUNITY LEGISLATION FOR TOURISM

Decisions taken in Brussels are becoming increasingly important to the tourism industry in the Member States of the European Community. Moreover, the advent of the Single Internal Market can only add to the growing amount of Community legislation already having a major impact on the conditions and regulations under which the tourism industry operates within Europe.

This chapter examines:
- The structure of the European Community
- Tourism policy within the EC
- Action on tourism already undertaken by the Community
- Future Community action to assist tourism

THE STRUCTURE OF THE EUROPEAN COMMUNITY

In 1957, the founder members of the European Community (EC) signed the Treaty of Rome, which laid the foundations of the Community and the internal market, by moving towards the establishing of customs union between the six countries involved: West Germany, Belgium, France, Italy, Luxembourg and the Netherlands. In 1973, Denmark, Ireland and Britain joined the Community, followed by Greece in 1981. In 1986, the EC became the 'Europe of 12', with the joining of Spain and Portugal.

Within the EC, there are three main decision-making institutions: the European Commission; The Council of Ministers; and the European Parliament.

1 The European Commission. The Commission is presided over by 17 members, including at least one citizen from each Member State, who act in the interests of the Community itself, do not receive instructions from any national government, and are answerable only to the European Parliament.

The Commission's three principal tasks are to:
- make proposals for European laws and policies, after consultation with interested parties in Member States
- implement EC policies based on treaty provisions or Council decisions
- ensure that EC rules and principles are followed by Member States

Within the Commission, there are 23 Directorates-General (DG). These are similar in function to national government departments. Within each DG, there are Directorates dealing with specific matters, including one with responsibility for tourism.

2 The Council of Ministers. The Council is composed of ministers from each State. Its role is to consider Commission proposals and pass laws – either by majority voting or by unanimity. For a proposal to be adopted by the majority voting system, it must gain at least 54 out of a possible 76 votes. The votes are held as follows:

Britain, France, Germany, Italy	10 votes each
Spain	8 votes
Belgium, Greece, Netherlands, Portugal	5 votes each
Denmark, Ireland	3 votes each
Luxembourg	2 votes

The presidency of the Council is held in turn by each Member State, for a period of six months.

3 The European Parliament. The three principal tasks of this institution are to:

• debate EC legislation proposed to it by the Commission

• propose legislative amendments for the Council

• perform a supervisory and consultative role

The European Parliament has 518 members, elected by the constituencies of the Member States. There is a system of committees, established to consider particular issues. Although the bulk of Parliament's work goes through the official channels of political groups and standing committees, an increasing number of important initiatives are led by inter-groups, an example of which is the Transport and Tourism Inter-Group. These unofficial groupings within Parliament provide a forum for cross-committee coordination.

TOURISM POLICY WITHIN THE EC

The Treaty of Rome does not confer any specific powers upon the Council to act in the field of tourism. Thus, the Commission does not give a Treaty base for Community involvement in this field, but instead cites a 1984 judgement by the European Court, which confirmed that Community nationals going abroad within the Community for the purpose of tourism are regarded as 'recipients of services'. All EC actions on, and policies for tourism proceed on this justification – that tourism, as a service, is covered by the terms of the original Treaty.

Nevertheless, tourism has only recently attracted the attention of the EC institutions, as awareness has grown concerning tourism's ability to promote closer relations between EC Member States, its importance as an economic activity within the Community, and the large number of Community policies which, directly or indirectly, have an impact on this industry. These policies range from the free movement of persons, through passenger transport and regional development, to the numerous measures preparing for the internal market.

As an indication of the Community's changing attitude towards tourism, the Tourism Directorate, which used to be in the Commission's Transport Directorate-General, was formally transferred on 17 February 1989, together with Small Firms, Consumer Protection and Crafts, to a newly-created Directorate-General for Small and Medium-sized Enterprises, entitled DG XXIII. This move clearly acknowledged tourism as an important area of economic activity, and heralded the beginning of moves towards the formulation of an EC policy for tourism.

Since 1988, the Community's Ministers for Tourism and the Commission have held regular meetings to exchange information on tourism policy in each Member State and discuss the approach to Community action in their field. At their meeting in November 1990 in Brussels, the Ministers asked the Commission to put forward guidelines for a Community action programme on tourism. Consequently, in April 1991, the Commission presented its Community Action Plan To Assist Tourism. The strategy contained in the Commission's Action Plan will determine Community policy and involvement in tourism over the next few years.

However, before a consideration of the details of the Action Plan, it is worth reviewing the actions already taken by the Community which have had and which continue to have a considerable impact on tourism in Europe.

ACTION ON TOURISM ALREADY UNDERTAKEN BY THE EC

Many measures aimed directly at tourism have been adopted by the European Parliament or are currently in the process of passing into European law. These measures may be divided into:

1 General measures connected with the completion of the internal market; and

2 Indirect actions resulting from the application of Community policies.

General measures connected with the completion of the internal market

In July 1987, the Single European Act came into force, to prepare for the creation of a single, internal market throughout the EC. The Act defined the internal market as:

'An area without frontiers in which the free movement of goods, persons, services and capital is ensured in accordance with the provisions of the Treaty'
(Single European Act, July 1987)

The key benefits of the internal market, as identified by the Commission, are: improved competitiveness via lower costs; trade creation; and closer coordination of monetary and economic policies.

The target date for the completion of the single, internal market is 31 December 1992, by which date, most of the remaining barriers to trade within the EC – physical, technical and fiscal – should have been removed.

The Act included 300 proposals to remove these barriers to trade within the Community. Many of these proposals have a direct bearing on the tourism industry as a whole, (although their impact may not in all cases be beneficial). The principal measures affecting tourism are: frontier controls; sales of duty-free goods; harmonisation of VAT rates; deregulation of air travel; and deregulation of coach travel.

Frontier controls

The Commission aims to abolish all intra-Community frontier controls. However, a General Declaration attached by Member Governments to the Act states that the provisions of the Act will not affect the rights of Member States to take such measures as they consider necessary for the purpose of controlling the problems of drug trafficking, terrorism, crime and illegal immigration. Already, Member States have chosen to exercise their rights under this Declaration in quite contrasting ways. France, Germany, the Netherlands, Belgium and Luxembourg, known as the Schengen group, are committed to the complete removal of frontier controls. Thus, since 1985, EC nationals displaying a green 'Nothing to Declare' disk on their car windscreens have been able to cross the borders between these countries, subject only to spot checks carried out in special bays so as not to obstruct traffic flows.

The British government, on the other hand, remains adamant that customs and immigration checks must continue, to combat the problems of terrorism, etc, and looks set to exercise its right to impose these controls as defined in the Declaration. Thus, while all other Member States allow customs and immigration checks to be carried out on trains, the British government is insistent that customs checks will be imposed at points of arrival for those travelling to Britain on Channel Tunnel trains (although it has been agreed that immigration formalities, the major cause of delays, will be carried out on all British Rail trains travelling through the Channel Tunnel to British destinations). With the possible result of increased delays and inconveniences for tourists entering Britain, the British tourism industry may suffer if controls are much more stringent than those adopted by other Member States.

Sales of duty-free goods

The proposed ending of duty-free sales for intra-EC travellers at ports and airports is one of the most controversial moves envisaged by the Commission. Commission officials argue that after 1992, the logic for duty-free sales will disappear with the removal of internal Community customs barriers. This step has yet to be approved by EC governments, many of whom are voicing rising concern over the issue.

Duty-free sales represent an important source of revenue for ports, ferry companies, airports, and airlines. A report for the International Civil Airports Association by consultants Coopers & Lybrand estimates that duty-free goods worth 1.6 billion ECU were sold by EC airlines and airports alone, in 1988, 1 billion ECU of them, to intra-EC passengers. Airports, which normally receive a share of the turnover of duty-free shops, would be particularly vulnerable to the abolition of intra-EC sales. For example, these currently account for around 15 per cent of income at Amsterdam's Schiphol airport, while BAA, formerly the British Airports Authority, earns about a fifth of its annual profits from duty-free sales. The BAA estimates that ending intra-EC sales would halve these profits, and that such losses would lead to a rise in airport handling charges, with the consumer ultimately paying more for air travel – between 1.1 and 2.3 per cent extra on intra-EC scheduled services, according to Coopers and Lybrand.

In 1988, charter operators on intra-EC routes sold 230 million ECU worth of duty-free goods on flights. Many only made a profit because of these sales, and these operators would be particularly hard hit if they were to lose revenue from in-flight duty-free sales. For the traveller, the cost of package tours would inevitably rise as a result, by between 1.5 and 2.3 per cent.

The ending of duty-free sales for intra-EC passengers would also create costs for airports towards the refurbishing of their facilities, since intra-EC travellers would have to be separated from those travelling to or from non-EC destinations (who would still be able to buy duty-free goods). Airports claim that this would necessitate extensive alterations to terminal buildings.

Harmonisation of VAT rates

In 1989, the Commission put forward a package of measures designed to harmonise indirect taxation between Member States. In essence, these recommended an alignment within three Community VAT (Value Added Tax) rate bands, for all Member States: a minimum standard rate, a reduced rate of four to nine per cent, and a limited zero rate. However, this proved to be a controversial proposal, with Member States remaining divided on this issue. Disagreement continues over what the standard rate of VAT should be, and even over whether VAT alignment is a pre-requisite of the Single Market.

The Commission's original proposals stated that the reduced rate should be imposed on passenger transport, along with other basic necessity products such as food, publications, and energy for heating and lighting. If this is accepted, it would lead directly to an increase in fares for airlines, trains, ferries, etc, since passenger transport is currently zero-rated for VAT (i.e. no VAT is charged) in some Member States. Similarly, acceptance of the proposal to introduce VAT at the reduced rate on publications would lead to increased costs for tourism promotional and sales literature in countries where no VAT is currently payable on such products.

The European tourism industry is showing considerable concern at the prospects of VAT being introduced on passenger transport and publications, since this would inevitably lead to price increases for their products. As with the case of duty-free sales, travel to destinations outside the EC would be unaffected, since this does not incur VAT charges. It is feared that this could distort travel movements to the detriment of intra-EC tourism.

Deregulation of air travel

Traditional rules for air transport traffic sharing within the EC do not meet the needs of the Single Market Europe of 1992. Through a long-established system of privileges and uncompetitive practices, large European airlines operating scheduled services have been able to retain control of almost all high intensity, high profitability routes, creating huge obstacles to real competition in Europe. The small, independent airlines have faced unfair competition from the big national flag carriers, most of which, including Lufthansa, Air France and Alitalia, are state-owned and heavily subsidised by their governments. As a result, for example, Lufthansa has an 80 per cent grasp on former West Germany capacity, and British Airways, a 68 per cent grip on British airline traffic. The domination of the market by Europe's national carriers is shown in Fig 2.1 on p 28.

Consequently, some of the most expensive air routes in the world are to be found in Europe. For example, the scheduled standard London–Nice return fare with Air France is over £400 for a 2064 km round trip, compared with Virgin's £350 fare for a round trip of 10 880 km on the deregulated London–New York run. Where deregulation has been tried before, and smaller airlines have been allowed to compete fairly for passengers alongside the national flag carriers, cheaper air fares have always been the result. For example, the cheapest ticket between London Heathrow and Dublin fell from £94 to £58 between 1985 and 1990, as a result of opening up that route to smaller airlines. On the London–Amsterdam route, the price fell from £91 to £84 for the same reason.

In order to create the conditions for improving the international competitiveness of European carriers and to give users of air transport the benefit of more numerous connections and lower fares, the Commission has, since 1987, introduced two sets of liberalisation measures. A third set, due to take effect from January 1993, will complete the EC's barrier-free single market for air transport. By that date, a number of important new rules will govern air transport traffic sharing within the EC, opening up all major routes to direct competition:

● airlines will be able to charge the fare that they wish to between destinations in two

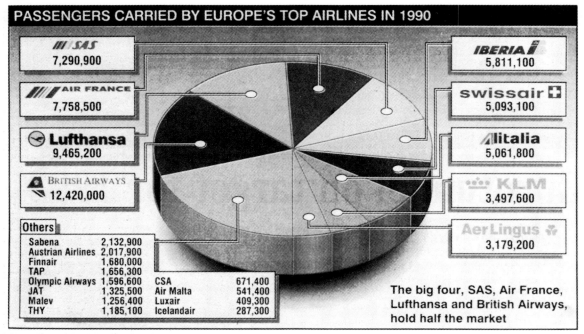

PASSENGERS CARRIED BY EUROPE'S TOP AIRLINES IN 1990

SAS 7,290,900

AIR FRANCE 7,758,500

Lufthansa 9,465,200

BRITISH AIRWAYS 12,420,000

Others

Sabena	2,132,900		
Austrian Airlines	2,017,900		
Finnair	1,680,000		
TAP	1,656,300		
Olympic Airways	1,596,600	CSA	671,400
JAT	1,325,500	Air Malta	541,400
Malev	1,256,400	Luxair	409,300
THY	1,185,100	Icelandair	287,300

IBERIA 5,811,100

swissair 5,093,100

Alitalia 5,061,800

KLM 3,497,600

Aer Lingus 3,179,200

The big four, SAS, Air France, Lufthansa and British Airways, hold half the market

Fig 2.1 Passengers carried by Europe's top airlines in 1990 (*Source: Association of European Airlines*)

Member States. Currently, the approval of both Member States is required.

● governments will no longer be able to protect the revenue of their national carriers by guaranteeing them a fixed percentage on key routes or by vetoing price-cutting by smaller rival carriers.

● currently, the rules dictate that an airline must be substantially owned by one European nation before it is allowed to fly from that country. By 1993, this ownership rule will be amended to allow any European-owned airline to operate throughout Europe, giving, for example, an Italian-owned airline the possibility of offering services between Germany and Spain.

● the Commission is planning regulatory changes which will make it easier for new airline companies to get slots at congested airports. At the moment, these are dominated by the national carriers.

The Commission believes that its measures will create a powerful core of major airlines, with a strong second layer of regional and smaller carriers, and better prices for passengers. However, they have already met with substantial resistance from national carriers who see their dominance of the market severely threatened by such measures.

The immediate response of leading airlines in Europe has been to take fast action to protect themselves from competition. The action they have taken is in many cases in direct opposition to the spirit and principles of the Commission's moves towards a more deregulated European airline environment:

● they have rushed to sign 'non-aggression' pacts with each other, forming agreements not to compete with each other in the future on specific routes. Deals between British Airways, Sabena and KLM, and between Air France, Lufthansa and Iberia are examples of this trend. EC officials in charge of competition regard these non-aggression pacts and alliances between large carriers as direct attempt to pre-empt the EC's efforts to liberalise European air transport, and are determined to stop them if they interfere with this legislation.

● they have begun a series of takeover of smaller national rivals: Air France has taken over UTA and Air Inter, thus effectively wiping out all domestic competition in France, and KLM has bought up the Dutch company Transavia. This trend towards greater concentration in the European airline industry is a major cause for concern among the smaller, independent airlines, who regard certain of the takeovers of the 1990s as being in no way in the interests of consumers or of the independent airlines themselves.

● some have embarked on a series of practices which are regarded by the Commission as blatantly predatory and designed to squeeze out smaller airlines. These include: providing so much capacity on a route that other airlines find it difficult to sell their services on the same route (in 1990, British Midland Airways accused British Airways of using this tactic on their Glasgow–London Heathrow service); charging fares which are appreciably below the carrier's full cost; and making unfair inducements to travel agents to encourage them to sell their products. The national carriers, being heavily subsidised by their governments, are able to conduct business in these ways, which are not open to fully commercial operators.

The continuing fear of Europe's smaller, independent airlines is that many European governments, such as France, are fundamentally opposed to the operations of companies such as themselves, favouring instead the concept of national carriers. The question of national pride is an important issue, since so many national airlines are regarded as important symbols of their countries abroad. Smaller airlines fear also that the large-scale restructuring currently taking place within the European airline industry will effectively make the liberalised trading climate meaningless, as the large carriers buy out their rivals and forge alliances so powerful that smaller operators will be unable to compete effectively. Their concern is expressed in the article shown in Fig 2.2.

The tourism industry as a whole would benefit from a system which created lower air fares for the public, and, therefore, increased incentive to travel. The capacity of these agreements to bring down air fares in the short term will certainly be limited by the pressures to raise air fares due to changes in VAT and duty-free regulations. However, they do provide for a potentially more open and market-orientated environment within which Europe's airlines will learn to operate, and, therefore, the long-term effects are likely to be beneficial to the

Independents fear crash landing

Julie Wolf in Brussels

COME 1993, small, independent airline companies will have been forced out of the European skies by mega-carriers like Air France, British Airways and KLM.

This is the dire scenario painted by Trans European Airways, Belgium's second largest charter company. TEA wants to see European regulators act now to prevent such predictions coming true. TEA's fears are echoed by other small carriers in Europe, some of which have already been gobbled up.

At stake is access to the deregulated air transport sector expected to result from the EC's drive to create a single market after 1992. EC countries have already enacted a first package of measures to inject more competition into the highly regulated market, where routes and profits have traditionally been shared out by national carriers. A second set of measures is under negotiation now and expected to take effect in 1993.

But in between, a dangerous void has been created, according to TEA. "What you have is a halfway situation where the mega-carriers will take advantage and consolidate their dominant position.

"We fear that by 1993 these carriers will have killed the independent carriers," says Thierry De Coster, managing director of TEA Holding. Should this happen, the large airlines will be in a position to carve up the market and raise prices, with the consumer losing out.

Mr De Coster and others cite the fact that until 1993, national governments can continue to give their flag carriers exclusive traffic rights. In Belgium's case, Sabena holds a monopoly on scheduled routes, limiting TEA to charter flights. At the same time the big carriers are increasingly moving into the charter business or offering cheap APEX tickets.

To stay competitive, "we need to get into the scheduled air flight business," says Mr De Coster. He advocates the speeding up of EC deregulation so that all carriers are given access to the market. In the meantime, TEA has filed suit with national and EC authorities against the Sabena monopoly.

Another worrying development for smaller carriers is the increasing consolidation of the airline business.

So far, for example, BA has taken over British Caledonian; Air France has acquired UTA, and Lufthansa is in talks with the small carrier, German Wings. Furthermore, a number of joint ventures have been launched, including the BA-Sabena-KLM deal, currently being investigated by the EC and Britain's Monopolies and Mergers Commission.

Fig 2.2 (*Reproduced by kind permission of* The Guardian, *2 April 1990*)

consumer, and all sectors of Europe's tourism industry.

Deregulation of coach travel

Coach operators in the EC can already take passengers to other countries and travel freely through these countries. The Commission's proposal for coach travel means that in future coach operators will be able to provide 'cabotage' services in other EC countries, i.e.

operate regular services outside the country in which they are based. The ability of coach operators to benefit from this new right will be limited by several factors, however:

● In certain Member States, the viable coach/bus network is already highly developed, offering little room for newcomers. This is the case in Britain, for example, where the coach/bus sector has already been deregulated for ten years, and is generally more cost-effective and competitive than its counterparts in other Member States.

● Some Member States (for example, France, Germany, the Netherlands and Italy) have invested heavily in rail infrastructure, and their governments are fundamentally opposed to encouraging a transfer of traffic to roads: first because their rail networks may become under-utilised, and second because rail is usually considered to be a more environmentally acceptable form of transport.

● Driver/operator regulations differ consider-ably from country to country, with those of certain Member States, such as Britain, being much stricter than those applied elsewhere. In theory, operators must comply with the regulations of the countries in which their services operate, but in practice, this may present considerable administrative difficulties for operators.

● Operators may also be deterred from expand-ing into other countries by the costs of having to establish offices abroad to service customers' needs and vehicle servicing facilities, etc.

Consequently, practical difficulties may mean that instead of a completely deregulated market, a system of bilateral agreements between Member States, for coach/bus services may evolve. This system of partners looks attractive as it will minimise operators' costs (and, therefore, fares) as contract boundaries will be formally agreed, and companies will be able to make us of each others' marketing outlets, vehicle servicing facilities, etc.

Free movement of labour and the mutual recognition of qualifications

Increased geographical mobility for those working in the tourism industry will inevitably result from the Commission's moves towards a system of EC-wide mutual recognition of educational and training qualifications. As a transitional measure, from 1 January 1991, a general system was introduced for the recognition of higher education diplomas awarded on completion of professional education and training of at least three years' duration. A system for the mutual recognition of vocational training given at secondary education level and short higher education courses, as well as for certain occupations requiring experience rather than a qualification, will be the next step towards full mutual recognition of qualifications within the EC.

Countries experiencing skill shortages will eventually be able to seek workers from abroad, but there will be increasing competition among Member States for tourism employees at all levels, as demographic changes mean that there is a shrinking supply of young workers, particularly in northern European countries.

Company law

Because of the often transnational nature of some tourist activities, the Commission's proposals on company law are of major importance for tourist businesses. With a view to completion of the internal single market, the Commission is concentrating its efforts on creating a Community framework for company law. The Commission's efforts are focusing on the closer harmonisation of national law, the removal of legal obstacles to cross-border mergers, and harmonisation of the procedures to be followed as regards take-overs and other general bids.

The internationalisation of tourism can also be assisted by the setting up of businesses or carrying on an activity in another Member State. A number of 'freedom of establishment' and 'freedom to supply services' measures already adopted apply to the tourist trades, such as restaurants, cafés, hotels, camping sites, couriers and travel agents.

Indirect measures resulting from the application of certain Community policies

Many areas of Community activity, although not aimed exclusively at tourism, have a tourism dimension, and, therefore, an impact on the industry in general. Such areas include: regional policy; consumer protection; measures to develop rural areas; cultural development in the Community; environmental policy; and education and training.

Regional policy

Because certain forms of tourism are traditionally found in less urbanised, less industrialised areas, these offer great scope for bringing prosperity and life back into those regions of a country which have been left behind in terms of development. Therefore, just as individual countries are beginning to use tourism as a means of developing particular regions, so too is tourism within the EC regarded as one way of boosting the economy of certain regions, as well as bringing social benefits to the people who live there.

Some of the EC's most important impacts on the development of tourism in Europe have been through financial contributions made from its Structural Funds. Through these, the Community has contributed to the development of tourism in those areas within the Member States designated eligible for regional development. This has been done mainly by providing financial assistance for infrastructure works (roads, electricity, water supply), the construction of facilities (e.g., yacht marinas, conference centres), and training programmes.

The Structural Funds from which tourism businesses in the Community most benefit are the European Regional Development Fund (ERDF) and the European Agricultural Guarantee and Guidance Fund (EAGGF).

1 The European Regional Development Fund. In terms of tourism development, the ERDF has proved the most significant source of funding. Since its creation in 1975, a growing proportion of this fund has been allocated to tourism: in 1984, specific allocations to tourism from this fund rose from less than one per cent to over three per cent; between 1986 and 1988, about five per cent of the ERDF was allocated to projects or programmes for the development of tourism in the EC.

The five objectives for the use of the ERDF are as follows:

1 Promoting the development and structural adjustment of the less developed regions

2 Converting the regions, frontier regions or parts of regions seriously affected by industrial decline

3 Combatting long-term unemployment

4 Facilitating the occupational integration of young people with a view to reform of the Common Agricultural Policy

5 (a) Speeding up the adjustment of the common agricultural structure; and

(b) promoting the development of rural areas.

The Commission has identified eligible areas under Objective (1) as being those where the Gross Domestic Product per capita is less than 75 per cent of the EC average, together with a limited number of special regions.

For such areas, specific priorities for the expansion of tourism have been proposed and these qualify for a substantial financial contribution from the Community. ERDF support usually takes the form of financial assistance of up to 30 per cent of the capital costs for tourism projects initiated by public sector bodies in these assisted areas.

For Ireland, Spain and Greece, 188.6 million ECU , 182 million ECU, and 166.7 million ECU respectively have been allocated to tourism. For Objective (5)(b) (rural development), the overall figure is 176 million ECU; and for Objective (2) (regional conversion), the Community support frameworks provide assistance of 267 million ECU for tourism activities in the period 1989–91.

Of the numerous cases of ERDF assistance for tourism, the following are a few examples:

● Development of Glenveagh National Park in Ireland

● Improvements to the road and air infrastructures of Ponta Delgada, in the Azores

● Restoration of the Theatre Royal in Newcastle, Britain

● Laying on of water supplies and construction of a sewerage system in Portugal's Alentejo region.

2 The European Agricultural Guarantee and Guidance Fund. The EAGGF also intervenes indirectly in assisting tourism in the EC. It achieves this through funding improvements to the infrastructures of certain rural areas and forest regions, in particular in Italy and France. EAGGF funds have been widely used to train farmers for tourist-related jobs, and to promote farm tourism and rural craft industries.

Apart from the Structural Funds, other sources of EC finance are widely used to the benefit of tourism:

1 The European Investment Bank: The EIB contributes to the growth of the tourism industry within the EC by making loans at a reduced rate of interest for the development of transport infrastructures, as well as tourist facilities. Between 1980 and 1986, loans totalling 350 million ECU were made to over 1000 tourist projects. This money was used towards the setting up of many small and medium-sized tourism and leisure businesses, as well as the construction of hotels, holiday villages, and ski-lifts.

In recent years, the EIB has contributed to the extension of Athens airport, the construction of yachting harbours in Calabria, Italy, and the improvement to the tourism infrastructure of the Canary Islands.

2 Integrated Mediterranean Programmes: Launched in 1986, the IMPs have as their objective the modernisation of the economy of Greece and certain Mediterranean zones of France and Italy. A major part of the 6600 million ECU earmarked for IMPs is to be used towards the improvement of the tourism facilities of these regions. For example, out of the 470 million ECU allocated to the island of Crete between 1986 and 1992, 10% was used towards tourism facilities and 23% towards the infrastructure.

Consumer protection

Measures have been taken in the following two fields:

1 Package tour holidays. The national laws of Member States concerning package travel, package holidays, and package tours show many disparities, and national practices in this field are also markedly different. The establishment of common rules on packages will contribute to a common market throughout the EC, thus enabling tour operators established in one Member State to offer their services in another, and Community consumers to benefit from comparable conditions when buying a package in any Member State.

The EC directive on package travel is designed to eradicate the disparities in the rules protecting consumers in different Member States, by establishing a set of common rules applicable throughout the Community. It means that, from 31 December 1992, tour operators and travel agents have to accept total legal responsibility for the services which they offer. The directive is designed to give consumers access to compensation when things go wrong with their package holidays, and contains precise rules governing tour operators' liability.

Holiday brochures will have to state clearly the tour price and will be subject to strict rules about the information which must be given to customers. Contracts, too, will have to follow certain guidelines and the price agreed on the document cannot be changed within 20 days before the departure date. In cases of cancellation, consumers will be able to transfer the package to somebody else; and they will be guaranteed a refund if the organiser changes an essential part of the arrangement – particularly the price.

Operators will have to take out insurance against bankruptcy, so that, in the event of a company going out of business, its clients would have the cost of cancelled holidays refunded, or, if necessary, be flown home. The cost of package holidays will almost certainly rise as a result.

2 Denied-boarding compensation system. The practice of overbooking is widespread among airlines, who tend to sell more seats on flights than the number available, on the principle that there will always be a few 'no-shows' – passengers who do not turn up for the flight. When the system backfires and all of those who have tickets for the flight appear, unlucky passengers find themselves being 'bumped' – obliged to wait until the next available flight. Under new EC regulations, those denied boarding in this way, on flights of up to 3500 km can expect to receive about US$100 in compensation if delayed for up to two hours and about US$200 for longer delays.

Rural development

A wide range of Community measures is available to rural tourism businesses, in particular under the EC's Common Agricultural Policy. For example, a 1985 Council regulation on improving the efficiency of agricultural structures provides for a system of aid which extends to investment in tourist and craft activities on farms. EC measures for rural tourism are described in Chapter 9.

Cultural development in the Community

Since 1986, the Commission has identified cultural tourism – tourism connected with the artistic and cultural heritage of a region – as one of the main fields for community action in the realm of cultural development. Measures have included the following:

• support for pilot projects relating to the conservation of the architectural heritage

• actions concerning European Cities of Culture

• a programme to encourage cultural events with a European dimension.

Environmental policy

The increasingly vocal concern that tourism should develop in harmony with the environment is reflected in various EC policy statements, including a Resolution on mass tourism adopted by the European Parliament in July 1990.

The Commission, in formulating the rules governing the use of the EC's Structural Funds, has made efforts to ensure that Member States take account of the environmental impact of the investment projects they propose for Community financing. According to these rules, Community funds must be used to support investments and projects which are in accordance with Community policy on the environment.

Otherwise, a number of environmental measures which the Community has adopted or planned to adopt will have an impact on tourism. Included in these measures are Community legislation on impact assessment of environmental projects, the quality of bathing water, waste management and the control of industrial or other emissions. The Commission's Green Paper on the urban environment underlines the need to develop a planning strategy for urban tourism.

Education and training

In every Member State, major resources have been made available for basic and further training in the field of tourism.

Similarly, since the early 1990s, the Commission has boosted and diversified its work in the field of training while pursuing the general objective of improving skills in order to keep pace with economic, technical, social and cultural change. The use of the Structural Funds emphasises the relationship between training programmes and development needs, and, as a result, tourism training programmes have been established in many of the regions identified under Objective (1) for the use of these funds. Similarly, the problem of training in rural tourism has been studied under Objective (5)(*b*).

Since 1987, through the Community's European Social Fund, special programmes have been implemented which explore the demand for training: transnational cooperation between educators, promoting the mobility and exchange of students and university staff, as well as the exchange of experience, through programmes such as COMETT, ERASMUS and EUROTECNET.

FUTURE COMMUNITY ACTION TO ASSIST TOURISM

Community policy for tourism during the 1990s will be shaped by a detailed Action Plan drawn up in 1991 by the Commission. In the document containing details of their Community Action Plan to Assist Tourism, the Commission makes the following statement:

'In response to the needs of the tourism industry resulting from changes in the business environment and shifts in demand, the Community should implement a coherent plan to supplemen' initiatives already undertaken under common policies or specific programmes.

The plan will cover all aspects of tourism and will aim to:

• achieve an all-round improvement in the quality and competitiveness of tourism facilities and services on offer in the Community;

• facilitate awareness of the demand for tourism; and

• satisfy that demand'.

Thus, the measures covered by the Action Plan aim essentially to help tourist businesses adjust (*a*) to the changes in the business environment resulting from completion of the internal market and economic and monetary union, and (*b*) to the shift in demand towards diversification and better quality, in a context of growing international competition.

The following extracts from the Action Plan indicate the Commission's priority areas of activity over the next few years.

1 Cultural tourism. 'Tourism in Europe faces a two-fold challenge: diversification in order to meet continually growing demand, and the need to cater for an increase in activities without destroying the European cultural heritage. Cultural tourism . . . is attracting growing numbers, from both inside and outside Europe. The development of different forms of cultural tourism contributes to the staggering of tourist visits, to a better balance in intra-Community tourist flows, and to the promotion of new tourist destinations.'

Proposed Community measures in favour of the development of cultural tourism include:

• support for the elaboration of new European cultural tourism routes and their promotion

• creation of a European prize for the best cultural tourism products

• European competition for museums which offer a complete tourism package in association with a tourism partner (tour operator, tourist office, local authority, etc)

• improvement in the welcome and the services offered to foreigners in European museums and sites, by the availability of information in several languages and the improvement in signposting.

2 Tourism and the environment. Proposed Community measures to strengthen the link between tourism and the environment include:

• support for the establishment by Member States of an inventory of European tourism resources in order to identify the regions with potential for developing new forms of tourism in harmony with the environment and those which require better management and protection

• elaboration of a code of behaviour for tourists, in order to provide ecological guidelines and ethics of behaviour

• drawing up a practical guide for the use of operators, containing recommendations which will make it easier to take environmental factors into account when devising tourism products and facilities.

3 Rural tourism. Details of proposed Community measures for rural tourism are given in Chapter 9. They include:

• elaboration of a harmonised European signposting system aimed at facilitating access to tourism products in rural areas

• improving the information available to operators in rural areas by the publishing of documents explaining existing Community support available in this field

• pilot actions in favour of the creation and promotion of new rural tourism products, emphasising partnership between operators at local, regional and European level.

4 Social tourism and youth tourism. Social tourism (*see* Chapter 7) is a means of making holidays accessible to those in the population who, for various reasons – e.g., disability or low incomes – would be unable otherwise to take a break away from home. Young people, because of their limited budgets also require special treatment to bring travel within their means. The Community's proposed measures to increase access to tourism include:

• publication of a guide, *Accessible Europe*, aimed at the disabled as well as managers of facilities, in order to encourage them to make their facilities accessible to the handicapped

• specific actions on the special factors concerning tourism for the elderly

• support for extension of the Youth Card which gives reduced prices to facilities and travel in Europe.

5 Vocational training. Expanding tourism in the Community and in Europe, and thus maintaining Europe as the leading world tourist destination, depends on a supply of quality products and services capable of meeting the increasing demands of consumers of tourist products. This in turn depends on the human resources available and their level of training. The following measures are designed to improve the quality of tourism services through vocational training:

• encouragement of the participation of tourism businesses in existing Community action programmes for training

• support for the cooperation between universities and tourism schools and tourism professionals

• pilot actions for specific training in this sector: in rural, social, cultural and environmentally aware tourism.

6 Promotion in third countries. As Europe continues to lose its world market share of tourism, the Community must step up its promotional activities aimed at 'third countries' – countries outside the EC. The Commission proposes to strengthen promotional actions in the North American and Japanese markets.

7 Staggering of holidays. The excessive concentration of tourists in particular areas at particular times of year has a serious impact on the industry's supply side: transport delays, overbooked accommodation and transport, overcharging and frequent deterioration in overcrowded regions. The staggering of school and workplace holidays would help alleviate this problem, and the Commission will undertake to:

• introduce a range of measures to encourage national authorities to stagger holidays more successfully

• publish and distribute information on pilot schemes testing innovative ideas to encourage the staggering of holidays within single Member States.

8 Improving the knowledge of the sector. In order to ensure the greatest consistency between the different measures taken to assist tourism and achieve the greatest possible impact from the measures contained in the Action Plan, an accurate picture of the tourism industry as it stands at present is necessary. To this end, the Commission proposes the following measures:

• follow-up action to the Community programme set up in 1990 to improve tourism statistics within the EC

• a programme of studies to evaluate the impact of existing Community policies in favour of tourism

• studies to analyse the emergence of new forms of tourism in Europe and the best ways of promoting them.

9 Transnational actions.

• cooperative tourism initiatives between border regions

• development of commercial links with Central and Eastern Europe through the transfer of know-how

• putting into operation new forms of tourism and technical cooperation between towns.

Community funds are best put to use where a strategic *plan* for the development of a region has been drawn up, as a result of discussions between all responsible authorities, developers, entrepreneurs and social partners. A recent report by the EC's Economic and Social Committee, **Tourism and Regional Development**, recommends that: 'the Structural Funds of the Community should only be made available for assistance and support where there is evidence of . . . a plan in which the participants are prepared to make a substantial commitment. There should not, with few exceptions be support for isolated projects or piecemeal development'.

The report gives the following as an example of the kind of development plan which would qualify for assistance from the EC funds for this purpose:

CASE STUDY
THE ALGARVE REGIONAL DEVELOPMENT PROGRAMME

The Algarve Regional Development Programme is a programme of investments established for the five-year period from 1986 to 1990, with the aim 'to integrate and harmonise public-sector actions with those resulting from private initiative, in order to promote balanced socio-economic development in the region'.

Background

The Algarve, which covers an area of 5000 square km, with its semi-arid climate and nearly 330 000 inhabitants unevenly distributed throughout the territory, is the principal tourist region of Portugal, receiving around 1.5 million visitors during the holiday period.

Tourism and related activities are now a major source of revenue and are economically dominant, absorbing a substantial proportion of regional resources (labour force, capital, land). Its predominance partly explains why other sectors are underdeveloped and fail to reach their full potential. The scarcity of water for irrigation, the technological obsolescence of fishing vessels and equipment, insufficient marketing infrastructures, limited diversification and the lack of efficiency in industry are the main problems concerning the other sectors. Another problem common to all of them concerns vocational training, which is tech-

Fig 2.3 The Algarve

nically and technologically backward and in short supply, thus further reducing their competitiveness.

A fundamental cause for concern is the gap between existing infrastructure and real needs – both those which derive from economic activities and those of the resident and tourist population. Despite significant efforts in recent years, there are still major deficiencies in basic sanitation (infrastructure and the treatment of used water) and transport.

The economy is being weakened further by stagnation in the fisheries and industry sectors, the low level of development in the cultivation (with and without irrigation) of vegetables and fruit, and the haphazard development of tourism, resulting in a decline in the quality of tourist services on offer. Tourist services are unplanned and undiversified, and the demand is, therefore, lower than it might be. Investment

is mainly in accommodation: 90 per cent of tourist accommodation in the area is concentrated on the coastline of only five 'conselhos' (administrative districts).

The economic trends described above mean that at least 28 200 jobs must be created in order to totally absorb the employment demand for the period 1986–90. Meanwhile, inter-regional imbalances are being exacerbated, accelerating population outflows from the mountainous area of the Algarve and causing ecological and economic problems.

Plan of action for the development of the Algarve

Details of a Regional Development Programme for the Algarve are given in the EC publication, *Tourism and Regional Development*. The priority objectives of this programme are:

● to reinforce the economic potential and the productive base through the diversification of the economic structure, which will require better use of existing local resources and the improvement of the integration between sectors, the aim being to strengthen competitiveness and reduce the seasonal nature of the main economic activities.

● to obtain a satisfactory level of employment and profits and better geographical distribution, by creating new jobs and improving professional training.

● to reinforce basic infrastructure and adjust it to the needs of industry and the resident and non-resident population. This objective requires support for the productive structure, better access to, and better communication within, the region, and the necessary infrastructure for residents and tourists.

● to ensure the conservation of the environment and natural resources by combatting erosion and degradation of natural resources, and by cleansing polluted rivers and the sea.

● to coordinate and integrate public sector measures to assist the productive sector and to promote the construction and maintenance of infrastructure.

Priority actions and projects in the public sector

The following are essential to the region's development:

• Creation of centres for professional training

• Improvement of road networks; construction of a bridge over the Guadiana river

• Enlargement of Faro airport and of various fishing ports

• Intensification and expansion of forestry

• Aid to aquaculture

• Supply of equipment and construction of infrastructure for the removal and treatment of used water in several towns, and construction of water mains

• Enlargement of the electricity grid

• Development of telecommunications

• Promotion of alternative tourism, especially golfing holidays, tourism in the mountainous regions of the Algarve, and holidays in spas.

The implementation of this Regional Development Plan calls for coordinated actions and initiatives by the public sector (central administration, public enterprises and local authorities) and private sector. Implementation will be monitored by the 'Commissão de Coordenacao da Região do Algarve' – the Algarve Regional Coordinating Committee.

Tourism

To realise the objectives established in this sector, the private and public sectors and the national tourism enterprise, ENATUR, will all have to contribute through various activities.

It is necessary, in the first place, to carry out infrastructure projects in the main tourist areas, because if sanitation and water supply schemes are not completed, tourism in the Algarve will not be competitive. It is also necessary to consider the tourist potential of some of the mountainous regions in the interior.

Action to promote tourism can be subdivided as follows:

1 Action by central and local administrations

• Drawing up of a Tourism Development Programme by the RTA (Região de Turismo do Algarve)

• Promotion of the region as a tourist destination through travel agencies, presence at international tourist fairs, etc

• Preservation and restoration of the historical and cultural heritage of the region

• Building of sports facilities for tourists, such as swimming pools, tennis courts, golf courses, marinas, etc

• Construction of accommodation facilities such as camp sites, hostels in the grounds of castles and other historic buildings

2 Action by ENATUR. ENATUR will expand and modernise the inns of S Bras de Alportel and Sagres and the hotel facilities in the spas of Caldas de Monchique, including the conservation of the source and the modernisation of the mineral water processing plant.

3 Action by the private sector. There are 64 projects under way in the following areas:

• accommodation (hotels, apartment hotels, inns, tourist villages, etc)

• sports facilities (golf courses, harbours, parks, etc)

• cultural amenities and conference centres

If only *half* of the aforementioned investments were made in the five-year duration of the Regional Development Programme, the result would be 20 000 more beds and 2600 new jobs in tourism.

CASE STUDY

AN ASSESSMENT OF EUROPEAN TOURISM YEAR 1990

Origins and objectives of EYT

1990 was European Tourism Year. This was decided by the Council of Ministers of the European Community, responding to a suggestion made by the European Parliament with the support of the European Commission. The justification for the project was two-fold:

1 Intra-European tourism enables people, particularly the young, to enrich their knowledge of the cultures and lifestyles of the 12 member countries of the Community, thus becoming more aware of what Europe is really about.

2 Europeans should be made aware that tourism is an economic sector of prime importance for the Community, and is one of the Community's main job-creating industries.

There were three main objectives:

1 To prepare for the establishment of the frontier-free Community;

2 To develop the integrating role of tourism in order to create a People's Europe; and

3 To stress the economic and social importance of the sector, in regional development and job creation.

The specific themes of EYT which were set by the Council of Ministers were:

● the promotion of greater knowledge among the citizens of the participating countries, especially young people, of the cultures and life-styles of other participating countries.

● the staggering of holidays

● the development of new tourist destinations

● exemplary character, meaning that it could serve as a pilot for similar projects in other regions or countries

● environment-friendly character in tourism, meaning tourism which embellishes, or at least does not damage, the natural or man-made environment.

EYT organisation and budget

The European Commission was given the task of organising EYT, and was assisted by a Steering Committee composed of one or two representatives from each Member State. Representatives of the European Free Trade Association were also invited to meetings, as the Community ministers responsible for tourism insisted on the need to approach the task on a continental scale. The Community and EFTA Member States each established a national committee to identify and propose projects for Community co-financing, to examine their suitability for sponsorship or patronage, and to support the preparation of various events, including the launching of EYT in each country.

The entire operation was coordinated by a special Management Unit set up by the Commission and based within the Tourism Division. The Unit was comprised of officials of the Commission, experts seconded from the National Tourist Offices of seven Member States and two EFTA countries, and executives from Euro Conseil, the management consultancy contracted by the Commission to support the activities of EYT.

The Management Unit reported to and consulted with the Steering Committee, which met twice in 1989 and four times in 1990, with further meetings in 1991.

The total budget allocated to EYT for 1989 and 1990 was ECU 8 142 457, which included a contribution of ECU 566 374 from the EFTA countries. In the field of sponsorship, the American Express organisation lent its support on three levels: research, publicity and conferences.

Promotion of the Year

The logo as shown in Fig 2.4 was chosen as the symbol of EYT.

Widely distributed, in 13 languages, the logo appeared on all EYT promotional material, from carrier bags to T-shirts, as well as many tourist publications in the 18 participating countries. The success and widespread use of the logo has persuaded the Commission to retain it on a permanent basis as the logo for European tourism.

Fig 2.4 European Tourism Year's logo

Two members of the Management Unit team were given special responsibility for press and public relations: responding to information requests from journalists, associations and the general public, and producing a special newsletter, *Eurotourism 1990*. The press coverage of EYT was more or less consistent throughout the year, with peaks after well-publicised events such as the inauguration ceremony.

Special events

In order to promote EYT, a number of special events were organised, or used to generate publicity for the Year. These included: the launch of EYT in Strasbourg in December 1989, and its inauguration in Dublin in January 1990 which were both attended by journalists from all over Europe as well as the USA; the Eurovision Song Contest, during which each song was preceded by a video showing European tourist destinations and ending with the EYT logo; and, 'The Wall', a rock concert performed in Berlin's Potsdamer Platz in July 1990, with EYT participation – EYT flags and posters were displayed around the concert area and the EYT hot air balloon was tethered in the grounds.

Competitions

The aim of the EYT competitions was to attract the attention of professionals and students of tourism, and, where possible, the general public. Ten competitions in all were held, for the best poster, best kept village, best tourist facilities for the handicapped, etc. The European finals for each competition were held in different countries, organised by the national EYT committees. For example, the Tidiest City competition had its European final in Bruges, Belgium, where the city of Aalborg in Denmark was declared the winner, with Bruges second and Bergen third. In addition to these competitions, the 'World Tourism Games' took place in the Austrian province of Burgenland during summer 1990. This meeting of sports enthusiasts from the tourism sector around the world will be repeated every two years.

Monthly activities

To emphasise the different aspects of tourism, a different activity was highlighted each month in EYT participating countries: January – walking; February – winter sports; March – heritage; April – angling; May – rural tourism; June – cycling; July – camping/caravanning; August – photography; September – water sports; October – golf; November – equestrianism; and December – the arts.

According to these themes, a wide variety of special events was organised. For example, in April, the Scandinavian countries arranged several activities for Angling Month, including a World Ice-fishing Championship competition in Inari, Finnish Lapland, and an 'Angling Day' of special fishing events held in Sweden.

EYT Projects

The original Council decision over the EYT highlighted the need for coordinated action to encourage a greater awareness by the citizens of the Member States, and especially young people, of the cultures and life-styles of other Member States. It also emphasised the need to promote the development of alternative forms of tourism and intra-Community tourism, as well as tourism from third countries. During EYT, these areas were largely encouraged through the co-financing of projects which formed the basis of the Year, and which were grouped according to the themes of youth tourism, cultural tourism, rural tourism, and tourism and the environment.

Youth tourism

Statistics indicate that young people constitute by far the greatest proportion of tourists, and, therefore, the Commission's efforts during EYT were geared towards expanding the existing product base for the young tourist. Over 40 projects dealing with the promotion of youth travel were selected for co-financing under the EYT budget, including the following examples: **Flottiglia Magna Grecia**: a fleet of eight yachts was chartered to take 50 young Europeans on a sailing trip which retraced the itinerary of the Greek settlers in the south of Italy. Also on board were archaeologists, travel agents and journalists who, with the young people, visited archaeological sites and cultural centres *en route*. Flottiglia Magna Grecia was a pilot project to test the feasibility of establishing this as a tourism programme. This has now been accomplished and the tours were launched at travel trade fairs in spring 1991.

Rassemblement des Jeunes: at the invitation of the French national committee, 350 young people from 25 countries were invited to France to participate in a three-day colloquium. All the participants were currently taking courses or working in tourism. The objective of the conference was to accentuate the movement of youth and the repercussions on the European tourism market.

Cultural tourism

Under EYT, the Commission co-financed a total of 83 cultural projects, pan-European and national, with a contribution amounting to over ECU 1 000 000. These projects included festivals, guides on cultural tourism, exhibitions, workshops, and conferences on tourism, culture and restoration. The development of a wide range of national and pan-European itineraries and heritage routes were also co-financed under this heading, including: the **Via de la Plata**, the Silver Route, a Spanish project to rehabilitate the ancient Roman route used for commerce, extending from north to south Spain. The realisation of this route by 1992 includes the improvement of the necessary infrastructure, the production of a map, and its promotion through travel agents. A second example, taken from a Commission publication is given in Fig 2.5.

Rural tourism

The Council Decision on EYT expressly designates rural tourism as an alternative form of tourism to be encouraged and developed. Several projects focused on the promotion of rural tourism, such as the production of a new brochure to promote agritourism (tourism on the farm) within the Community. Other projects concerned the development of new products and packages, including a 320 km cycle ride to discover Flanders, and the renovation of local rural dwellings for tourism in the mountains of the Canary Islands.

Tourism and the environment

An estimated 50 000 ECU was allocated to co-finance some 50 projects directly related to tourism and the environment, ranging from the designation of a cross-border national park between Hungary and Austria, through travelling exhibitions on themes relating to the problems of tourism and the environment, to a pilot project conducted by German Federal Railways catering services, through which plastic crockery in their railway buffets was replaced by edible plates and containers made from a cereal base!

Conclusions

Certain difficulties were encountered at the time the Year was launched, due to too short a preparation period (the Council's decision to declare 1990 the European Year of Tourism was taken in December 1988, leaving the Commission

Fig 2.5 An example of a cultural project funded by EYT

Sur la trace des Celtes

Production d'une affiche faisant apparaître les principaux centres d'intérêt celtes en Europe ainsi que les festivals celtiques, les auberges de jeunesse et les voies de chemin de fer. Ce projet est mis en place en France, Angleterre et Irlande avec le concours de la Fédération Européenne des Auberges de Jeunesse et Interail. Son but est de montrer les liens historiques entre les pays européens, principalement aux jeunes générations et de les encourager à voyager hors saison pour découvrir les centres d'intérêt celtes.

EUROPE ■

On the trail of the Celts

Production of a poster/map displaying the major sites of Celtic interest in Europe including celtic festivals, youth hostels and railways. This project in France, England and Ireland is being organised with the International Youth Hostels Federation and Interail. It aims to demonstrate the links between European countries especially amongst the youth population, and to encourage travel by young people during the off peak season to visit areas of Celtic interest.

EUROPE ■

Auf der Spur der Kelten

Entwurf eines Plakats mit den wichtigsten keltischen Kulturstätten in Europa, den keltischen Festspielen, den Jugendnerbergen und den Eisenbahnen. Dieses Projekt wird in Frankreich, in England und in Irland unter Mitarbeit des europäischen Verbandes der Jugendherbergen und von Interrail in die Wege geleitet. Seine Zielsetzung ist es, die historischen Beziehungen zwischen den europäischen Ländern zu zeigen, und besonders die jungen Leute dazu anzuregen, ausserhalb der Saison zu verreisen, um die keltischen Kulturstätten aufzusuchen.

EUROPA ■

only 12 months to prepare the Year), insufficient staff taking up their posts too late, and a limited budget. The numerous activities which took place in such diverse areas of activity also meant that it was difficult to exercise control over the smooth operation of all of them and to ensure their promotion to the general public.

Despite these drawbacks, the EYT Steering Committee, during their meeting in February 1991 in Brussels, declared their unanimous satisfaction with the results obtained during the course of the Year.

The achievements of EYT can be assessed in four respects:

1 The usefulness of exchanging information and pooling experience between the Commission and those involved in tourism, and within the Commission itself: EYT encouraged closer links to be developed between national and local administrations, trade associations and representatives of the industry, and between all of these and the Commission. Closer cooperation also grew up between the different Commission departments responsible for information, the environment, and social and regional policy, through the joint organisation of specific measures.

2 The need for a broader framework for the development of new initiatives and the exchange of experience between Member States: in most of the specialised branches of tourism, EYT encouraged the development and implementation of projects aimed at diversifying and improving the supply of tourist services and placing this supply in a European dimension. For example, the cultural projects demonstrated a need for a more effective information policy, for improved cooperation and for Europe-wide networks for the exchange of experience.

3 An innovative approach to action to assist tourism: one of the aims of EYT was to support national schemes or pan-European projects. The Year showed that transnational cooperation in the tourism field is particularly beneficial, particularly in as yet relatively undeveloped areas (e.g., urban tourism) or where the need for transfer of experience and know-how is considerable (as in the case of cooperation with Central and Eastern Europe).

4 The importance of making operators inside and outside Europe more aware of the richness and diversity of European tourism: many of the EYT promotional activities drew attention to European tourism, the nature of the industry and the conditions in which it can be further developed. The very extensive use of the EYT logo could prove fruitful in paving the way for introducing the concept of a *European* tourism product to supplement what is already on offer in the different Member States.

CONCLUSION

After many years of occupying a place of only minor importance within the EC institutions, tourism has recently been accorded more prominence within the European Commission. The launching of a European Year of Tourism was a testament to the growing realisation at the level of European policymaking that tourism plays an important part in the economic and social life of the Community.

The advent of the single internal market will facilitate certain aspects of travel for individual citizens within the EC and will streamline tourism business practices. Certain changes, however, notably in duty-free and VAT regulations, may make travel more expensive for the consumer. The Community Action Plan for Tourism represents an extensive direct intervention in tourism by the EC, and may help to maximise the benefits of this industry, both for those active in it and for the citizens of Europe themselves.

ASSIGNMENTS

1 Compiling a regional development plan
Valuable financial resources from the EC's Structural Funds can be instrumental in assisting the tourism industry of particular regions, by providing the means for improving infrastructure, tourism training, the protection of the environ-

ment, and the promotion of certain tourist products. All of these developments can bring economic and social progress to the less favoured regions of Member States.

However, funds for this purpose are limited and are most likely to be allocated to regions which produce a sound Regional Development Plan, to support their application for assistance from the EC.

Taking as an example the Algarve Regional Development Programme, compile a development plan for a region in your own country, or another country you know well. The region should qualify under one or more of the five objectives for the European Regional Development Fund, and should be capable of being developed for tourism.

Make the plan as detailed as possible, and include:

• background information on the region and its problems
• priority objectives for its development
• proposals for public sector projects
• suggestions of tourism products for the region
• a list of the main partners in the region.

2 Transnational cooperation in tourism.
Throughout European Tourism Year and beyond, a common theme within EC tourism policy has been the importance of transnational cooperation in tourism, in particular the setting up of tourism products which bring together two or more Member States of the Community.

Many examples of this kind of product already exist: a 'Vincent Van Gogh' cross-border tourist route for walkers and cyclists following the artist's travels in Belgium and the Netherlands; the establishing of a tourism 'Euroregion' between Kent County Council and the Nord Pas de Calais, the two regions joined by the Channel Tunnel; and a French, British and Irish project based on the major sites of Celtic interest in Europe.

Devise a project for a new transnational tourism product which would bring together your country with another. It could be based on a cultural connection, such as an artist, for example; or it could be some historical connection or a natural feature which covers the two countries. Give an indication of who the market for this product would be, and how it would be marketed.

CHAPTER 3

SHRINKING EUROPE: THE EUROPEAN HIGH-SPEED TRAIN NETWORK AND THE CHANNEL TUNNEL

As the skies over Europe become increasingly congested, and advances in technology mean faster and more comfortable trains, rail travel on Europe's expanding network of high-speed lines is already cutting journey times substantially between major cities. This chapter examines the impact on tourism of the European high-speed train network, and the Channel Tunnel, Britain's link with the network.

This chapter examines:
- The growth of Europe's high-speed train network
- The impact of the high-speed train network on tourism
- Changing patterns of tourism due to the Channel Tunnel

THE EUROPEAN HIGH-SPEED TRAIN NETWORK

The shape of the network

By the year 2000, those choosing to travel around Europe for business or leisure will be able to do so on trains travelling at over 300 km per hour along high-speed rail links bringing most of the continent's major cities within a three-hour trip of each other. Far from being a futuristic fantasy, high-speed train travel is already a reality in parts of continental Europe, and the impact on inter-city communications has been as great as that created by the appearance of the first ever passenger train, which travelled between Manchester and Liverpool at 45 km per hour, in 1830.

A continent-wide high-speed train network for the rapid transportation of tourists around a Europe without frontiers grows nearer by the day, as individual countries extend their own national railway systems, to accommodate the technologically advanced trains. Work is already

well underway in some countries: **France** was the first European country to develop a high-speed train link, the famous TGV – *train à grande vitesse* – between Paris and Lyon, in 1983. Travelling at 270 km per hour, the TGV halved the journey time to two hours. Following the success of this link, came the TGV Atlantique line from Paris to Le Mans (in 1989) and Tours (in 1990), using trains travelling at 300 km per hour. The TGV Nord line is being constructed to link Paris with the Channel Tunnel, via Lille, in 1993. An extension to this line is planned, to Brussels, then Amsterdam, then, by 1998, to Cologne and Frankfurt.

In **West Germany**, two fast-speed lines are in use, linking cities in the north with cities in the south: Hannover with Wurzburg (300 km), and Mannheim with Stuttgart (100 km). A Cologne to Frankfurt line is due to be completed in 1995. The Rome to Florence *direttisima* is the first high-speed train link in **Italy**, with extensions to Naples in the south and to Milan in the north already underway. The final proposed link is to be between Turin and Venice, via Milan. **Spain** is currently constructing the first line for its *tren* *alta velocidad*, or TAV, between Madrid and Seville, with completion scheduled to coincide with the Expo '92 trade fair in Seville in 1992. Further lines are envisaged that would link Madrid to Lisbon and speed passengers between the main cities of the Basque country.

By the end of 1989, 14 different European national railways, inside and outside the European Community, were planning high-speed links. It is planned that a European high-speed train network similar to that shown in Fig 3.1 should be in place by the year 2005.

The European Community's role in the high-speed train network

The EC is involved in the development of the high-speed train network through the Treaty of

Rome's requirement that Member States should introduce a Common Transport Policy, for all forms of transport. Work in this field is undertaken by the **European Transport Commissioner**, whose role it is to develop and coordinate a coherent European plan for all forms of transport, including rail.

It is the EC, as opposed to individual Member States, which maintains the overall vision of a Community-wide network of high-speed trains. The parts of this network which are already in place have been constructed by individual countries, principally to fulfil their own domestic transport requirements. The EC, therefore, concentrates its own activities on promoting the connecting up of the various national systems into what will be an integrated, international system of rail transport.

The European Transport Commissioner's ally in this aim is the **Community of European**

Fig 3.1 Europe's high-speed rail network (*Source: Community of European railways*)

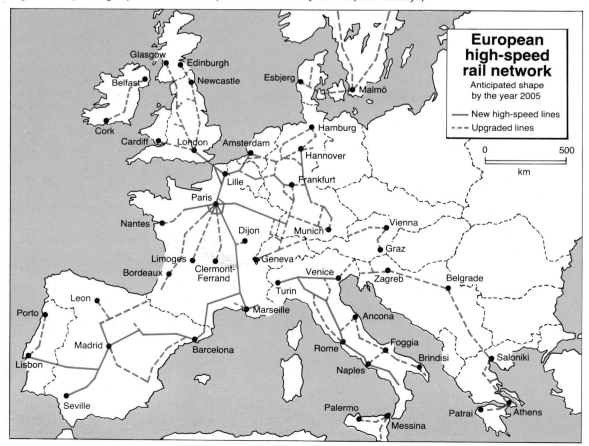

Railways (CER), a body bringing together all the railway authorities of the EC countries plus those of Switzerland and Austria. This organisation, representing all of the individual railway authorities, also aims to join up lines in different countries to make a continent-wide high-speed network. It, therefore, presents a useful body with which the EC can negotiate on this issue.

Through the European Transport Commissioner, the EC's activities concerning the railways fall into two categories:

- assistance for new high speed lines; and
- solving regulatory issues.

New lines

In 1989, the EC proposed the setting up of a new Transport Infrastructure Fund. The Fund was to be used for financing new lines, in particular those which would bring benefits to the Community as a whole by providing the 'missing links' in the emerging high-speed train network. The justification for proposing such a fund was that some such lines would involve very high construction costs for the particular Member State on whose territory the link lay, but that their overall benefit was to the whole Community. By 1990, certain countries, including Britain were still opposed to the idea, and the EC was considering going ahead with the fund, but excluding those countries which refused to contribute. Obvious candidates for eventual financial backing from the EC fund would be:

- Alpine rail passes linking northern Italy to the main central European rail system; and

- routes through the Pyrenees to improve Franco-Spanish links.

Regulatory issues

As the number of high-speed lines grew, the EC, anticipating the emergence of a pan-European network, saw the need for technical and administrative harmonisation of the various national rail networks involved.

Consequently, by the end of the 1980s, the EC had set a range of proposals before the national railway authorities, for their consideration. These ranged from harmonisation of railway track gauges and accounting methods to a plan to stimulate competition by allowing railway authorities to run their own trains on any national railway system within the Community, for example, to allow the SNCF to operate passenger services between London and Edinburgh, in competition with British Rail.

These proposals had only a very lukewarm reception from most railway authorities, who perceived a potential threat to their established operating methods. However, by 1990, the EC, in full knowledge that the Treaty of Rome commits the Community to a Common Transport Policy, including freedom of competition, was continuing to work on its plans for complete rail harmonisation and integration.

Competition with other forms of transport

Rail traffic on the line between Paris and Lyon grew from 12.2 million trips in 1980 to 19.2 million in 1985, with the arrival of the TGV. Of the extra seven million, the SNCF, Société Nationale des Chemins de Fer, estimates that 33 per cent was diverted from air travel, and 18 per cent from road travel.

If the impact of the SNCF TGV service proves to be typical of the new high-speed train links between European cities, then one major result of the network will be the diverting of traffic from air and road travel. The train and the plane are in competition with each other for passengers on journeys of 500 to 1000 km in length. Below 500 km, the train has the advantage, and over 1000 km, the plane is the form of transport most often chosen.

However, within the competitive zone of 500 to 1000 km, travel by high-speed train offers the tourist several advantages over travel by air:

- Rail termini are usually situated in **city-centre locations**, unlike airports, which because of the vast area of land required and because of aircraft noise and safety considerations, are most often on green-field sites at some distance from the centre of the cities they serve. There is, therefore, a saving to the rail passenger in terms of time as well as money. There is a further saving in time for rail travellers in the sense that they do not have to check in for their journey half an hour or an hour in advance of their departure time, as air travellers do.

- **Delays** in air travel are, on average, much longer than those in rail travel. Business travellers, in particular, find flight delays extremely frustrating, and, as the pressure on Europe's airports and flight paths grows, delays caused by a missed take-off or landing slot are becoming increasingly common. Moreover, despite great advances in technology in recent years, air travel is still much more sensitive to weather conditions than the various forms of surface travel, including rail.

● In terms of **fares**, trains usually have the advantage over air travel, with lower standard fares and the ability to offer a range of discounts and deals to travellers. Price is less of an issue for business travellers, who most often are not themselves paying; but for leisure tourists, cost is an important consideration.

● The **rolling stock**, or the carriages, used by the high-speed trains offers more scope for flexibility of design than the traditional plane structure does. The ability of trains to adapt their design to serve the needs of a wide range of travellers was addressed by Christian Sagnac, the Head of International Marketing for the SNCF, at a conference entitled 'Rails into Europe', held in London in May 1988. He said:

Functionality – the adaptation of vehicles for individuals or groups of passengers – will be essential. There is already a growing requirement for family coaches with adapted seats and space; basic coaches for youth parties; group trainsets providing a convivial atmosphere – as well as the traditional need for separate first class vehicles for professional classes which can offer privacy, conviviality and meal service as required.

Computers are capable of making specific types of reservations to satisfy various preferences and group sizes, and we will provide on-train activities such as hi-fi music, video and television entertainment, telephones (and possibly Minitel, provided that radio transmission problems can be overcome). Specially adapted catering services will involve the removal of on-board cooking, the creation of inviting dining-rooms providing a modern service based on vacuum-packed food heated in steam ovens, and a wide choice between regional, classical or international gastronomies.'

It is this capacity of trains to provide a highly flexible range of services to passengers which makes them attractive to those who may otherwise use road or air travel. The advantages to business and leisure tourists of a high degree of reliability and flexibility are clear. Business tourists will be able to hold on-train conference sessions as they speed towards their destinations, and will have at their disposal many of the business facilities found in their own offices. For leisure tourists, the journey itself will become part of the holiday, which will begin as soon as they board the train.

Rail holiday packages

The advent of high-speed train travel also brings with it attractive possibilities for the development of new holiday packages of the type on offer from tour operators such as TUI, Touristik Union International, whose experience underlines the importance of another train facility – the **motorail** service, which is described in the following case study.

CASE STUDY

TUI AND MOTORAIL HOLIDAY PACKAGES

TUI is one of the premier German tour operators, but is better known under its trade marks, Touropa, Scharnow Airtours, Hummel Seetours, and Dr Tigges. In 1986/87, its total volume of passengers reached 2.64 million, with a turnover of DM 3 billion.

In the years before charter flights developed, TUI had up to one million passengers per year using train travel as part of their holiday packages. By the mid-seventies, the volume had dropped to 250 000. TUI's management, therefore, was faced with having to make a decision about the future of train-combined holiday packages.

They decided to continue offering the packages to see what could be done to make them more attractive. They took this decision for various reasons:

● TUI still had a large volume of clients choosing their train-combined holiday packages.

● Their employees' know-how concerning train services was considerable.

● By continuing to back the rail packages, TUI could diversify their risks between their other air and sea travel products.

Part of the problem was that the couchette coaches of the German national rail company, Deutsche Bundesbahn, in which passengers were carried had not changed in design since

1952; but the needs and expectations of TUI's customers had changed considerably over the years. New, modernised rolling stock was needed, but no investment funding was available to DB for this purpose.

In 1978, therefore, TUI, demonstrating their commitment to their rail-based product, solved this problem by investing in their own rolling stock – TUI's own train comprising 30 couchette coaches and three club coaches, at the cost of DM 35 million. It was a great success. The train began running in 1980, transporting 100 000 TUI clients a year from Germany to Austria, Switzerland and the Mediterranean. When, four years later, the volume of passengers began to drop, TUI realised that what was needed to complete the package was the introduction of motorail services, which would enable tourists to take their cars with them on the train.

The motorail service was introduced in 1985 and developed in a very positive way, bringing back to train travel many holidaymakers who, for 10 or 20 years, had been driving their own cars to their destinations. TUI's passenger surveys found that more and more car drivers were interested in travelling safely, without stress and strain on themselves and their cars, and gaining two extra days' holiday time, by covering, in some cases, over 1500 km by train during the night. The continuing success of the TUI train, now with a capacity of 280 000 passengers per year, is based on catering for clients who enjoy train travel and who want the convenience of having their own cars to drive at the end of their journey.

As well as highlighting some of the advantages of train travel over car travel, the TUI experience also draws attention to the opportunities for the creation of new holiday packages using high-speed trains with motorail facilities. In 1988, Klaus Dietsche of TUI said:

'Huge tourist streams go by private car or by air to the South. Tour operators know the needs of these people. They have the building blocks to create new products for holidaymakers travelling around by their own car. And they have the means to take care of them in the holiday region, giving them advice and assistance.

Why should it not be possible to come to a fruitful cooperation between railways and tour operators in creating a European network of motorail holiday trains?'

A final indication of the flexibility of the services which the high-speed trains will offer is given by the SNCF's plan to offer TGV **night services**, using seats designed for overnight journeys, similar to those found in long-haul flight planes. In his paper presented to the 'Rails into Europe' conference in 1988, Christian Sagnac announced this plan and, looking forward to an established Europe-wide high-speed train network, raised the possibility of using such trains for overnight journeys from London, Brussels or Amsterdam to Marseille, Nice, or Barcelona, for example. He also spoke of slower, but larger capacity trains with double-decker sleeping cars, running at 200 or 220 km per hour, for overnight journeys.

CASE STUDY
ENVIRONMENTAL CONSIDERATIONS

Spain's tren alta velocidad (TAV)

Despite the obvious benefits of high-speed train travel to passengers, those who live near the routes of the inter-city links often protest strongly about the harmful impact which the lines have on the environment. Residents' resistance to having high-speed train lines passing close to their homes was dramatically illustrated by the reaction of the people of Kent, who initially rejected all four routes for the London to Channel Tunnel link proposed by British Rail in 1988.

However, there has also been much concern over the harmful impact of high-speed lines on the natural environments through which they pass, even when these are far from people's homes. Spain provides an example of how potentially damaging such lines can be.

In 1992, people from all over the world will travel to Spain to visit the Expo '92 trade fair in Seville. From Madrid, they will take Spain's first high-speed train, the tren alta velocida or TAV, which will carry them at 270 km per hour to Seville. In the train, they will have access to video, telephones, telefaxes, a business centre, bars, and a boutique. These passengers, however, may be unaware of the intense controversy over the route chosen for the TAV. Figure 3.2 shows the route proposed by RENFE, the Spanish state-owned railway company. The line passes directly through the Sierra Morena, the 'Dusky Mountains' which separate the Spanish tableland from the lush south of the

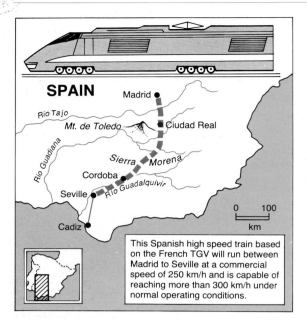

Fig 3.2 Spain's TAV: the chosen route

SPAIN
Madrid
Rio Tajo
Mt. de Toledo   Ciudad Real
Rio Guadiana
Sierra Morena
Cordoba
Seville   Rio Guadalquivir
Cadiz

0   100
km

This Spanish high speed train based on the French TGV will run between Madrid to Seville at a commercial speed of 250 km/h and is capable of reaching more than 300 km/h under normal operating conditions.

country. This region is a wildlife paradise, unique in Europe, a breeding-ground for lynxes, wolves, wild boars, black vultures and Imperial and Golden eagles. It is the impact of the TAV on this region which has led to the controversy and to the clashes between the Spanish government and ecologists, on this issue.

There was no mention of the Madrid to Seville link in the government's Railway Transport Plan presented in 1987. This was aimed at modernising and extending Spain's extremely inadequate 12 700 km rail network by the year 2000, and was endorsed by ecologists. But by 1990, according to AEDENAT, the Spanish Association for the Defence of Nature, many of the projects in this plan were already being sacrificed in order to finance the building of the 1500 billion pesetas TAV. They claimed, for example, that a much-needed commuter line to the Madrid dormitory town of Alcalá de Henares had been suspended because of cost overruns on the TAV.

Spanish ecologists declared the Madrid-Seville route the greatest onslaught on the environment in Spain of current years. Apart from its impact on the Sierra Morena breeding ground, they claimed that the route had detrimental effects even before it arrived there. It passes through the only sizeable recreation park in the poor south of Madrid; it cuts through the country's

largest breeding ground for lesser kestrels on the outskirts of the capital; and it crosses the Toledo Hills, where ecologists fear that the noise of construction alone will have interfered with reproduction among the area's rare lynxes.

In early 1990, the Spanish Transport Ministry and the RENFE published the results of an impact study, the first to be carried out in Spain for a railway project. The study acknowledged that action was needed, and, in the light of its findings, the sum of four billion pesetas was being set aside to lessen the environmental damage. Ecologists maintained, however, that this was too little, too late, and that time would eventually prove them to have been justly concerned over the environmental effect of the line.

THE CHANNEL TUNNEL

All going according to plan, the Channel Tunnel will open for business in 1993, joining the British and Continental European rail networks. This major feat of engineering will provide Britain with a vital link with the emerging European high-speed train network, and will enlarge that network to embrace a nation of 55 million people.

The 50 km of railway line passing through the Tunnel will profoundly change the map of rail services in Europe. London will be 3 hours from Paris, 2½ hours from Brussels, and only one night away from Madrid, by train. Figure 3.3 shows the distances of major cities from the Channel Tunnel, and compares journey times from London to Paris using the Tunnel and using the other forms of transport currently available.

The design of the Tunnel

The Channel Tunnel will allow two different kinds of train to pass through: **shuttle trains** and **through trains**:

● Shuttle trains will operate between the British and French terminals at either end of the Tunnel itself, one near Folkestone in Kent and the other at Coquelles, near Calais. These will carry passenger vehicles and freight vehicles in two different kinds of specially-designed wagons. For tourism, it is the passenger wagons which are most important. These will carry cars and coaches, which will drive straight on to the

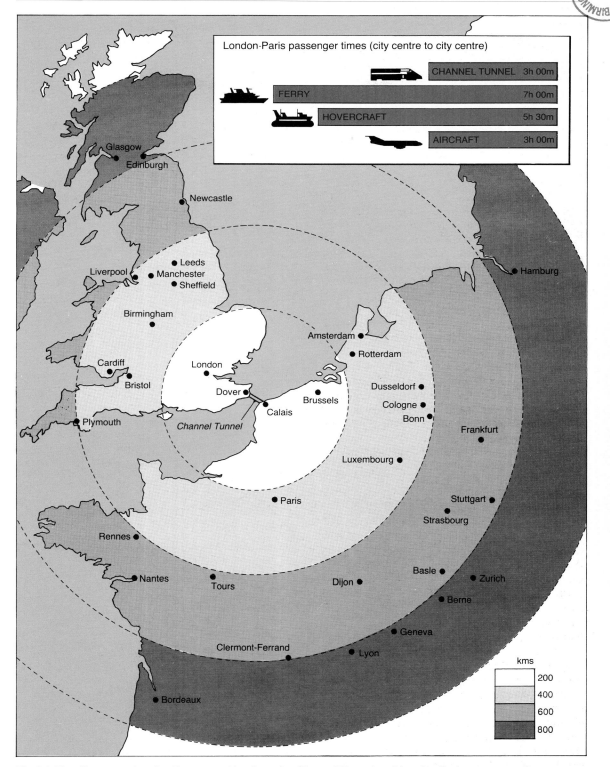

Fig 3.3 The distances of major European cities from the Channel Tunnel and London-Paris passenger times

shuttle trains, after paying at the terminal. There will be no need to book in advance. During the journey, passengers will stay in their vehicles, and at the destination terminal, cars and coaches will drive off the shuttles and out of the terminal area to continue their journey. According to Eurotunnel, the Anglo-French company constructing the Tunnel, passenger shuttles will depart approximately every 12 minutes at peak times, crossing from one terminal to another in about 35 minutes.

● Through trains – for passengers travelling without vehicles, and for freight – will be operated by British Rail and the SNCF between British, French and other destinations in Europe. Passengers will board these trains in one city and disembark in another city, having travelled through the Channel Tunnel. Hourly or more frequent through services are planned during the day between London and Paris and London and Brussels. It will be trains of this type which will link Britain and the Channel Tunnel with the enlarged European high-speed train network.

In total, in 1993, up to 200 trains per day are expected to pass in each direction through the Channel Tunnel, representing an average of one shuttle or through train every seven minutes.

The impact of the Tunnel

The impact of such a service on travel and tourism will be immense. British Rail estimates that within two years of the opening of the Tunnel, about 13 million passengers per year will be travelling on international trains between Britain and Continental Europe. The impact of this volume of traffic will not be confined only to London and the South-East of England; approximately 30 per cent of these passengers will come from, or will be travelling to, destinations beyond London.

Both the railway companies and Eurotunnel, the company which as well as constructing will also operate the Channel Tunnel, consider that the international passenger train services using the Tunnel will capture their market from existing services: those crossing the Channel by air, by rail and sea, and by coach or car and sea.

Figure 3.4 shows the volume of passengers crossing the Channel in 1986, the last year for which comprehensive data is available.

Fig 3.4 Volume of passengers crossing the Channel (1986)

		Passengers (million crossings)
By sea	by car	8.7
	by coach	6.1
	by foot	7.7
	Sub-total	22.5
By air		31.9
	Total	54.4

With the opening of the Tunnel, two new means of cross-Channel crossing will be available to travellers:

● by **rail** through the Channel Tunnel; and

● by **road vehicle** using the shuttles through the Channel Tunnel.

It is inevitable that the Tunnel will compete with both ferry and air travel. With the shuttle's daily capacity of up to 25 000 passenger cars, capacity on the Straits of Dover crossings to France will double in 1993.

A survey in 1988 by independent consultants made the following forecasts for the Channel Tunnel:

● It will divert virtually all the present rail-linked traffic in to the through trains.

● It will carry two-thirds of all car traffic between Britain and Continental Europe.

● It will capture over 80 per cent of current cross-Channel coach passengers: 50 per cent on coaches carried on the shuttles, and 30 per cent diverted to the through rail services.

● It will take three-quarters of the day-excursion traffic, in the form of coach tours.

Competition with the ferries

In the face of this impending competition, the ferry companies were, by the end of the 1980s, already preparing themselves by developing attractive new products for the market. In 1989, the principal companies, P&O European Ferries and Sealink British Ferries, introduced new ferries, larger and faster ships, with much more emphasis on comfort. For example, P&O introduced the 26 400 tonne, two 300-passenger and 650-car Pride of Dover and Pride of Calais

Fig 3.5 P&O's superferry, *Pride of Calais*

ferries. Plans were also being made to streamline operations to match Eurotunnel's, so that ticket purchase, check-in, loading and unloading would all happen much more rapidly. The companies were assisted in this by the port of Dover, which by 1990 had invested over £50 million in improvements to its own facilities, to improve efficiency. In marketing terms, the ferries' plan was to differentiate themselves, in image terms, from Eurotunnel, by emphasising the leisurely aspect of crossing the Channel in this way. The ferries of the 1990s, then, will incorporate attractions such as shopping facilities, cinemas, and children's play areas. Fares may also come down, particularly on routes where the new, larger-capacity ships are used.

These changes will not be confined to the short Dover or Folkestone to Calais routes. Even though the effect of the Channel Tunnel on ferry services outside the Dover and Folkestone area was relatively unknown by the end of the 1980s, all the ferry companies involved, such as Sally Line, Olau Line and Brittany Ferries, had followed a similar strategy of investing in new, larger ships with superior on-board passenger facilities and terminal improvements where necessary.

Competition with air services

The air services from Paris and Brussels to London have always been among the busiest in the world, with both British Airways and Air France carrying more passengers on the Paris to London route than any other airline. The 1988 survey by independent consultants forecast that about 16 per cent of all air passengers between Britain and Continental Europe would divert to the Channel Tunnel's through rail services, a total of 5·8 million passengers per year. However, as early as 1990, there were several reasons for concluding that by 1993 air services would be in a stronger position to compete with the trains:

● The Single European Act will be in force, deregulating fares, allowing free competition between carriers, and leading to the growth of charter flights.

● The Heathrow Express link to London's Paddington station will be in place, with a journey time of 16 minutes.

● There will be more routes into regional airports in Britain.

● Larger aircraft may be in use, increasing the total capacity on the market.

The high-speed trains through the Channel Tunnel will, therefore, come into operation at a time of strong competition between all forms of cross-Channel transport. In the short term, at least, the consumer is likely to benefit from this situation, as competitive pricing is likely. All the competing carriers will make massive efforts to secure more business, for example by running more intensive campaigns advertising short-breaks to a variety of destinations, including the major cities in the north of Europe. A rise in the amount of tourist activity in that region is certain.

CASE STUDY

THE CHANNEL TUNNEL'S EFFECT ON BRITAIN, FRANCE, BELGIUM AND THE NETHERLANDS

The vast majority of Tunnel travellers will be French, Belgian, Dutch, German or British. Anticipating a higher level of tourist activity between these countries in 1993 and beyond, the national tourist organisations of these countries began planning for the Tunnel's impact as soon as construction work began.

The **British Tourist Authority**, the organisation responsible for promoting Britain as a tourist destination, realised that the opening of the Tunnel would present Britain's tourist industry with a serious challenge. While providing a new gateway into Britain for tourists from France, Belgium, the Netherlands and Germany, the Tunnel would also make it much easier for British people to leave Britain to spend their holidays and short-breaks in Continental Europe. In terms of tourist numbers, it was feared that Britain might lose more through the Channel Tunnel than it gained.

The situation looked difficult. In 1988,

4.6 million visitors came to Britain from the following four countries:

France	1 756 000
Germany	1 599 000
Netherlands	769 000
Belgium	496 000

However, in the same year, 8.1 million British tourists travelled to these four countries – 76 per cent more than the 4.6 million who came to Britain from there. Northern Continental Europe was clearly more popular with the British than vice versa. Moreover, if holiday-taking trends continued, the BTA estimated that by the year 2000, 16 million Britons would be visiting France, Germany, the Netherlands and Belgium by the end of the century. Would the Channel Tunnel turn out to be a huge drain for British tourists, to the detriment of British domestic tourism, and to the benefit of these four countries listed above?

To prevent this from happening, the BTA in 1988 set itself the bold challenge of equalising the two-way tourism traffic between Britain and these four countries, by the year 2000: to attract as many tourists from France, Germany, the Netherlands and Belgium, as the British tourists visiting these countries.

An extensive marketing strategy was planned, using the BTA's offices in Paris, Frankfurt, Brussels and Amsterdam, to promote Britain as an attractive tourist destination and to increase the public's awareness of the Channel Tunnel. The strategy included the following action points:

● joint marketing schemes over a five-year period from 1991 to 1996 in conjunction with a wide range of carriers and interests including Eurotunnel and the national railways.

● promotional programmes to enhance awareness of alternative transport from Europe by ferries and airlines.

● an intensifying campaign, starting in 1988, to promote awareness of the Tunnel.

● a programme starting in 1990 to educate the Continental travel trade about the Tunnel, concentrating on through rail links, coach shuttle and car shuttle.

● a publicity and marketing campaign to exploit the Tunnel's novelty value for the 1993 to 1996 seasons.

By 1990, the marketing strategy was already being implemented, beginning with a market assessment of the four countries involved. The following extracts from the assessment give an indication of the steps to be taken by the BTA, in the run-up to the Channel Tunnel's opening:

There is still concern in **France** that we drive on the left, a reassurance campaign will be necessary to allay these fears. Although visitors travelling by car will represent a significant element of the market, the majority of French are still expected to travel independently either by air or by rail, particularly from the region around Paris and north of the capital.

In **Germany**, we shall concentrate on car-borne traffic. The Germans view the Tunnel symbolically as drawing Britain closer to Europe, and making this country a more easily accessible destination. Since a large proportion of Germans use their cars for their holidays, this will be an important market for development.

The **Dutch** market has shown a significant shift in the past few years from sea-borne to air-borne traffic. Being a maritime nation, ferries are popular, so it is possible that the Tunnel will not capture a significant share of that market in the early years.

The market should be strong in **Belgium**, particularly if a motorway link is built between the Belgian border and the Tunnel entrance. Prices will need to be competitive, since the Belgians are very cost-conscious.

Infrastructure and tourism developments

Tourists using the shuttle trains to transport themselves and their cars across the Channel will drive through the regions of Kent in Britain or the Nord Pas de Calais in France, on disembarking. The opening of the Channel Tunnel will, therefore, present both these regions with an excellent opportunity of receiving more tourists. By 1988, tourists were already being drawn to these areas to see for themselves the progress which was being made as the Channel Tunnel was drilled out from both sides of the Channel. At both the French and British ends of the Tunnel, special visitor reception and exhibition centres had been built to provide day-trippers with information on the project.

Both regions will hope to be more than simply the places which tourists drive through on their way to more distant destinations, and by the end of the 1980s, ambitious schemes to tempt tourists to spend time in Kent or the Nord Pas de Calais regions were already underway.

The French regard the Tunnel as an important generator of commercial growth in the Nord Pas de Calais, a relatively depressed area with higher than average levels of unemployment. Consequently, the development of the Tunnel inspired, in part, the formation of the Nord Pas de Calais Regional Plan, to make sure that the region gains the maximum benefit from the Tunnel. The framework of the Regional Plan includes points for development of the seaside resorts of Bray-Dunes/Zuydcoote. It calls for: improvement of urban infrastructure; accommodation, including the extension of camping and caravanning facilities; and an increase in the number of bed and breakfast places, a relatively new concept in France. Also planned are improvements to reception facilities for visitors, and tourism infrastructure such as the development of bridle paths, local signposting and a new Tourist Information Centre.

Further along the coast, attractions are being developed from industrial and naval heritage sites. One major project in Dunkirk includes redevelopment of the industrial wasteland surrounding the dockyard, to include a leisure complex and a marina. On the Calais coast, attractions are being enhanced: a lace museum is to open in a former lace factory building. The area around Fort Nieulay in Calais is to be expanded to include a footpath network and reception area; and Fort Risboin's sailing centre will be modernised and a 60-bed youth hostel added in time for the opening of the Tunnel.

A National Maritime Centre, developed as complementary to the Channel Tunnel, opened in Boulogne in 1990, comprising several exhibition rooms, a testing area for boats, a media centre and cafe, souvenir shop and shopping precinct.

While it is important to the inhabitants of the Nord Pas de Calais region that tourists spend some time there, it is also important that tourists are able to drive easily through the region if that is their intention. Therefore, much of the work in progress leading up to 1993 concerns road access. By the end of the 1980s, the A26 road between Reims and Calais had been completed, and the A1 Paris to Lille road was being widened from two lanes to three. The coast road from Calais to Le Havre was also being up-graded, and the A8 Brussels to Lille road was due for completion by 1993.

CONCLUSION

The transport links between European cities will become progressively improved, and choice for travellers extended, as Europe's high-speed train network is assembled over the years to come. The combination of this network and the opening of the Channel Tunnel will radically change patterns of tourist activity in Europe's north-west region, as travel between Britain and continental Europe is greatly facilitated.

The added competition presented by this network and the Channel Tunnel offers the opportunity of developing a more efficient, better value, system of intra-European travel, as other forms of transport respond imaginatively to these new challenges.

ASSIGNMENTS

1 Look back at the section on the EC's role in the high-speed train network.

(*a*) What reasons do you think Britain may have had for opposing the idea of a Transport Infrastructure Fund operated by the EC? What possible advantages to Britain might there be in such a fund?

(*b*) Both Charles de Gaulle and Roissy airports in Paris are to be served by the TGV network. What possible impact could this have on the volume of passengers using Heathrow and Gatwick airports in Britain and Schiphol airport in the Netherlands?

2 Re-read the case study on environmental considerations for the Spanish high-speed link.

(*a*) The next high-speed link planned by the Spanish government will run from Madrid to Barcelona. Ecologists claim that the potential environmental impact of this line would be even greater than that of the Madrid to Seville link. Conduct your own impact study of this project, highlighting the principal environmentally sensitive regions and making recommendations as to how these could be avoided.

(*b*) In 1988, while some towns were fighting to keep high-speed trains *off* their territory, a bitter battle raged between Lille and Amiens, each town determined to have the TGV Nord pass through them on its route between Paris and the entrance to the Channel Tunnel. Research the reasons for this, and find out how the issue was resolved.

3 Look back at the BTA's marketing strategy for the Channel Tunnel's impact on p 53 and answer the following questions.

(*a*) Suggest some companies as examples of:

- 'a wide range of carriers and interests'; and
- 'the Continental travel trade'

in the context of Britain's Channel Tunnel promotion.

(*b*) One of the British Tourist Authority's objectives is to encourage the growth of *off-season* holidays and short breaks in Britain. How will the Channel Tunnel help the BTA in this aim?

(*c*) In 1988, the BTA made a series of recommendations to the British government, concerning the Channel Tunnel. One was that Customs and Immigration controls should occur on the Channel Tunnel trains, and that sufficient manpower should be allocated to ensure maximum effectiveness and minimum delay.

Why was this recommendation made? What was the government's response?

4 Qualitative research was carried out in 1989 by the British Tourist Authority and Eurotunnel to discover the views of Continental leisure car travellers about a trip to Britain. Figure 3.6 gives an extract from the findings of the survey.

As the BTA marketing manager based in Frankfurt or Paris, you are running a publicity campaign to promote short-breaks to Britain for tourists using their own cars to drive through the Channel Tunnel.

Draft the advertising copy for a one-page advertisement to appear in a German or French magazine. The advertisement should aim to emphasise the convenience of travelling to Britain in this way, while still preserving the 'exotic appeal' of Britain as somewhere slightly 'different'.

Write the copy in a language other than your own, if possible.

Perceptions of a Trip to Britain

The Channel is currently a physical and psychological barrier to Continental leisure car travellers as "with the sea there is a gap". The sea crossing is often perceived to be long, arduous and something that requires careful organisation by tourists considering a short or spontaneous cross-border trip. Therefore, "you do not go to Britain as to other European countries" as the journey is "very long and you have to wait" and "if you do not book, you cannot cross".

However, amongst people who have visited Britain before and those planning a longer trip, the sea crossing is considered as a pleasurable aspect of a trip to Britain.

Many Continental Europeans with experience of visiting Britain view it as an exotic short-haul destination – a concept which is reinforced by the need to cross the sea. This adds a quality of mystery and adventure which is not experienced by simply crossing a land frontier. This "exotic" appeal of Britain appears to be a unique feature amongst European destinations and one which we must protect after 1993. At present, tourists are attracted by a different culture which includes our heritage, bed and breakfast – particularly the hearty breakfast – and our pubs. Those who have not visited Britain may find the exotic appeal a negative factor and may therefore not wish to visit.

After the Tunnel opens, there is some concern amongst Continentals that Britain will lose its identity and become similar to mainland Europe as it will be "so easy to go there, you will not have the impression of being there".

Fig 3.6 (*Source: British Tourist Authority*)

5 Conduct your own research into the infrastructural developments taking place in Kent, in preparation for the Tunnel's opening. Collect evidence of the type given above for the Nord Pas de Calais, including new tourist attractions, accommodation, and access roads.

Are there any contrasts you can draw between Kent and the Nord Pas de Calais?

C H A P T E R 4

NEW TRENDS IN ACCOMMODATION

Europe's varied supply of accommodation plays a vital part in attracting visitors from other parts of the world, as well as encouraging Europeans themselves to travel around their own continent.

During the 1980s, the accommodation sector responded imaginatively to the changing patterns of tourism and leisure operating in Europe, resulting in the development of exciting new products for emerging markets set to continue expanding in the years ahead.

This chapter examines:
- Trends in hotel accommodation
- The growth of budget hotels in Europe
- The short break market
- All-weather holiday centres

HOTELS IN EUROPE

The importance of hotels as a form of holiday accommodation is shown in the results of the survey, *Europeans and their Holidays*. For main holidays and other holidays taken, the question, 'What sort of accommodation did you stay in?' was asked. The answers are shown in Fig 4.1.

For most EC countries, hotels are the form of accommodation most often chosen for holidays. Germany and Luxembourg show the largest percentage of holidaymakers staying at hotels, while for the French, Spanish and Portuguese, the most common holiday accommodation option is staying with relations of friends, going back to their family roots. For the Dutch, camping and caravanning holidays lie just ahead of those spent in hotel accommodation.

If the general EC average for using hotels as holiday accommodation is around one in three (32 per cent), the figures for those using hotels for travel outside their own countries are much higher. Figure 4.1 shows that on average, the further away the holidays taken the greater percentage of holidaymakers staying at hotels. For intra-EC European travel, the figure is closer

to one in two, at 44 per cent, while for travel outside the EC the use of hotels is even greater. The distribution of hotel accommodation throughout the EC countries is shown in Fig 4.2. Europe's supply of hotels is divided between individually owned hotels, which are often

Fig 4.2 Distribution of hotel accommodation in EC Countries

Country		No of hotels Total	Bed capacity (Hotels and similar estab.)	Bed capacity %
B	Belgium	2175	89137	1.4
DK	Denmark	941	79004	1.2
D	Germany	18642	1127884	17.2
E	Spain	4410	1034621	15.8
GR	Greece	3728	375367	5.7
F	France	20136	1042100	15.9
IRL	Ireland	664	/	
I	Italy	38717	1700000	26.0
L	Luxembourg	234	/	
NL	Netherlands	1923	114011	1.7
P	Portugal	320	135549	2.1
UK	United Kingdom	34094	850716	13.0
Total		125750	6548389	100.0

Source: Eurostat, Europe in Figures, Edition 1989/90 and WTO)

Fig 4.1 Accommodation arrangements

(a) Hotel
(b) Rented villa/bungalow/chalet etc
(c) Own weekend home or holiday cottage etc
(d) Staying with relations or friends
(e) Staying as paying guest in private house
(f) Camping/caravanning
(g) Holiday village
(h) Youth hostel, boat/cruise, other

	(a)%	(b)%	(c)%	(d)%	(e)%	(f)%	(g)%	(h)%
Belgium	30	21	2	16	3	17	5	4
Denmark	26	10	10	23	1	18	1	11
Germany	43	17	5	12	10	10	1	3
Greece	38	2	15	19	22	8	—	1
Spain	21	13	14	32	5	13		4
France	19	17	7	33	2	22	4	2
Ireland	33	18	3	30	6	9	1	3
Italy	33	17	11	21	7	12	1	2
Luxembourg	53	20	7	9	—	10	2	4
Netherlands	30	16	12	8	1	31	—	6
Portugal	13	16	9	42	5	19	—	3
United Kingdom	36	19	2	19	1	19	2	5
EC average	32	17	7	21	5	16	2	4
By type of location								
Seaside	23	20	7	15	4	21	3	3
Mountains	41	18	6	15	6	14	2	5
Other	22	9	8	42	6	9	1	3
By destination								
Own country	23	17	9	26	5	16	2	3
Other country	44	18	5	11	4	18	1	4
Non-EC Europe	54	15	3	8	6	11	3	5
Outside Europe	55	6	—	26	6	8	5	9

(1) Multiple answers bring the total to more than 100

family-run businesses, and chain-affiliated hotels – belonging to a hotel chain or group, often operating on an international basis. The distribution of chain-affiliated hotels throughout the EC is very uneven from country to country. Chain hotels account for a relatively high proportion of the total hotel capacity of certain countries, such as Belgium, where their market share is 66.3 per cent, France (20.3 per cent) and Spain (18.5 per cent). By contrast, in countries where individually owned hotels predominate, chains account for a much lower proportion of the total: Denmark (5.1 per cent), Greece (5.4 per cent), and Portugal (7.4 per cent). In the EC as a whole, hotel chains account for 22.5 per cent of the total market.
(Source: Eurostat and OECD, 1988).

However, not all hotel chains operating in Europe are European in origin. In the past, the European market has been targeted by American hotels chains, and, increasingly, the Japanese. The table in Fig 4.3 shows the top 20 chains operating in Europe, ranked according to their 1988 annual turnover.

Despite the strong presence of the British and the French in particular, the penetration of the European market by American chains is clearly visible. This trend towards a significant non-European presence in the European hotel market is bound to accelerate as the advent of the Single Market streamlines business practices across the continent, making it even more attractive to hotel chain developers in other

Fig 4.3 Top 20 hotel chains operating in Europe

Chain Brands/country of origin	Total no: Hotels	Rooms
1 Accor Novotel, Sofitel, Mercure, Ibis, Urbis, Formule 1, Hotelia France	598	63315
2 Groupe Sol Melia Hoteles, Sol Hoteles Spain	133	34181
3 Bass Crest Hotels, Holiday Inn GB	151	26987
4 Trusthouse Forte Little Chef, Travelodge, Viscount, Excelsior, Forte Hotels, Post House, etc. GB	254	27500
5 Groupe Taittinger Campanile, Concorde France	202	14468
6 Seibu Inter-Continental, Forum USA	41	16177
7 Steigenberger Germany	31	5266
8 Ciga Hotels Italy	40	5185
9 ITT Sheraton USA	18	12024
10 Groupe Wagons-lits Pullman, Altéa, PLM Azur, Arcade, Primo 99 (et associés) FR/Belgium	148	18490
11 Queens Moat Houses Queens Moat Houses GB	123	12500
12 Marriott Marriott Hotels/Resorts, Marriotts Suites, Residence Inn by Marriott, Courtyard by Marriott, Fairfield Inn by Marriott USA	6	5290
13 Rank Organisation Rank Hotels GB	7	2348
14 Center Parcs Netherlands	12	21070
15 Scottish and Newcastle Thistle GB	33	4212
16 Air France Méridien France	11	4212
17 Mount Charlotte GB	68	9150

18	**Hoteles Unidos-Husa** Spain	120	20500
19	**Ladbroke** Langham Hotels, Hilton Int GB	62	18000
20	**Ital Jolly** Italy	34	5642

Source: Neo Magazine April 1989

parts of the world. Already, many of the larger hotel chains, realising the potential inherent in the European market, have initiated pan-European expansion programmes, and spearheaded them by taking their head office operations into Europe. Examples of this include Inter-Continental Hotels which transferred all operations to Britain, and Holiday Inns which moved to Brussels. Japanese investors have also become very active, with companies such as Aoki Westin attempting to buy the Swissotel group, and the Adachi Enterprise group joining forces with Marriott to undertake an expansion programme in Europe.
(Source: Pannell Kerr Forster Associates, Eurotrends 1990).

TRENDS IN HOTEL ACCOMMODATION

The two trends which dominated the European hotel industry during the 1980s look set to continue, and accelerate, during the 1990s. Product segmentation and polarisation are the two (related) trends which have characterised much of the activity in the accommodation sector over the past decade, thus changing the face of the hotel industry in Europe, and beyond.

Product segmentation

The use of product segmentation in a field of commercial activity means that the producer deliberately gears products to very specific and separate markets, resulting in a range of clearly identifiable, branded, products designed for clearly identifiable and specific markets.

In terms of the hotel sector, product segmentation involves designing the entire product (the hotel) in such a way that it responds to the needs of a very specific clientele. These needs may be in terms of price, location, level of provision of facilities and services, standard of luxury, and so on. Hotel groups most often use product segmentation to carve out and expand for themselves market niches which can be easily and identifiably targeted for marketing purposes.

Large hotel groups can use this technique as a way of differentiating their various products for the client, by giving each product a very clearly specified pricing and facility provision. The ACCOR group, for example, has several clearly differentiated brands of hotels:

● **Sofitel** luxury hotels, aimed at the international business traveller in search of a sophisticated atmosphere, at the same time personal and relaxed.

● **Novotel** mid-range, comfortable, city-based hotels, mainly for business travellers during the week and, increasingly, a family clientele at the weekend.

● **Mercure** hotels' speciality is their diversity. Hardly resembling a chain at all, they all differ as to their architecture, surroundings, and decoration. All very individual in character, they appeal to clients who like a warm, personal service.

● **Ibis-Urbis** budget hotels, offering a simple formula of accommodation and basic catering at a very reasonable price.

● **Formule 1** basic hotels providing basic but comfortable accommodation and minimum catering, at very low tariffs.

● **Hotelia** semi-residential hotels with medical facilities, designed for senior citizens.

This kind of segmentation of the hotel product is an effective method for hotel companies to maintain or expand their market share, and even, in some cases, to create new markets. The market response to product segmentation in the hotel field as a whole has been very positive, with brand loyalty becoming an increasingly important factor in clients' choice of hotel. Product segmentation also makes possible **market segmentation** – a selective (and, therefore, more economic) marketing strategy involving the promotion and distribution of the product to the clearly defined group of potential customers for whom that product (in this case a hotel) was designed. Once established, the market image of a particular brand or chain of hotels helps increase consumer awareness, making it easier and more economical to market to the clientele for which it is intended.

Polarisation

In most European countries during the 1980s, there was a degree of polarisation in their hotel businesses, as most activity and development focused on the extreme ends of the hotel spectrum – the **luxury** sector and the **budget** sector. It is at these extremes that product segmentation works best, since the market for each can be clearly delineated, and easily recognisable standards applied rigorously. Some of the most exciting and innovative developments of the 1980s took place in these two sectors.

The luxury sector was extended as hotels increasingly sought to cater for the needs of the business traveller and leisure travellers – in particular the over-50s, a group with a growing amount of disposable income, in Western Europe in particular. Weekend breaks in luxury country house hotels were among the fastest growing areas of the British hotel industry for example.

Refurbishment has played an important part in the tendency towards polarisation, as mid-range hotels have increasingly upgraded their facilities and services, installing sports facilities, en-suite bathrooms, and 'extras' such as refrigerated mini-bars, video televisions and trouser presses. The motivation behind such improvements was often the possibility of attracting more business tourists, the more demanding holidaymaker and clients on weekend breaks. In this way, a substantial proportion of Europe's supply of independent and chain-affiliated hotels moved up, out of the mid-priced range.

This phenomenon helped the growth of the budget sector which in many ways filled the price-gap caused by the refurbishment and upgrading of mid-price hotels. At this end of the spectrum, especially in continental Europe, new, basic but clean and comfortable hotels were operating at tariff levels easily within the reach of most budgets. In budget hotels, it is possible for parents and two children to be accommodated in a room with a private bathroom, colour television and tea and coffee-making equipment, for less than £25 a night. This development represents little short of a revolution in the European hotel business.

BUDGET HOTELS

Also known as 'economy hotels' or 'lodges', budget hotels have been defined as:
'limited service lodging establishments offering the benefit of good value for money in standardised, modern accommodation.' Their aim is to provide good quality, low-priced accommodation, for leisure and business tourists who are looking for guaranteed standards at affordable prices.

Before the arrival of budget hotels, 'affordable' prices were to be found most commonly in the kind of two-star hotels which were usually individually owned and family-run, as opposed to being part of a known hotel chain. But, even with the benefit of hotel classification, standards of comfort, cleanliness, catering and value for money in these hotels varied enormously. Consequently, for potential guests considering booking this type of accommodation, there was always the risk that the product would be disappointing and unsatisfactory. On the other hand, those customers seeing the security of guaranteed standards of quality were obliged to use the more expensive three- or four-star hotels belonging to the recognised chains.

Budget hotels have the marked advantage of being able to offer both guaranteed standards and attractive prices. Quality in budget hotels is usually as good as that found in three- or four-star hotels, but tariffs are much lower. The guest receives the essential elements of the hospitality industry – accommodation, food and drink – in simple, modern surroundings which are comfortable but without the 'frills' and extras found in more expensive hotels, such as video televisions in the bedrooms, extensive 'à la carte' menus in the restaurants, and a high staff to guest ratio, for example.

Distribution in Europe

In Europe, the French dominate the budget hotel market, with their broader and longer experience of this sector. Several factors have favoured the fast growth of budget hotels in France:

● The French have long summer holidays during which there is an exodus along major road routes from the north to the south of the country. France also attracts car-borne holidaymakers across its boundary frontiers with Germany, Spain, Italy, Belgium, and Switzerland, and also from Britain. This expands the market base for the budget hotel product.

● The majority of the French population remains within their own country and many take budget holidays.

● The French are also more committed to spending their money on food and drink, and prefer to spend rather less on accommodation.

● In contrast to Britain, the French budget chains have benefitted from reduced land rents, low construction costs, and easy availability of good development sites.

(Economist Intelligence Unit, Travel & Tourism Analyst)

In France, budget hotels are recognised as the fastest growing sector of the market, already representing around five per cent of the total room stock, with brands such as Campanile, Arcade, Ibis, Urbis, Formule 1, Balladins, Fastotel and Lune Etoile becoming increasingly common names in French towns and beside motorways. The success of these brands has encouraged the hotel groups to expand into neighbouring countries. For example, out of 25 new Ibis/Urbis openings in 1989, 15 were in France, and the rest abroad, in countries including Germany (Nuremberg), Britain (London) and Switzerland.

Not content to leave the entire budget hotel market to the French, hotel groups based in other European countries, however, have begun to develop their own budget products, such as Little Chef Lodges, owned by Trusthouse Forte, or Italy's MotelAgip chain.

Economy measures

What enables budget hotels to offer such competitive tariffs and still make a profit? Writing on this topic in *Leisure Management*, the Surrey University lecturers, D Gilbert and L Arnold give the following reasons:

The various economies they make, in construction and operating methods, create savings, the benefits of which are passed on to the customer in the form of lower tariffs:

1 Savings in construction costs. Within each budget hotel chain, there are great similarities to be found between all of the hotels in that chain. A very high degree of **standardisation** means that economies can be made through the use of mass construction, with much prefabrication taking place away from the actual building site. The emphasis is placed on the building of the bedroom accommodation, as opposed to lavish public areas. Budget hotel rooms, themselves, as well as being simply designed and furnished, are usually highly standardised, meaning that cost savings can be achieved through bulk-buying of fixtures, fittings and furniture. Finally, many budget hotels are built on out-of-town sites in industrial estates or beside motorways, where land is cheaper.

2 Savings in operating costs. Staffing in budget hotels is kept to a minimum, through the use of simplified procedures for the checking-in and out of guests, housekeeping, and catering. There is extensive use of automation; for example, guests programme the alarm in their rooms for early morning calls, instead of requesting this service from a member of staff. Buffet breakfasts are widely used, and standardised menus further restrict the need for large numbers of catering staff.

The market for budget hotels

The market for budget hotels includes, but is not restricted to, people on limited budgets for accommodation. Families, retired people, self-employed business travellers, touring sports teams, and young travellers make up a large proportion of the market. Many people in these categories represent the hitherto untapped market of those who, because of financial restraints, would not usually stay in hotels, but would use some other form of accommodation such as bed and breakfasts, youth hostels or friends' and relatives' homes.

Budget hotels in Europe have already succeeded, therefore, in introducing new sectors of the population to the regular use of hotel accommodation. With still only about ten per cent of the population of most European countries regularly using hotels, there is clearly great potential for encouraging more tourists to use this form of accommodation.

The marketing emphasis of most budget hotel chains is placed largely on their convenience, consistency, and value-for-money. By using a promotion strategy emphasising consistency in standards and value, an appeal is made to those seeking familiarity and risk-reduction, as opposed to the gamble of booking a room in an unknown, individually owned two-star hotel. As consumers become more used to the security of using standardised leisure products (such as fast-food establishments, for example) budget hotels look set to benefit from the kind of brand loyalty which often accompanies this trend.

The impact of budget hotels in Europe

The budget hotel is a new product with an appeal to a much broader market than the clientele of traditional hotels. They provide for a new market, and as such have an educational role to play, introducing new sections of the population to the 'hotel habit'. It is probable that the hotel industry as a whole will eventually benefit from this enlarged client pool. However, more immediately, the emergence of this dynamic new sector will necessarily present a challenge to existing 'traditional' hotels in Europe. As their numbers grow, budget hotels will increasingly exert pressure on mid-priced hotels, especially those in the two- and three-star categories, which are neither cheap nor particularly luxurious. Many such hotels are old, poorly sited, and with a long history of under-investment. How will the traditional hotel sector cope with this new competition? In Fig 4.4, the opinion of one man, the British Chairman of the Best Western hotel chain is given.

In general, the tourism industry in Europe stands to benefit from the development of this new accommodation sector. Tourist activity depends on the availability of affordable accommodation, and the emergence of budget hotels can only act as an incentive to more people to travel more often. This applies as much to tourists from other continents coming to Europe as it does to intra-

European tourism. The growing stock of budget accommodation in Europe will inevitably make a holiday in this continent more attractive to cost-conscious leisure travellers from other parts of the world.

Future prospects

Several characteristics of budget hotels appear to ensure their continuing expansion in Europe during the 1990s.

● They are well-placed to benefit from the increasing popularity of short-breaks in Europe. For a holiday lasting only three or four days, the fact that the rooms are small and furnished in a basic manner is not so important to the client.

● Their lower construction costs mean that budget chains are more likely to grow, since the lower investment means a reduced business risk. Chains are more likely to take a chance on building a budget hotel on a particular site, when, with modest construction costs, the stakes are lower.

● As Eastern Europeans travel increasingly within their own countries and into other parts of the continent, they will discover that the budget hotel product suits their requirements for low-cost accommodation.

CASE STUDY

FORMULE 1 BUDGET HOTELS

A notable pioneer in the budget hotel business in Europe is the Accor group, who, through their subsidiary, Hotec, have developed a network of basic, modern and convenient hotels under the trade mark 'Formule 1'. Accor now has over 200 units in Europe. Most of these hotels are situated in France, but 1989 saw the start of a European breakthrough, when two hotels were opened in Belgium. Since then, Formule 1 hotels have opened in Britain, Germany, and the Netherlands.

Formule 1 tariffs are among the lowest in Europe, originally set at 110FF per room, for one, two or three people, when Accor launched the chain in 1988. (In 1991, the price per room was raised to 130FF.) In order to offer rooms at this price, which were exceptionally low, even by budget hotel standards, the entire Formule

Budget — or quality?

WITHOUT a doubt, budget hotels are expanding at such an enormous rate that they are bound to cause some concern to the established hotel market. However, there are a number of factors which perhaps should be taken into account before we all start to panic and go into liquidation.

Firstly we have to consider what one means by "budget hotels". On the whole these are purpose built hotels, built to a price and specification, and in a location which has a very high passing trade. Budget hotels offer tariffs which are seen to be competitive against more traditional hotels and are usually in the £20-£30 bracket.

James Bowie, national chairman of Best Western Hotels, tackles the question

tion, use hotels at present. Only about 10 per cent of the population regularly use hotels (i.e. once or more a year) and only some 25 per cent of the population have ever used a hotel.

So there is obviously a huge market of people who have never, or do not consider using hotels at all.

While, without doubt, budget hotels will put pressure on the traditional hotel industry it may well offer hotel accommodation at what one might term "entry level", to a large portion of the population who do not at present consider hotels at all.

Expansion

However they may be as low as £12 according to the French hotel chain "Accor", or as high as £35 in some situations. The important thing to note is they are designed to cater for a one night passing traveller.

The great expansion of budget hotels has occurred most notably in perhaps France and USA. The growth of the budget hotels in the USA has been considerably assisted by very generous government tax allowances towards capital building.

This has meant that the USA has a massive overbuilding problem in all sectors of the hotel industry, not least the budget chains.

In Frvance, again a country where road distances are much greater than our own in the UK, budget hotels have

sprouted up on new motorways and new trunk roads. These hotels are, on the whole, much more compact and much more "budget", in design of style than perhaps their American equivalent.

In the UK, the great growth of budget hotels has definitely been motorway locations and out of town trunk road locations, where convenience to the passing traveller is the most important factor.

Progressive

However, the history of hotel keeping in these three countries is somewhat different in that, in the UK, there has been investment in hotel development throughout the country consistently over the last 25 years and indeed it is fair to say that British hotel companies are among the most progressive in the world.

France on the other hand would not

have seemed to develop their traditional industry in the way the UK has and while there is a considerable amount of good quality one and two star accommodation in the towns, it is neither corporately owned or marketed in any aggressive way, and tends to be very much the family run business. The USA, on the other hand, has a huge heavily developed hotel industry across all sectors where the pressure to achieve occupancy has kept rates artificially low. This meant that the "budget chains" have been hard pressed because the middle market is offering ratres only just above budget rate but with better amenities.

Remarkable

So what of the future in the UK? First of all, it must be remembered what a remarkably small number of people, as a percentage of the popula-

Pressure

Certainly the middle market under pressure will be forced to decide where their standards must be set. The public who may start to use hotels will expect a lot more for their money when moving to the mid-market and up-market hotels and so the pressure will be on hotels in the mid-market and up-market bracket to offer a more sophisticated, more comfortable environment but above all much better service.

While budget hotels will have an effect on the market place, quality hotels offering quality service with a smile and obvious client loving care, with good marketing and aggressive selling should not see budget hotels as a threat, but as an opportunity to expand the hotel buying public.

Those quality hotels with personal service and a welcoming attitude are the sort of hotels that Best Western in Europe is offering and will continue to offer.

Fig 4.4 (*Source: Travel GBI*)

1 concept called for great innovation on many fronts: in the construction and maintenance methods, in the approach to the hotel market, and in the services it provides for guests.

Construction and maintenance techniques

In order to offer Formule 1 rooms at 110FF per night, it was necessary to construct each room at a price *less than half* that of constructing the average two-star hotel bedroom. This was the challenge which Accor put to construction companies, most of whom said that this simply could not be done. Finally, three different companies using three different techniques were chosen for the ingenuity of their designs. These

three basic designs are still those in use today. The feature they all have in common is off-site **prefabrication**. Standard bedrooms are constructed off-site, delivered complete with carpet, furniture, plumbing and electrical fittings, and finally assembled very quickly at the site. The finished product is shown in Fig 4.5.

The rooms are all identical and have all the same contents:

- a double bed
- a single bed
- a washhand basin with mixer tap
- a small table
- a desk and chair
- a wardrobe and luggage rack
- a colour television with built-in alarm clock.

Fig. 4.5 One of the Formule 1 hotels developed by the Accor group © David Lefranc

The construction and assembly process for these rooms means that all the furniture and fittings are fixed to the walls and floor as an integral part of the structure. This feature has additional cost-saving consequences: since there is no need to move furniture around in order to clean the room, six such rooms can be cleaned in one hour, as opposed to the two and a half rooms which can be cleaned in the same time in a traditional hotel.

Despite their highly functional nature, Formule 1 rooms are also extremely attractively designed, comfortable and well sound-proofed. The fittings and furniture, although simple in design, are of a high quality and very robust.

There are no private facilities (i.e. showers and toilets) in the bedrooms – with the one exception of Formule 1 hotels in Germany, where the market is such that private facilities are essential. Elsewhere in Europe, Formule 1 hotels offer shared facilities, with one shower and one toilet for every four bedrooms. The advanced maintenance techniques employed in connection with the showers and toilets mean that they are cleaned automatically after each time they are used. A powerful spray of a water/disinfectant mix ensures that the facilities are kept clean and hygenic for the next user.

Operating and management methods

Formule 1's strategy is to develop as a network of concessions. Therefore, each Formule 1 hotel is operated as a separate company by its owners. Most hotels are owned and managed by young couples, who themselves undertake the vast majority of the tasks involved in running the hotel and the business side of the subsidiary. They man the reception desk between 6.30am and 10.00am, and between 5.00pm and 10.00pm. Outside these hours, the front door of the hotel is locked and there is no staffed reception. Guests arriving during these periods gain access to the hotel and their rooms by using the hotel's automatic vending machine, situated beside the front door. Using their credit cards, guests reserve and pay for their room, and are given a receipt by the vending machine. No keys are issued, even when the reception desk is manned. Instead, the guest's receipt for payment, issued either by the receptionist or by the vending machine, contains a number which, when tapped into the keyboard panel beside the front door to the hotel or the bedroom door, causes the doors to open automatically. In the absence of keys to be issued and collected, the guests can come and go freely, without having to meet a receptionist.

This system of access into the hotel was chosen as the most economic way of keeping staff costs down, as it allows Formule 1 hotels to function without a round-the-clock receptionist and night-porter. It means that these hotels can be manned by two people, as opposed to a staff of six, who would be required in a traditionally staffed hotel of comparable size. Otherwise, the cost of these employees' salaries would have had to been added to the price of the rooms.

Catering in Formule 1 hotels is limited to breakfast, which is offered on a self-service basis. This is a 'continental' breakfast of bread, butter and jam, with hot drinks, taken in a small dining area close to the reception desk. Guests requiring food or drink at other times have the choice of eating in a nearby restaurant (Formule 1 hotels are always placed close to a restaurant or at least an outlet selling take-away food), or using the automatic vending machines in the hotel, for snacks and drinks.

Formule 1 hotels are open 365 days a year. If the owner/managers want to take a break or a holiday away from the hotel, they have to recruit – and pay – another couple to act as relief for them during their absence. There are a number of couples who instead of having their own hotel move around, standing in for others in this way.

Staff training

Despite the low cost of its rooms, the Formule 1 chain of hotels is by no means synonomous with low standards of service. Rigorous staff training is the company's key to high quality service, since, with so much responsibility being concentrated in the hands of the couple who run each hotel, it is vital that their skills and knowledge are first class.

In 1990, Formule 1 spent six million FF on staff training – about 2½ per cent of their annual turnover – an exceptionally high percentage for any company. Over 200 people followed the intensive training programme, which in the space of four weeks gives each couple the practical and theoretical skills they need to manage a Formule 1 hotel: marketing, management, maintenance, reception, etc. After this initial four-week training period, the managers spend between one week and four weeks working under supervision in a Formule 1 hotel finally t bring their skills up to the standard required to run a hotel independently.

Analysis of the Formule 1 market

The market at which these hotels is aimed is, for the main part, a totally new one, but with great scope for development. The idea from the outset was to appeal to people who use hotels either rarely or never.

Formule 1 hotels are aimed at the short or medium-length stay market. This market is essentially composed of a number of specific groups – commercial travellers, sales representatives, travelling workmen and supervisors, lorry drivers, sports groups, people attending conferences, and those on touring holidays.

A recent survey showed that, of all Formule 1 hotel guests:

- 76 per cent were men
- 58 per cent were between the ages of 26 and 34 years
- 61 per cent were travelling for work-related purposes
- 63 per cent habitually spent one night or more per week in a hotel
- 42 per cent had chosen Formule 1 because of personal recommendation
- 74 per cent had chosen Formule 1 because of the price.

There was unanimous agreement that these hotels offered excellent value-for-money. Their cleanliness, the quality of the reception, and the signs to help guests find their way around inside the hotels were also seen very positively. On the other hand, there were criticisms of the road signposting which guides guests to the hotels. This was felt to be insufficient, making certain hotels difficult to find.

Pricing policy

As the least expensive of all hotel chains in Europe, Formule 1 is proud to display its tariffs, not only in the rooms themselves and at the reception desk, but in figures two metres high on signs just outside the hotels, where they can be seen from nearby roads and motorways. This novel way of communicating with potential customers has begun to be tentatively copied by other budget hotels, even though their tariffs are inevitably higher.

Formule 1 also like to point out that their tariffs apply to all hotels in the one country, and that there is no supplement for a second or third person in the room, or for the television.

Formule 1 expansion

Since 1988, a new Formule 1 hotel has opened every week in France. Now with over 200 units, in France and in other European countries, the chain is well on its way to achieving its basic objective which is to have 1000 hotels in operation by the year 2000. To reach this target, the chain aims to have a presence in all European towns of over 30000 inhabitants. If reached, this will give Formule 1 a ten per cent share of the market for budget hotels and other hotels at a comparable price level.

The extent of the chain's success can be seen, not only in their rate of development, but in their occupancy rate. In a recent year, this reached 74 per cent, even though many of the hotels included had not been open for the whole 12 months of the survey.

Finally, as a variation on their theme, the chain has collaborated with the petrol company, ELF France, to construct a network of 'hotel/service stations'. Under this formula, the managing couple not only runs the hotel of 32 or 50 bedrooms, but also manages the service station on the same site. Fifty such units are planned, and the first opened in the Vosges region of France in July 1989.

Problems ahead?

Could Formule 1 be a victim of its own success? Already, a number of imitators have sprung up, operating along similar lines, but with slightly higher tariffs. The higher tariffs are usually justified by the addition of features not offered in Formule 1 hotels, such as telephones in the bedrooms, en-suite facilities, and so on. There is the strong possibility that a significant part of the budget hotel market will 'trade up', opting not necessarily for the cheapest product but, instead for a 'basic plus extras' formula.

The distinctive hi-tech design of Formule 1 hotels, with their bold use of geometrical forms and features in primary colours, looks up-to-date and fresh now. However, in the future as architectural styles change, there is the possibility that they will come to look old-fashioned and dated – are the construction techniques flexible enough to evolve with changing tastes in design?

THE SHORT BREAK MARKET

A short break is normally defined as a stay away from home for leisure/tourism-related purposes lasting one, two or three nights. For a number of years now, the number of short breaks taken in Europe has continued to rise, while the average length of holidays has fallen. The emerging trend is one of shorter holidays, taken more often, and further away.

Several socio-economic factors have produced this trend, which is fully expected to continue during the years ahead. Speaking at a conference organised by the French consultants, BIPE Conseil in 1989, Françoise Poitier of INRETS mentioned the following factors:

- Europeans have seen increases in the numbers of paid holidays allocated to them, numbers already high by comparison with the Americans or the Japanese, for example. The practice of adding single days to weekends in order to take a long weekend break away from home is becoming increasingly widespread.

- The amount of discretionary income available for spending on travel and leisure has, on average, risen in most European countries during the past decade.

- Transport infrastructures are advancing rapidly, making it easier and faster to travel around within Europe. High-speed trains, the Channel Tunnel, and better roads through the Alpine and Pyrenean mountain ranges are examples.

Despite the economic importance of the short break market, its importance has only recently been recognised by the tourism industry as a whole, notably by:

● Ministries of Tourism and local authorities alerted to this general trend and keen to benefit from it

● Tour operators eager to make sales during the low season

● Airline companies and hoteliers attracted by the possibility of attracting extra clients, particularly at the weekends, when they cannot rely on custom from business tourists.

Accor, Europe's biggest hotel group illustrates this last point well. The occupancy rate in the European hotels during the week is around 90 per cent, but it falls to between 40–45 per cent during the weekend.

Statistics covering the short break market in Europe as a whole are scarce due to the recent nature of interest in this phenomenon; but the rise in popularity of the short break has been well charted by individual European countries. The examples which follow underline the importance of this expanding market.

Figures supplied by the **German** tourism analysts, Studienkreis für Tourismus, show that the percentage of the West German population taking one or more short breaks has risen from 20 per cent in 1975, to 25.7 per cent in 1980, and to 34.1 per cent in 1987. This accounts for a total of 16½ million people taking over 40 million short breaks. Showing the predominantly *domestic* nature of this form of tourism in certain countries, around 75 per cent of the short break destinations were in West Germany. Austria and France represent the leading foreign destinations for short breaks taken by Germans.

A similar picture is presented by the **Dutch** tourism office, the NRIT, whose figures suggest a 73 per cent growth rate in the proportion of the population of the Netherlands taking a short break, between 1981 and 1989. The proportion rose from 18 per cent of the population in 1981 to 29 per cent in 1988 to 31 per cent in 1989. In 1989, 4.2 million people took a total of around ten million short breaks.

According to the **Belgian** national tourism office, 18.5 per cent of the Belgian population took a short break in 1988, representing 26.3 per cent of all holidays taken away from home. Most of the short breaks were taken in Belgium (63.1 per cent), and most were taken during the summer months. France was the principal foreign short break destination, with 14.4 per cent of the total, followed by Germany (8.4 per cent) and the Netherlands (6.2 per cent).

With their many public holidays and their long-established habit of having short breaks away from home, the **French** are the European leaders in terms of the number of short breaks taken every year. INSEE (the French national institute of economic and statistical information) figures for 1989 show that 152 million short breaks were taken by French people that year – an average of 2.8 short breaks per head of population. The tendency is highly domestic, with a least 50 per cent of the population, from more than half the regions of France taking short breaks in the regions in which they live. The INSEE figures also provide some interesting insights into the make-up of this market. Its research showed that:

● the more heavily urbanised the place of permanent residence, the more likely the inhabitants were to take a short break. Rural inhabitants took least short breaks while Parisians and those living in other large cities took most.

● the further someone had gone in their level of studies, the more likely they were to be part of this short break market. Those with a higher education were the most likely to take a short break.

● the age range most likely to take a short break is that between 21 and 30 years: 57.9 per cent of those in this age group took a short break.

CASE STUDY
CENTER PARCS

Responding to the growth of short break holidays taken by Europeans, the Center Parcs concept is based on the concept of 'holidays at any time of the year'. Clients opt for either a weekend break, a 'midweek' (four days between Monday and Friday), or an entire week's stay in a centre combining high-quality accommodation and unique all-weather leisure facilities. To date, all Center Parcs establishments have been built in northern Europe, where the large centres of population and changeable climate are both factors which have favoured the success of this particular product.

Company history

Originally developed by the Dutch leisure company, Sporthuis Centrum, Center Parcs was bought up by the British company Scottish and Newcastle in 1989. By that time, the innovative Center Parcs concept was already well-established in northern Europe, with 13 establishments in the Netherlands, Belgium, Britain and France.

In Europe, Center Parcs is by far the market leader in all-year-round holiday centres. The concept has been developed and refined over the past 20 years, ever since Piter Derksen, the Dutch founder of Center Parcs, decided to create tropical paradises in places where nature never intended them to be.

Derksen was the owner of a chain of 20 shops selling sports and camping material, when he bought up some plots of land to develop as camping sites, with purpose-built leisure facilities for the clients. In 1968, he opened his first 'ideal holiday village' at De Lommerbergen, in the Dutch province of Limbourg: a collection of attractively appointed cottages sited around sports facilities, aimed primarily at a family clientele. Following on from the success of the De Lommerbergen village, he built others along the same lines in the southern and eastern regions of the Netherlands.

In 1980, the Sporthuis Centrum group entered a new era of development, with the opening of its first tropical paradise at De Eemhof. The De Eemhof village was the prototype for all of the Center Parcs to be built during the decade following its opening.

The Center Parcs product

The immediate and continuing success of the tropical paradise holiday centres was due to their combination of the three principal features which make Center Parcs unique in Europe:

1 **Location**. Each Center Parcs village is situated in between 100 and 300 hectares of woodland and water. The natural environment must be of prime quality: if there are not sufficient trees and shrubs, then these are planted.

2 **Accommodation**. Each contains accommodation in the form of several hundred self-contained high-quality bungalows. The bungalows have been designed in such a way that each overlooks water, and not the neighbouring bungalows. Central heating, open fireplaces, private terraces, and satellite and video television are standard features.

3 **Special feature**. Center Parcs' unique selling point is the central 'tropical paradise', a recreational complex of water-based activities including an artificial wave pool, waterslides, waterfalls, jacuzzi, and a running stream – all surrounded by real tropical plants such as banana trees, palms and orchids. Each park's tropical paradise is protected from the northern European climate by a huge glass dome or pyramid, inside of which the temperature is maintained at a steady $30°$ – equivalent to the daytime temperature of Mediterranean countries in summer.

An interior view of a bungalow and a Center Parcs tropical paradise are shown in Figs 4.6 and 4.7.

Shops and restaurants surround the artificial environment of the recreational complexes, with supermarkets, boutiques, banks, and a range of dining facilities, from fast-food outlets to gourmet restaurants. In addition to bungalows, certain Center Parcs have hotels. The Thetford Forest Park in England has a 98-bedroomed hotel, and the Normandy park, with its 'Résidence du Lac' hotel, which, among its 89 bedrooms, has three honeymoon suites complete with circular jacuzzis.

The Center Parcs' package price includes accommodation and free entry to the tropical paradise recreation complex. Beyond these two elements of the holiday, clients can choose from a range of activities, such as tennis, horseriding, mountain bikes, sauna, and so on, for which there is an additional charge. With golf currently enjoying an immense wave of popularity in France, a golf course was added to the Center Parcs village in Normandy which opened in 1988.

Operating methods

Center Parcs' emphasis is on the high quality of their product, and one of their methods of ensuring that standards remain high is to run all the services themselves, with the exception of golf and horseriding lessons where these are provided. The high standards of service and accommodation are matched by an emphasis on

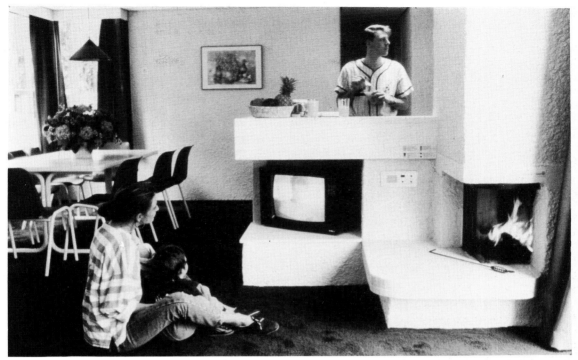

Fig 4.6 An interior view of a bungalow at a Center Parcs village (*Reproduced by kind permission of Center Parcs*)

Fig 4.7 A tropical paradise at a Center Parcs village (*Reproduced by kind permission of Center Parcs*)

an excellent physical environment in the centres, and a major contributing factor in this respect is the absence of motor vehicles inside the centres.

Center Parcs do not operate a system of overbooking, but prefer to be in a position whereby they can accept last-minute reservations. Clients can make bookings up to a year in advance, but in practice a substantial proportion of clients book at the last minute, sometimes following a turn for the worse in weather conditions. On average, each Center Parcs establishment receives around 4000 calls a week from clients, 25 per cent of which result in immediate reservations.

Direct booking is by far the most commonly used method of reserving Center Parcs short breaks. The average rate of direct bookings for countries outside France is 75 per cent, most of the rest being made through travel agents. In France, 96 per cent of reservations are direct bookings. While all of their centres are open to all clients, regardless of nationality, Center Parcs have a policy of reserving a proportional share of the places in any park for those living in the country in which the park is situated. In this way, around three-quarters of the clients of any park will be nationals of the park's host country.

Word-of-mouth recommendation is the most common route by which clients come to purchase a Center Parcs short break. On average, over half of the company's clients have learned of Center Parcs through family or friends. The remainder have booked in response to the company's press and television publicity.

The Center Parcs market

The clientele is essentially a young family one (in the Netherlands, for example 70 per cent of the clients come with their children). The majority of client families have a head of household at the middle or senior management level. Business tourists also comprise part of the Center Parcs market, with the hosting of seminars and conferences. To avoid any clash between the business and family clienteles, meeting rooms are situated underground for maximum peace and quiet.

The average amount of money spent per client per day, beyond the cost of the accommodation itself is around £12, spent primarily on meals, followed by shopping in the boutiques, then

sports facilities – i.e. tennis, squash and sauna.

Center Parcs' clients are drawn mainly from the surrounding region of its location. Each of the parks is situated in a region with a catchment population of between five to eight million within a two hour drive of the park. Generally, people are disinclined to travel vast distances to a short-break destination.

Compared with most hotel accommodation for example, Center Parcs' occupancy levels are extremely high: in 1990, the occupancy level of British Center Parcs reached 95 per cent, in Belgium, 92 per cent, and in France and the Netherlands, 90 per cent. On the whole, the clientele seems to be largely satisfied with the product: in a recent survey carried out in a French Center Parcs establishment, 57 per cent of the clients said that they had found the product to be even better than they expected, and 75 per cent said that they intended returning to the park in the year ahead.

Company expansion

In 1981, the company began its exportation of the tropical holiday village concept, by opening a centre in Belgium. Expansion abroad has continued to the point where there are now 14 Center Parcs in northern Europe, with a total of 40000 bedspaces. The parks' locations are shown in Fig 4.8.

The construction of an average Center Parcs establishment requires an investment of around £50–£75 million. The product is a uniform European one found across Europe, regardless of in which country it is placed. Only the choice of food changes according to the host country.

Between them, the 14 Center Parcs create employment for over 6000 people. The company's policy is to employ local people to the greatest possible extent. As a result, typically 90 per cent of staff employed come from an area contained in a 30 km radius around the park.

In 1989, the year of its takeover by Scottish and Newcastle, the company had a turnover of just under £190 million, an increase of 27 per cent over the previous year. The annual turnover and net profits of the company are shown in Fig 4.9.

In 1990, Center Parcs announced their intention of building a second French park of 650 bungalows and a 80-bedroomed hotel at

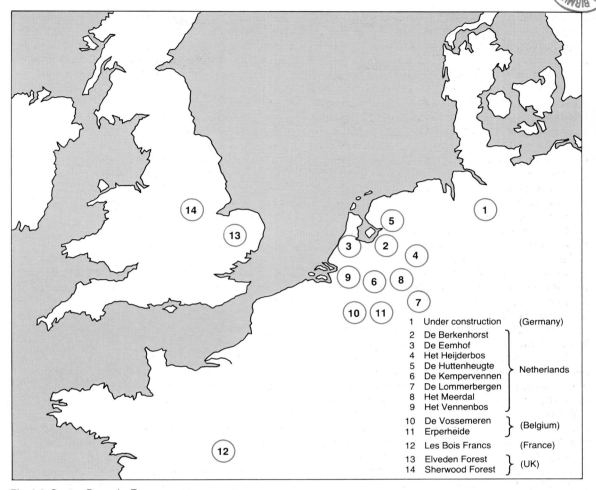

Fig 4.8 Center Parcs in Europe

Legend for map:

1 Under construction (Germany)
2 De Berkenhorst
3 De Eemhof
4 Het Heijderbos
5 De Huttenheugte
6 De Kempervennen — Netherlands
7 De Lommerbergen
8 Het Meerdal
9 Het Vennenbos
10 De Vossemeren — (Belgium)
11 Erperheide
12 Les Bois Francs (France)
13 Elveden Forest — (UK)
14 Sherwood Forest

Fig 4.9 Center Parcs' annual turnover and net profits

Annual turnover	£million
1985	76.5
1986	84.6
1987	111
1988	148
1989	188.4
1990	243

Annual profits (net)	£million
1985	12.3
1986	14.7
1987	18
1988	18
1989	20.7
1990	28.4

Chaumont-sur-Tharonne, in the Sologne region, to be opened in 1993. Three further parks are planned for France alone between now and the year 2000, with priority being given to the Nord-Pas-de-Calais region, the location of the French end of the Channel Tunnel. Finally, Center Parcs are looking beyond Europe, across the Atlantic, where negotiations are going on between them and an American hotel group concerning a possible joint venture establishment near New York.

CONCLUSION

In the highly competitive accommodation sector of the tourism industry, budget hotels have recently arrived to change the face of the hotel industry in Europe. Budget hotels have already become widespread in France, one of the two least expensive countries for hotel accommodation in the EC. As they expand throughout Europe, the budget hotel chains are presenting a serious challenge to the traditional hotel trade, and are, at the same time, 'democratising' the industry by widely extending its clientele.

All-weather holiday centres are another new product, adding to the consumer's choice of accommodation. Their success is, in part, due to the timely nature of their arrival in Europe, as the short-break habit gathers pace and as the taking of second holidays becomes more generalised for the wealthier nations. The very existence of all-weather holiday centres in the less temperate countries of Europe will accelerate this trend.

ASSIGNMENTS

1 Accor's expansion strategy in Europe. You work as Research and Development Manager in the Head Office of a major international hotel group. You have received some information giving details of the future expansion strategy of the hotel group Accor, your principal competitor.

Using the information given in Fig 4.10, write a report for the General Manager of your company. Outline the main points of the rationale behind the strategy, using your knowledge of current and future trends in Europe.

Fig 4.10

Category	France Price	%	UK Price	%	West Germany Price	%
Budget	<300 F	20	<30 £	1	<90 DM	2
Mid-scale	300/600 F	74	30/60 £	45	90/180 DM	62
Up-scale	600/800 F	3	60/80 £	35	180/240 DM	26
Luxury	>800 F	3	>80 £	19	>240 DM	10
		100		100		100

Europe	Hotels 1989	1991	1995	2000	Rooms 1989	1991	1995	2000	Hotels 2000/1989
Sofitel	29	46	70	97	4 553	7 356	11 902	16 452	334
Novotel	209	256	326	421	28 940	36 360	45 450	58 400	201
Mercure	109	174	262	386	10 745	17 796	27 516	40 566	454
Ibis Urbis	275	366	515	676	25 624	36 710	51 355	67 925	246
Formule 1	119	254	651	1 150	7 996	17 142	46 342	76 903	966
Hotelia	13	32	80	146	1 488	3 665	8 890	15 040	1 123
Atria	1	7	29	44	129	920	3 750	5 910	4 400
Total Europe	755	1 135	1 933	2 920	79 475	119 949	195 205	281 196	387

Regions	Hotels 1989	1991	1995	2000	Rooms 1989	1991	1995	2000	Hotels 2000/1989
France	572	776	1 109	1 432	52 565	72 253	98 377	123 300	250
Germany	62	90	203	350	8 131	10 942	23 136	33 231	565
Austria	11	17	24	33	1 537	2 220	2 950	4 170	300
Belgium	16	33	50	60	1 934	3 521	4 976	6 206	375
Spain	5	23	81	241	723	2 828	8 420	22 240	4 820
Netherlands	16	26	55	68	2 510	3 314	5 750	7 200	425
Italy	15	29	50	115	2 650	4 936	7 436	13 349	767
Portugal	8	18	29	40	1 048	2 050	3 300	4 500	500
Britain	30	67	211	377	4 490	8 105	19 400	33 690	1 257
Switzerland	6	10	18	33	647	1 210	2 100	3 830	550
Eastern Europe	10	35	76	121	2 628	6 550	13 540	20 510	1 210
Rest of Europe	4	11	27	50	612	2 020	5 820	8 970	1 250
Total Europe	755	1 135	1 933	2 920	79 475	119 949	195 205	281 196	387

In particular, discuss:

• The principal areas of expansion, by brand and by geographical regions. Why these particular brands? Why these regions? (*See* the descriptions of Accor's brands on page 59.)

• The differences between market segmentation in France, Britain and Germany. To what extent are these differences reflected in the expansion strategy?

• The assumptions which the strategy makes about future trends in Europe.

2 Center Parcs' competitors.

(*a*) The success of Center Parcs' all-weather holiday centres has led to the arrival of competitors offering similar products in northern Europe. Undertake some research to find out:

• who these competitors are, and

• how their products compare with that of Center Parcs.

(*b*) All-weather holiday centres are not the only accommodation option for Europe's short-break market. Investigate and report back on the range of short-break products available in your region. Cover as wide a range as possible of products aimed specifically at the short-break market.

THEME PARKS IN EUROPE

Loosely defined as 'large-scale amusement or leisure parks, grouping rides and attractions into specific 'themed areas', theme parks now feature among Europe's foremost day-trip destinations. With the arrival of Euro Disney, a new chapter in the history of European theme parks will begin. But this is a history which has already shown that this particular type of visitor attraction, in a class of its own, can meet with dynamic failure as well as success.

This chapter examines:

- The history and geographical distribution of theme parks in Europe
- Their distinguishing characteristics as visitor attractions
- The design and management of theme parks
- The impact of theme parks on European tourism

INTRODUCTION

It is a remarkable fact that, despite Europe's dozens of theme parks on its own territory, many of which attract over one million visitors per year, the theme parks best known to most Europeans are those sited far off in California and Florida. It was in the USA in the 1950s that the term 'theme park' was originally coined to describe Walt Disney's creation, Disneyland, which, at the time, he described as, 'a magical little park where children and adults could have fun together'.

If this description has an uncharacteristically modest ring to it now, it has long since been supplemented by the many superlatives and glowing tributes to Disney's genius which are liberally employed in any investigation into the world history of theme parks. For, despite their many imitators, in the USA and elsewhere, the Disney Theme Parks still hold the top positions for attendance, well above all the other themed attractions and amusement parks in the world. In the USA, where there are about 30 theme parks (each of which attracts over one million visitors annually), any *one* Disney theme park hosts more than *twice* as many visits per year as its closest competitor.

In 1992, the doors to Disney's first European theme park will open, on a site 32 kilometres east of Paris, and a new chapter in the history of theme parks in Europe will begin. However, the theme park as a unique form of visitor attraction is already well established in many European countries.

HISTORY OF THEME PARKS IN EUROPE

Theme parks are essentially large-scale, permanent, out-of-town day-visitor attractions, offering a range of individual attractions and facilities, including fairground-type rides, shopping and catering. They appeal primarily to a family market and in Europe most operate during the warmer weather months only.

European theme parks' closest predecessors may be found in the 'pleasure parks' which appeared at the end of the 19th century in many European capital cities, such as the Prater Park in Vienna or Copenhagen's Tivoli Gardens. These were permanent attractions, offering a range of features in the one place: trees and lawns, roundabouts and 'big wheels', cafés, bars and concerts. Some of these, such as the Tivoli Gardens, still exist, but most disappeared between the two world wars.

The first generation of modern theme parks in

Europe appeared in the 1960s, and had much more modest beginnings than their American counterparts. Most were small affairs, starting their existence as small family businesses, and growing gradually each year, as new rides and attractions were added.

The example of the Bagatelle Park near Berk in northern France is typical of the evolution of the earliest European theme parks. Opened on the site of their holiday home by a family of wool merchants, Bagatelle was established about 30 years ago as an open air café, with mini-golf and some animals in cages. The owner, Francois Parent, gradually extended it through the years, adding rides and other, more elaborate attractions, according to the profitability of each year's trading. Today, the Bagatelle Park operates on a relatively modest, but successful, basis, attracting about 300 000 visitors per year, mainly from the surrounding region.

The vast majority of Europe's major theme parks have been created or extended to their present size within the last 20 years, partly assisted in their growth by the spread of private car ownership and changing socio-economic conditions. The use of the family car for getting to theme parks led to the expansion of existing theme parks' catchment areas, and to the possibility of new theme parks being constructed on low-cost, out-of-town sites. Improvements in the general standard of living and the average amount of free-time available for leisure have also contributed to theme parks' growth during the past two decades.

GEOGRAPHICAL DISTRIBUTION

The growth has not been evenly distributed throughout Europe. Theme parks remain a largely *northern* European phenomenon. The main reason for this imbalance is that it is in the northern half of the continent where the large centres of population vital to the profitability of theme parks are to be found. Derek Oliver, Head of Sales and Marketing for Thorpe Park in Britain, has estimated that, in order to succeed, a theme park must be placed on a site with a population of 15 million people within 1½ hours' driving time. Naturally, motorways greatly extend the numbers of those within this driving time, and for this reason, many theme parks are

to be found close to these major axes of communication.

There are other reasons for the geographical concentration of theme parks in northern Europe. This is where the most prosperous populations of the continent live; and this is where the unpredictable climate creates a need for the kind of all-weather attractions which are usually a feature of theme parks.

Figure 5.1 shows the principal theme parks currently operating in Europe.

The Netherlands and Germany have been the theme park centres of Europe for the past 20 years. The Netherlands, with its great density of population has about 15 'major' theme parks, of which De Efteling attracts the most visitors. In Germany, where its 15 theme parks attract an average of 15 million visitors a year, standards are set by Europa Park and Phantasialand. Britain's Alton Towers receives most visitors per year of all Europe's theme parks.

DISTINGUISHING CHARACTERISTICS OF EUROPE'S THEME PARKS

Taken together as a group, what are the features which Europe's major theme parks have in

Fig 5.1 Theme parks in Europe attracting 300000 visitors or more annually		
The Netherlands	*Germany*	*Belgium*
De Efteling	Europa Park	Walibi
Duinrell	Phantasialand	Meli Park
Pony Park	Panoramapark	Bellewaerde
	Heide Park	Bobbejaanland
	Holiday Park	
	Fort Fun	
United Kingdom	*France*	*Denmark*
Alton Towers	Bagatelle	Legoland
Thorpe Park	OK Corral	Tivoli Gardens
	Astérix	
	Big Bang	
	Schtroumpf	
	Futuroscope	
Sweden	*Spain*	
Liseberg	Tivoli World	

Fig 5.2 De Efteling Family Leisure Park (*Reproduced by kind permission of the Netherlands Board of Tourism*)

common, making them unique among visitor attractions?

1 Setting and facilities. They are constructed in 'greenfield' locations, well outside any towns and cities; on-site, they offer everything required during the day's visit: entertainment, catering and shopping facilities.

2 Range of attractions. Large-scale 'white-knuckle' rides (so called because of the riders' tendency to hold on tightly, for security!) are the best-known feature of theme parks; but these are always complemented by other rides for younger or less adventurous members of the family, as well as other attractions, such as performances of live theatre, cinema, or music. Increasingly, highly sophisticated technology – holographs, lasers, interactive games and robots – are used in theme park attractions.

3 An identifying theme, and planned themed areas. Many parks have a familiar character or group of characters who act as an overriding theme for the attraction. In Europe, Astérix and the Smurfs are among the characters currently attracting visitors to theme parks and accompanying them throughout their visit.

The other sense in which these parks are **themed** concerns those sections of such parks

which are constructed as various 'themed areas'. These provide variety by giving visitors the impression of passing from one very distinctive 'land' to another. For example, visitors to Phantasialand near Cologne travel through the oriental temples and sculptures of Chinatown, to the Wild West town, Silver City, then to a reconstruction of Old Berlin in the year 1900, and on to the Space Center. The theme of each area determines the choice of catering, rides, live entertainment, and even shopping facilities.

4 High standards of product and environmental quality. Theme parks are designed and managed to ensure that the visitor's experience is of the highest quality. All aspects of the visit contribute to this kind of customer satisfaction: the absence of litter, the quality of the food, the provision of live entertainment for those queuing for rides, and the ease with which visitors can find their way around. How design and management systems help achieve these high standards will be examined later in this chapter.

5 'Pay-one-price' admission. Visitors' admission charges paid on entry, entitles them to use the rides without paying any extra. Parking is usually 'free' too, as research has shown that visitors do not like to pay out twice before entering the park.

High stakes, high-risk businesses

It is the *combination* of all the above characteristics which makes theme parks unique as visitor attractions for the whole family. However, another important characteristic setting them apart from other tourist attractions is their **scale**. Euro Disney will occupy a site one fifth the size of Paris itself, and elsewhere in Europe, theme parks of 150–200 hectares, the size of a small town, are not uncommon.

The immense dimensions of some of Europe's theme parks have led to them being called the 'heavy industry' of tourism, the service sector equivalent of a huge steelworks or car manufacturing plant.

Europe's most recently constructed theme parks, and those still at the planning stage, are vast. In France, the Smurfs park, Big Bang Schtroumpf, in Lorraine and the Astérix Park north of Paris, both opened in 1989 with a surface area of 160 hectares each. These parks and their contemporaries may be regarded as the 'second generation' of European theme parks. The principal difference between them and the earlier, 'first generation', parks lies in the initial magnitude of the new theme parks.

Most of the earlier parks in Europe grew gradually, expanding and reinvesting a little each year. In this way, a park's reputation evolved slowly but surely, and there was minimum risk involved in investing a proportion of each year's profits in order to expand the park or add new rides or attractions to entice visitors back the following year.

In contrast to this, the trend in Europe is now towards the instant construction of new, large-scale, theme parks, most of which are already larger on their opening day than 'first generation' theme parks which have been operating for decades. It is their physical size, as well as the vast numbers of jobs created by these new theme parks which gives them the characteristics of heavy industry.

Another characteristic which they share with heavy industry is the huge amount of initial investment required to construct them and get them operational. For example, the Astérix Park needed 800 million francs, and the Smurfs park, 850 million francs, of initial investment. The need for sums such as these means that the second generation theme parks cannot be family-owned and run, as their predecessors were. Funds need to be raised from a variety of investors prepared to put money into these enterprises but the risks involved in investing in this type of enterprise are extremely high, as the ill-fated Mirapolis and Zygofolis theme parks have demonstrated.

CASE STUDY

MIRAPOLIS AND ZYGOFOLIS

The French developed the theme park habit much later than the inhabitants of most other northern European countries. Major theme parks in Germany, Belgium, Britain and the Netherlands began operating successfully as novel tourist attractions in the 1960s and 1970s, when only small-scale theme parks were operating in France.

It took the all-important Disney decision, in 1986, to site Euro Disneyland near Paris, to convince French developers and financiers that theme parks could be a worthwhile venture in France. Investors in particular suddenly wondered why the market in France should be left only to the Americans. The result was that within the space of three or four years, French banks, construction companies and even public service companies rushed into the financing of six major theme parks, amounting to an investment of 2700 million francs.

During the same period, a dozen aquacentres were constructed in the hope of attracting the same market. Consequently, by the end of the 1980s, tourists and day-trippers in France could choose from the abundance of parks shown in Fig 5.3. The optimism was, to a large extent, justifiable. Despite not having a large selection of major theme parks in their own country, the French had in the past shown a great degree of interest in this form of tourist attraction. Europa Park, on the German side of the Rhine, and the Walibi theme park near Waterloo in Belgium each attract about one third of their total visitors from France. Yet the high-risk nature of investment in theme parks was to be clearly demonstrated by the fortunes of at least two of France's brave new theme parks. A recent article by Marc Amboise-Rendu in *Le Monde* takes up the story of Mirapolis and Zygofolis:

Mirapolis

France's first major theme park, Mirapolis, situated just north of Paris, opened on a wave of confidence and optimism. Trusting in American feasibility studies, and using an architect well-acquainted with the design of American theme parks, the owners of the park felt that its success was assured. However, it encountered problems even from its first day open to the public in Spring 1987. On day one, the park was invaded by fairground roundabout operators who caused a considerable amount of damage to the park, in order to draw attention to the difficulties of their own profession, which was faced with the threat of competition from theme parks.

However, that incident was only the beginning of Mirapolis' problems. Those visitors who made their way to the theme park found little to interest them: the rides were too widely dispersed, and still showed the damage caused

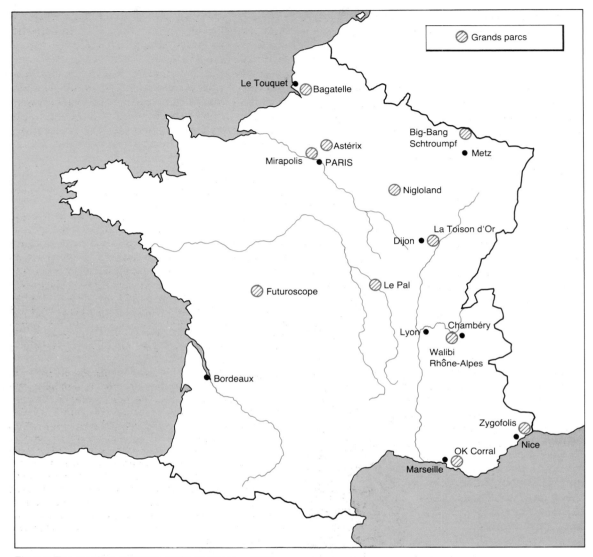

Fig 5.3 The location of theme parks in France, 1990

by the fairground operators; and the gardens and greenery had not yet grown into place. Despite the widespread dissatisfaction of visitors, 600 000 visits were made in the first year, and another million in 1988. But these figures were far from those hoped for by the park's investors, and operators, who had budgeted for two million visitors a year. Club Mediterranée were called in to mount a rescue operation on the park's fortunes. As a result, investors were asked to advance a further 150 million francs in order to improve the park. Charges in the park were reduced by 40 per cent, the parklands were brought into flower, and the food in the restaurants was improved. Finally, the fairground roundabout operators were invited to bring their rides and their specialist knowledge to the park.

Despite all of these measures, a promotional campaign organised by Club Mediterranée, and a long hot summer, fewer than 700 000 visitors turned up in 1989. By the end of that year, the park's survival was very much in doubt, together with the investors' fortunes, so optimistically piled into this venture. Finally, in 1991, Mirapolis was closed down completely.

Zygofolis

Further evidence that theme parks could be a high-risk investment was provided by the example of Zygofolis. In July 1987, the Zygofolis theme park, close to Nice, opened its gates to the public. At the end of its first year of operation, however, it had accumulated a deficit of 46 million francs, and one year later, it went into liquidation. The investors, including the French financial group Paribas and the Société Générale bank, lost over 300 million francs as a result.

Mirapolis and Zygofolis stand as reminders to all theme park developers and potential investors that this form of tourist attraction is by no means a guaranteed success.

What went wrong? Many tourism professionals have their own theories and opinions. They point to the poor design of Mirapolis, with the oversize gaps between rides, the lack of greenery, and the use of the unpopular Gargantua as the symbol of the park. In a country known for the high quality of its cuisine, the food on sale in the park was felt to be well below standard. The bleak concrete pathways, the all-too-visible overhead electricity cables and pylons, and the busy, noisy RN14 highway, clearly within view of the park, are also deemed to have spoiled the atmosphere of a park supposed to be providing fun and leisure for its visitors.

Zygofolis is believed by many to have opened too soon, before the park itself was fully operational. Delays in its construction meant that not all of the attractions were open to visitors during the first few weeks of operation. As a result, the all-important initial impression given to visitors was far from perfect. As part-compensation for its earliest visitors, the management of Zygofolis reduced the entry price during the first two weeks of opening. However, this brought the entry price down lower than the group tariff, previously billed as the best value. The vociferous complaints from those groups which had purchased their tickets in advance did little to enhance the park's reputation.

Similarly, the decision to site Zygofolis in a sunny, warm-weather region may have backfired. While the favourable Provence weather may have been a guarantee of a longer opening season for the park, compared to more northern attractions, the endless days of sunshine may also have made it more difficult for Zygofolis to attract tourists and residents away from the beaches.

Interviewed in 1989 by the editor of the magazine, *Leisure Management*, Dennis Speigel, President of the International Association of Amusement Parks and Attractions, based in the USA, gave his verdict on the failure of these parks:

'Both Paris and the Côte d'Azur are very good markets. It is the people who designed the parks and the people who operate the parks who had problems. They didn't know what they were doing.

From my professional standpoint, I think that the designers of Mirapolis park were not in touch with the public and didn't understand what makes a park function successfully. The attractions were spaced too far apart, the design of some of the attractions really missed the target, and people aren't going to be fooled. They'll come out once, but if it isn't right they won't come back. When you come to theme park design, it isn't what the designer wants, it's what the public wants. I think that was the problem in the Mirapolis park, because the people are certainly there and the market is there.

(Zygofolis) had problems with its management team, which in my estimation did not understand the business they were in. The didn't have a concise understanding of how to administer a park of this nature, both on the marketing and on the operating side. This isn't just something that a person sees and just decides to do on a whim; it takes professional experience and specific expertise to both plan and operate these parks. It isn't as easy as it looks. There is a very precise formula used to make these parks successful. It isn't a matter of "I've got $50 million, I can dig a hole and fill it full of rides and attractions and people will come." You have to know what you are doing. . . .

In France, these parks are like two "satellites" out of control and it is having an impact on the rest of the industry. People are saying it won't work in France, but that is silly. It will work. Developers have to change their attitude a little but it will happen.'

The risk inherent in this type of investment is made more acute by the fact that, with the exception of Euro Disney, European theme parks are currently only open for six or seven months of the year. Consequently, they only have just over half of every year in which to make the income they need in order to remain viable.

Moreover, constant **reinvestment** is vital to the survival of any theme park. In order to attract visitors back, year after year and to maintain market share, a constant programme of reinvestment in new rides and other facilities is required. A 1987 survey of European theme parks by the Economist Intelligence Unit (EIU), found that annual reinvestment for major parks varied between £1 million and £4 million. Furthermore, the new rides which serve to tempt visitors back, are far from cheap; for example, the thrilling 'Transylvania ride' which opened in 1990 at the part-zoo, part-theme park Chessington World of Adventures in England, cost £3 million.

Thorpe Park's Derek Oliver sums up the investment risk inherent in theme parks:

'Most speculators, entrepreneurs and property developers can usually work out a rule-of-thumb profit and loss account for any speculative development on the back of an envelope and, with a few notable exceptions, most get it right each time. The (theme park) business is not so predictable and has few proven formulae. It must still be considered, even though the concept is sound, as a risk venture.'

One reason for this is that, unlike the general property market, the leisure business is highly specialised and totally non-essential. Potential visitors can stay at home and be entertained and amused at far less cost and trouble. The choice is theirs.'

DESIGN AND MANAGEMENT OF THEME PARKS

Europe's short history of theme park success and failure, combined with observations of this kind of attraction in the USA, has enabled those responsible for their design and management systems to identify practices which are considered most likely to optimise a new park's chances of success.

Design and appearance

Regarding the **design** of theme parks, careful consideration must be given to the choice of theme, the arrangement, and the appearance of each park.

Since the identifying theme of the park will symbolise its actual image for potential visitors, it needs to be based on characters or stories which are universal, familiar, and popular. One reason often suggested as partly contributing to the failure of Mirapolis was the choice of Gargantua as the theme. This character from a story by Rabelais, it is said, provoked negative reactions in those young customers who had had to read the book at school!

On the other hand, those friendly Gauls who symbolise the Astérix Park are not only well-regarded, but almost universally recognised: according to a study by the French consultants, Sofrès, 97 per cent of Europeans under 35 years of age recognise Astérix. Similarly, the Netherlands' De Efteling park and the Verden park in the north of Germany use the popular fairy tales of Hans Christian Anderson and the Brothers Grimm as their identifying themes.

Mainly due to the endeavours of Disney in this field, there is now an established 'science' of arranging the various attractions and facilities within theme parks. It is an exact, rigorous science which draws on other disciplines ranging from architecture to psychology.

The most successfully designed parks are those which immediately delight visitors by giving them the impression that, on entering the park, they have moved into a different, better world, with its own rules and logic. The key to achieving this illusion lies in planning the layout of the park, and arranging the entertainments. The 'real' world must be firmly left outside, with the family car. Thus, most theme parks use grassy hillocks or trees to block out the surrounding roads and car parks from view. Inside the park, the objective of the planners is to never let go of the visitor's attention, even for one minute. The skilful planning of the theme park layout means that the visitor is subtly guided along a pre-determined path, without even being aware of it. Rides, boutiques and food outlets succeed each other with ever-increasing splendour, each ride, for example, being even more thrilling than the previous one.

Achieving the ideal **density** of attractions is vital, too. The problems of Britannia Park and Mirapolis are believed to have partly been due to the fact that the attractions in these parks were too few and too sparsely spaced. In other words, visitors' attention was not totally engaged as it ought to have been, and many of them left feeling dissatisfied. Naturally, there must be gaps between attractions. But the most successful parks take great care to fill these: for example, the antics of actors in costume can accompany visitors from one attraction to the next; and even in the queues for rides, the provision of live entertainment is one way of ensuring that the show is constant and total.

The skilful use of architecture and technology also serve to reinforce visitors' impression that they are in a fantasy world, completely removed from everyday life. Both aim to delight and disorientate visitors, by playing games with space and time. For example, visitors to the Heide Park in northern Germany might be forgiven for thinking that they are in some kind of timeless America, as they embark upon the 'Mississippi' paddle-steamer and sail past the (half original size) Statue of Liberty. By the time they move on to the electronic theatre where the trees sing, the flamingoes speak and the frogs dance, visitors must be entirely convinced that they have left reality far behind.

The actual appearance of theme parks is vitally important to their success. The impression given by the best is one of extreme cleanliness. The emphasis on high standards of cleanliness and absence of litter springs from the desire to give visitors the impression that they have come to a world which is closer to perfection than the one they have left behind – even if in most parks, the absence of litter is due more to the endeavours of the staff than to the behaviour of visitors.

Patterns and techniques of management

Staff working in theme parks are rightly regarded as one of the major contributors to a park's success. These are the people who come into direct contact with visitors, and it is their professionalism which determines customers' impressions of how welcoming, helpful and friendly they found staff to be, during their visit – a crucial element of the day-out. For this reason, those responsible for managing theme parks place great emphasis on staff training in customer relations skills and on careful recruitment. Seasonal staff as well as permanent staff undergo rigorous training in every aspect of dealing with the public. Managers need to know from hour to hour how things are going in their park, to identify any potential problems and solve them before they become evident to visitors. Management style, therefore, tends to be one of 'sleeves-rolled-up' involvement, as opposed to managing from a distant office, removed from day-to-day events.

The insistence on high professional standards for staff and close managerial involvement are two features of general theme park management designed to ensure the highest possible quality in all aspects of the visitor's experience of the park. Another is the emphasis on **management control** of the various facilities on offer in theme parks. Customer satisfaction depends above all on the quality of the principal three elements of any theme park: rides, food and drink, and shopping facilities.

The importance of catering and shopping for theme parks' income is shown in Fig 5.4.

The EIU survey investigated the ownership and control of rides, catering and shops in theme parks, and the results are given in Fig 5.5.

The vast majority of the parks wholly manage their own rides. This enables management to exercise complete quality control over this major element of theme parks.

Catering and retailing are viewed somewhat differently, with only about half of the parks wholly controlling all of their restaurants and shops. The alternative to direct management control of these facilities is to let them out as **concessions** to other companies. The problem with this method is that central management of the park has no direct control over the quality of the food or the products on sale in the shops.

Fig 5.4 Percentage income for theme parks (*Source: Disney*, Projection 2000)

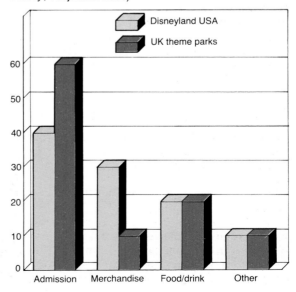

Fig 5.5 Operational patterns of European theme parks

| | Facilities operated by park management | | | | | | | | |
| | Rides | | | Catering | | | Shops | | |
	All	Some	None	All	Some	None	All	Some	None
Alton Towers	*			*			*		
Bellewaerde	*				*				*
Bobbejaanland	*				*			*	
De Efteling	*			*			*		
Duinrell	*				*		*		
Europa Park	*			*				*	
Heide Park	*			*					*
Meli Park		*			*		*		
Panorama Park	*				*		*		
Thorpe Park	*			*			*		
Walibi	*					*		*	

Source: The Economist Intelligence Unit

For this reason, about half of the parks surveyed have chosen to wholly control all their restaurants and shops. In this way, management is in a strong position to ensure all-over quality control for their parks' services.

THEME PARKS AND TOURISM

One reason often given for the development of theme parks is their ability to boost tourism in the region in which they are situated. Developers – and the local authorities who must justify their decision to give approval for their construction – emphasise theme parks' ability to attract visitors to the region and to encourage them to spend more time and money there.

However, what is the exact contribution made by theme parks to the level of tourist activity in their vicinity? In considering this, a number of questions present themselves:

1 To what extent do theme parks simply feed off the supply of tourists already visiting a region?

2 Is the proportion of tourists, as opposed to day-trippers, visiting theme parks sufficiently large to justify the claim that theme parks boost tourism?

3 Do theme parks play a role in stimulating international travel within Europe?

Surveys of theme parks in Europe suggest that the answer to all of the above questions could be that it depends on the theme park in question.

In reply to the first question, it is useful to distinguish between those theme parks sited in tourist regions and those placed close to large population centres. The former deliberately make their appeal, first and foremost, to holidaymakers. European theme parks in this category are usually sited close to seaside holiday resorts: Blackpool Pleasure Beach, Tivoli World on the Costa del Sol, and Benidorm's Europa Park are examples of theme parks which primarily attract those who are already visiting the region, on holiday, as opposed to the permanent local population (which, in most cases would be too small to sustain a theme park by itself).

Theme parks in tourist regions, therefore, directly feed off the supply of tourists already visiting those regions, on holiday. In this way, they are an asset to the region, but they are not usually a sufficient reason, by themselves, for tourists to decide to come there in the first place. However, such theme parks are in a small minority in Europe, and a more accurate impression of theme parks' impact on tourism is given by examining the visitor profiles of the more typical parks situated close to large centres of population. To what extent do these boost tourism in their regions?

Day-trippers, as opposed to tourists, undeniably constitute the vast majority of most European theme parks' clientele. The 1987 EIU survey found that, on average, 70 per cent or more of theme park arrivals were day-trippers, making the journey from their own home and back again the same day. The balance was made up of what might be properly termed 'tourists'

– i.e. those clients staying at least one night in the region on short breaks, holiday or on through trips. The predominance of day-trippers is easily explained by the fact that theme parks offer a range of attractions which can be fully enjoyed in the space of one day's visit. Clients go home at the end of the day satisfied that they have sampled most of what was on offer.

However, many theme parks do attract staying tourists into their regions, with a corresponding impact on the local economy. For example, after Alton Towers began advertising in the South East of England, there was a notable increase in demand for short breaks in its vicinity. Similarly, the construction of Europa Park in Rust has led to an influx of tourists into a region not previously considered as a tourist destination. Now, a sizeable proportion of those using accommodation in the region is composed of visitors to Europa Park, and camping facilities in Rust have doubled in surface area since the opening of the park.

A growing trend in theme parks will mean that the percentage of their visitors composed of staying tourists, as opposed to day-trippers, is set to increase. The trend involves the provision of accommodation by theme parks, to encourage visitors to extend their stay to longer than one day. The idea may have more than a little to do with Disney. The sheer size of Euro Disney, and its copious supply of on-site accommodation for visitors, will ensure that Euro Disney itself will lead directly to a sharp increase in overnight stays in the Parisian region. Many visitors will use Euro Disney as their base, spending several days in the Magic Kingdom theme park, but also touring around, visiting other attractions in or near Paris.

Other European theme parks, increasingly aware of the advantages of combining tourist accommodation with the main attraction, have begun either constructing their own accommodation, or arranging short-break packages with existing accommodation in the region. An increasingly common arrangement is that visitors to a theme park are given a discount in the associated accommodation, or users of the accommodation are given a discount for entry to the park.

Where the existence of a theme park leads to an increase in business for local hotels, and camping and caravan sites, for example, the parks can justifiably claim to be having a beneficial impact on their region as a whole, helping other businesses by providing them with additional clients. Where, on the other hand, theme parks are constructing their own accommodation, the impact on other, existing businesses may be negligible. When theme parks provide everything needed by the visitor – entertainment, shopping facilities and catering as well as accommodation – other tourism businesses in the region may well find themselves in the position of receiving crumbs from the table of these vast enterprises.

In response to the third question on p 82, (To what extent do theme parks encourage cross-frontier travel between different European countries?), once again, the situation differs greatly according to the location of the park in question. In Britain, separated from continental Europe by the sea, a very small proportion of theme park visitors are from beyond that country's frontiers, and their importance in generating international tourism to Britain is accordingly minimal. (However, theme parks in the southeast of England will be hoping that this situation may improve with the opening of the Channel Tunnel.)

On the continent, however, the opposite situation is found, particularly in the north-west of Europe, where close land frontiers make cross-border travel a frequent and effortless occurrence. The proportion of foreign visitors attracted to a park depends on two characteristics of the park: its closeness to its country's frontiers, and its size and reputation. Given the dimensions of Belgium, for example, any theme park in that country will be easily and quickly accessible from neighbouring countries. Parks there receive many foreign visitors from nearby France and the Netherlands. At the Walibi park near Waterloo, between 40 and 50 per cent of the visitors are from outside Belgium, with almost one third of the clients coming from France. The park's owner, Eddy Meeus, has so much faith in his French clientele that he has reached an agreement with the French railway company, SNCF, to run special excursion trains to his park from Paris.

The other characteristic which determines a park's ability to attract foreign visitors is its size. The best illustration of this effect may be seen in the Disney theme parks in the USA, which enjoy a worldwide reputation. At the other end of the scale, the clientele of small theme parks may be restricted to those living in the region in which the park is situated. Euro Disney's size will ensure it a reputation thoughout Europe and beyond. It has been predicted that 56 per cent of its visitors will come from outside France, many making the trip for the sole purpose of going to Euro Disney. For the time being, however, very few other European theme parks enjoy the renown required to encourage foreign visitors, or indeed domestic clients, to travel more than three or four hours to get to them. However, given their ability to stimulate cross-frontier travel into the countries in which they are situated, theme parks clearly do play a role in earning valuable foreign receipts for those countries – even if, for the moment, the vast majority of visitors continue to be day-trippers only.

CASE STUDY
EUROPA PARK, GERMANY

Europa Park is a major German theme park situated on the Rhine plain in the small community of Rust, about 30km to the north of Freiburg.

As the name suggests, the park has a European theme, with Italian and Dutch villages, and French, Scandinavian and German themed areas. The park has had a considerable impact on the development of the surrounding area, with the activities of several local businesses being linked to the park, directly or indirectly. Much of the merchandise supplied to the park is produced in the region, and Europa Park is also a major employer of local craftspeople. A relatively high proportion of the guests of local hotels, hostels, and camping sites have come to Rust specifically to visit Europa Park. Prior to the construction of the Park, tourism in that region was practically non-existent. In a recent study of Europa Park's market profile, Dr R Michna of Albert-Ludwigs University, Freiburg, gives the following reasons:

In order to get to the park, visitors make a journey of 1½ hours, on average, and the average distance travelled between the point of departure and the park itself is 87 km as the crow flies. In reality, the actual distances travelled by visitors vary greatly above and below this average. The catchment area is above

all found to be determined by the road network in general, and the motorway network in particular. National frontiers present no obstruction to this general pattern, neither encouraging nor discouraging visits to the park.

The vast majority of visitors are day-trippers, leaving their own homes in the morning and returning there at the end of the day. On the other hand, 16 per cent of visitors were found to be tourists. This group was composed mainly of French, German and Swiss holidaymakers who travelled to the park from their holiday accommodation. Most were found to have made the trip to the park from the zone 25–50 km around the park, this including the tourism centres in the Vosges mountains, the Black Forest, and some mountain resorts.

The proportion of foreign visitors to Europa Park, both day-trippers and tourists is approximately 45 per cent of the total, composed of 23 per cent French and 22 per cent Swiss.

The same study of Europa Park's clientele also investigated other criteria relating to the park's visitors. On the socio-economic front, for example, it concluded that the clientele was essentially an urban, middle-class one, with those from less favoured classes being hardly represented. Eighty-four percent of visitors came by car. Children and teenagers were found to constitute 32 per cent of the clientele, while there were hardly any visitors over the age of 65.

Regarding visitor behaviour and the differences between the three principal nationalities visiting the park, the study noted that the French and the Swiss on the whole spent more than the Germans, while the French were the most frequent visitors, with more repeat visits than the other two groups. They also spent longer at the park than the Swiss and Germans – on average, spending over 6½ hours.

Two-thirds of all visitors come with family or friends, in groups averaging four people. The remaining one-third come in organised groups, such as school parties, Scouts, etc.

CASE STUDY
EURO DISNEY

One of the most eagerly anticipated tourism projects in Europe of the 1990s is Euro Disney Resort, located 32km east of Paris in Marne-la-

Vallée, part of the Ile de France region. Due to open in 1992, Disney's first European enterprise will occupy a site of 1943 hectares, about one-fifth the size of Paris itself.

When it opens, Euro Disney Resort will include themed hotels, a campground, restaurants, shopping and entertainment facilities, championship golf, and at its centre, the Euro Disney Theme Park itself. Office, industrial and residential developments will also be constructed on the site.

The latest of the Disney theme parks, Euro Disney will join California's Disneyland, Florida's Walt Disney World, and Tokyo Disneyland, which currently hold the top positions for attendance over all other themed attractions and amusement parks in the world. Even in the USA, with its total of 1800 theme parks, each of the Disney parks attracts more than twice as many visits per year as its closest competitor.

The Disney success

What are the factors contributing to the ongoing success of the Disney formula, now about to be on offer in Europe? The company itself gives the following reasons:

- Disney theme parks are not designed just for children. They are designed to appeal to the young and the 'young-at-heart', enabling the whole family to enjoy the experience.

- A Disney theme park is not a collection of rides and games. It is a totally themed experience with unique attractions created with the latest technology and the newest Disney innovations

Fig 5.6 The new Euro Disneyland theme park (*Reproduced by kind permission of Euro Disneyland*)

to tell stories. They are also designed to be all-year-round attractions, regardless of weather conditions.

- Activities of The Walt Disney Company as a whole contribute to the success of each Disney theme park. Disney motion pictures, television, home video, publications and Disney character merchandising all assist in maintaining a high awareness of Disney and the Disney theme parks.

- Disney is committed to providing the highest quality entertainment experience: a clean, beautifully landscaped park, with friendly, helpful employees, all leading to visitors' perception of receiving the best value for their time and money.

Why Europe and France?

What were the reasons which led the Disney company to believe that their parks' successes in the USA and Japan could be repeated in Europe? And why was it decided to site Euro Disney in France? The decision was based on two main considerations, **market potential** and the extent of the **Disney appeal**.

Market potential

1 The **demographic profile** of Western Europe is favourable to the success of a theme park. More than 350 million people live in Western Europe, concentrated into a land area about one-half the size of the USA. Yet the American population of 240 million – nearly a third smaller – supports *two* Disney locations, with a combined total of almost 40 million visits per year.

2 **Per capita incomes** in Western Europe were considered to be sufficient to support this type of development. In France in particular, disposable income earmarked for leisure purposes is expected to grow by 12 per cent during the 1990s. The Ile de France region, too, has one of the highest income levels in Europe.

3 The Paris **location** offers exceptional access to millions of Western Europeans, as shown in Fig 5.3 on p 78. 17 million people live within a two-hour drive of Euro Disney Resort; 41 million within a four-hour drive, and 109 million within a six-hour drive. Most major European airports are within a two-hour flight of Paris, and Paris

is already one of Europe's major tourist destinations.

4 European leisure trends, too, are highly favourable. The Western European pattern of four to six weeks' holiday per year is greater than the American norm of two to three weeks. Fifty-six per cent of Western Europeans take at least one holiday per year, with 34 per cent of these taking two or more. In addition, the short-break and weekend markets are very active, as more leisure time becomes available. In France alone, time spent at work decreased by an average of 12 per cent during the 1980s. Second holidays, short-breaks and weekend breaks are taken throughout the year, creating advantages for an all-year-round attraction such as Euro Disney Resort.

Disney appeal

Western Europeans already demonstrate an enthusiastic acceptance of existing Disney entertainment products:

1 Disney **animated films** have consistently proven popular in Europe, with many becoming number one releases in different markets.

2 Disney **publications** income is more than three times greater in Western Europe than in the USA. Throughout Western Europe, readership of Disney publications approaches 15 million weekly.

3 Disney weekly **television programming** is now appearing in all Western European countries, to both critical and public acclaim. France's weekly 'Le Disney Channel' has won the prestigious '7 d'Or' award for Best Children's and Family Programming.

4 With sales nearly doubling from 1985 to 1987, Disney *Home Video* is now the top-selling family entertainment product on videocassette throughout Europe.

The combination of the strong market potential and the established appeal of Disney products in Europe has convinced the owners of Euro Disney, and its investors, that the park will attract year-round attendance levels comparable to the other Disney parks. Some **11 million** visitors are expected in the first year, with the average visit length being over two days. The visitor mix is projected to consist of: 44 per cent

from within France; 43 per cent from the United Kingdom, West Germany, Italy, Belgium and the Netherlands; and 13 per cent from other countries in Europe and around the world.

Transport to the park

Euro Disney Resort will be accessible by a variety of means of transport, private and public. The park is situated between two international airports, Roissy-Charles-de-Gaulle and Orly, and is connected to Paris by the autoroute A4, on which new interchanges are planned, to further increase accessibility. However, the master plan for the project, as agreed with the French government, calls for the RER (réseau express régional), part of Paris' underground train network, to be extended directly to Euro Disney Resort by opening day, with a new terminal station to be located within 150 metres of the Magic Kingdom's main entrance. To this end, line A of the RER, which crosses Paris from east to west will be extended a further 10 km to the east, to carry passengers from central Paris into the heart of Euro Disney Resort in half an hour.

Finally, a special TGV line will link Euro Disney Resort with the European high-speed train network.

The attractions

The centrepiece of Euro Disney Resort will be the Euro Disneyland theme park, a classic Disney theme park based on themes from Walt Disney's motion pictures. It will cover 57 hectares and will feature 29 major shows, rides and ride-through adventures, at least 36 themed shops, and more than 30 restaurants themed to the five major lands:

● Main Street-USA: a street in a typical town in turn-of-the-century America, with horsedrawn streetcars, 'horseless carriages', barbershop quartets and ragtime piano music.

● Fantasyland. Sleeping Beauty's castle will be the centrepiece of this zone of attractions based on Disney interpretations of legends and fairy-tales such as Pinocchio, Snow White and Sir Lancelot.

● Frontierland. The 'Big Thunder Mountain' runaway mine train will speed visitors through gold rush country and other folklore scenes from America's Wild West past, such as The Lucky

Nugget Saloon and the Rustler's Roundup Shooting Gallery.

● Adventureland. This land will provide an exotic, tropical setting for attractions based on Disney films such as 'Swiss Family Robinson', 'Treasure Island' and 'Peter Pan'.

● Discoveryland. Inspired by Jules Verne and other visionaries of past and present, Discoveryland will acknowledge man's achievements and contemplate the possibilities for the future, using 3-D film and other examples of state-of-the-art technology.

However Euro Disney Resort will be much more than a theme park. The Phase I master plan for the project includes six themed hotels, a campground, restaurants, shopping and entertainment facilities, housing, a championship golf course, as well as the Magic Kingdom Theme Park itself.

The six hotels will provide 5200 rooms, from budget to luxury standards. The Magic Kingdom Hotel, designed to reflect the charm and elegance of Victorian architecture, will be situated at the entrance to the theme park, close to the RER and TGV stations. This 500-room, luxury hotel will contain shops, restaurants and conference rooms. The other Euro Disney hotels – the Hotel New York, Sequoia Lodge, Newport Bay Club, Cheyenne Hotel, and Hotel Santa Fé – will reflect a diversity of American themes. Of the 64 000 hotel bedrooms currently on offer in Paris, about 40 000 are at the level of two stars or above, the same as Disney hotels. Therefore, the 5200 Disney rooms which become available in 1992 will represent more than one-eighth of the total Parisian hotel accommodation stock at this level.

Euro Disney Resort will also feature a 22 000 square metre entertainment centre, offering continuous entertainment, from high-energy discos and cinemas, to night clubs and Wild West dinner shows. Visitors to Euro Disney Resort, whether they come for business or for leisure purposes, and whether they visit the theme park or not, will be able to use the entertainment centre, the golf course, windsurfing and canoe centres, and the Hotel New York's ice-rink.

In this way, the entire project will have the potential to act as a magnet and a holiday base for tourists who want to sample several attractions of this region of France, and not only the Disney theme park. Many visitors will stay for a week or more, and will travel to places such as Rheims, or the Champagne region, to Paris' Orsay Museum or the Louvre, or even, having learned the theme park habit, to the nearby Astérix park. To encourage visitors to tour around, a Tourist Information Centre will be built in the Euro Disney Resort entertainment centre. There is no doubt that the impact of Disney's first European venture will be felt far beyond the Marne-la-Vallée site itself.

The impact of Euro Disney on other theme parks

What is the attitude of other European theme park operators to the arrival, in the heart of the continent, of the most famous name in the business?

The powerful combination of the Disney reputation, plus a central location well served by European transport networks, will provide Euro Disneyland with an extensive catchment area over which to exert its considerable pulling-power. Yet, surprisingly, the threat of competition from Euro Disney does not appear to be a source of preoccupation for the majority of existing theme park owners in Europe. Indeed, according to the most recent survey conducted by the Economist Intelligence Unit, in 1990, Disney is hardly regarded as competition at all. On the contrary, most theme park operators are of the opinion that Euro Disney Resort will create and sustain its own market, as opposed to competing for a market share with existing parks.

Most operators, then, are publicly expressing a positive attitude to the newcomer, and are preparing themselves to rise to the challenge presented by this latest arrival on the theme park map of Europe. They even maintain that Euro Disney will provide a boost to other theme parks, by increasing consumer awareness and consciousness about their benefits as day visitor attractions. There is also general agreement that Euro Disney will establish new standards of management and presentation in theme parks, thereby raising the level of what the public will expect and demand from theme parks. Euro Disney's standards will become the benchmarks used by consumers during their visits to any theme park.

Most parks have already begun formulating and implementing their **'response strategies'**. Two general strands to these strategies were identified by the EIU during its survey: investment in **product enhancement** and **marketing** sophistication.

Product enhancement

The majority of European theme parks are already reorientating their investment strategies, in order to prepare themselves. The emphasis is moving away from continuing large-scale investments in new rides, towards the improvement of the quality of appearance and presentation of what the parks already provide – i.e. consolidation of the existing product base, through enhancement of general quality and cleanliness of the park, more attention to detail, and increasing staff training in customer relations skills.

Investment in theme parks across Europe is also increasingly being channelled into **diversification**, usually into the provision of accommodation. For example, De Efteling plans to diversify in the period 1990 to 1995 by building a bungalow park, and a camping/caravan site, while investment in new attractions over that period will remain frozen.

Marketing

The second strand to theme parks' strategy in the face of Euro Disney is that of marketing. The EIU survey found that, increasingly, theme parks were becoming more aggressive and sophisticated in their marketing. Their aim is two-fold: to establish market shares in traditional markets, while at the same time exploring new market opportunities. In order to achieve this, promotional budgets are being vastly inflated. A typical example is provided by Alton Towers, whose annual marketing budget increased by 30 per cent between 1986 and 1988, to £926 000,

72 per cent of which was spent on television advertising.

A major part of theme parks' promotional budgets are being used to explore new market opportunities, beyond the traditional late spring and summer day-tripping families. Currently, two markets in particular are being targeted: the off-peak market, and corporate involvement. It is in these more marginal areas where potential market gains are thought to exist. Accordingly, theme parks all over Europe are found to be emphasising the all-weather nature of their attractions, to attract off-peak visitors, while at the same time attempting to interest companies in using the parks for corporate entertainment or conferences.

A third market also considered by some to offer scope for consolidation and development is that of repeat visitors. Currently, repeat visits constitute between 40 per cent and 65 per cent of theme park business, and many park operators are using marketing techniques to increase the percentage of visitors who return to the park.

CONCLUSION

Although theme parks are not a recent innovation in Europe, interest in them has rapidly grown since the decision to site a Disney park in the heart of the continent. Successful theme parks are high-quality products, catering for the family day-trip market, and having their own particular science of design and management.

The impact of Euro Disney began long before its gates opened to the public, as it sparked off a wave of theme park construction in France, and a general re-thinking of management and marketing strategies of theme parks all over Europe. As Euro Disney's standards become those by which Europeans evaluate all other theme parks in their countries, the best will survive and prosper while the mediocre will not.

ASSIGNMENTS

1 A new theme park. You are a consultant specialising in tourism and leisure. Your clients are a consortium of investors who have decided to build a new theme park in your country. Write a detailed report for them (including maps and

statistics where appropriate), giving answers to the following questions:

(a) *Where* should the new theme park be located? (Take into consideration existing transport networks, levels of population, potential for attracting visitors from other countries, climate, etc.)

(*b*) *What themes* should be used for the park? Suggest a character, or group of characters, or some other theme which would give a *name* and a suitable *image* to the park.

(*c*) How should the new park meet the challenge of *Euro Disney*?

(*d*) *What risks* are there for the clients, in investing in this theme park?

2 Recruiting and training theme park staff. You are the new personnel manager of a major theme park which is due to open to the public in six months' time.

(*a*) Write a one-page job advertisement, to appear in the local newspaper, for staff to work in the park. Mention the different categories of work available, together with the skills and qualification you are looking for.

(*b*) Draw up a staff training programme for reception staff. They are responsible for selling tickets, welcoming visitors, and informing them about the park's facilities. Include details of the topics of each training session, mentioning any opportunities for day-release training, in local colleges, for example.

C H A P T E R 6

BUSINESS TOURISM IN EUROPE

Because of the close association of the tourism industry with sunshine, leisure and pleasure, business tourism is the sector which is most often forgotten in any consideration of this industry. Yet business tourism in its various forms represents a very substantial share of all tourist activity in Europe, and brings many benefits to those destinations which excel in this sector. One major advantage is that business tourists are the highest spending tourists of all, which partly explains why so many towns and cities in Europe and beyond constantly make such strenuous efforts to attract this kind of visitor.

This chapter examines:
- The different forms of business tourism
- How business tourism differs from leisure tourism
- Business tourism facilities and services
- Business tourism promotion in Europe

Business tourism comprises several different types of events and activities. What all of them have in common is that they all involve travelling for work-related purposes.

BUSINESS MEETINGS

When people travel to meet each other to discuss business or to exchange information with others in the same profession or the same association, for example, they are engaging in business tourism. Meetings of this type can be divided into **corporate** meetings, when the aim of those attending is to do business with each other, or **associate** meetings, when people with a common interest or belonging to a local, national or international association meet to exchange ideas and information. The important feature is that people travel, and usually stay away from home, in order to attend them. It could be one business person travelling to meet colleagues in his or her company's branch office in another city, and staying overnight; or it could be several thousand delegates flying from another continent to spend a week together at their

annual conference in one of Europe's capitals.

Because they have the potential to bring visitors in large numbers, **conferences** or **conventions**, are big business and represent the prizes most sought after by destinations keen to be chosen as the venues for these events. The American Bar Association's members are lawyers practising in the USA. When they held their annual conference in London a few years ago, it brought 20 000 Americans across the Atlantic – the biggest 'invasion' since World War II. By the time they returned at the end of the conference, they had spent US $60 million in London. Figures of this kind explain why destinations spend so much time and money competing with each other to persuade conference organisers to choose them as places to hold their events.

A **congress** is the term often used to describe a large event, attracting delegates from many different countries – i.e. an international conference. Many such congresses are held by international associations with members drawn from all over the world. Some of the most reliable business tourism statistics available are those concerning the volume of congresses. These are produced by the Union of International Associations in Brussels, who every year publish figures on international (non-governmental) association congresses. The UIA identifies between 7000 and 8000 of these annually. Figure 6.1 shows the main countries chosen for these events in four recent, consecutive years.

The picture changes very little from year to year, but the importance of Europe as a destination for international congresses is clear. Taking 1990 as an example, as is always the case, the USA appears in top position. However, out of the 8559 events in the UIA's data base for that year, 5225 of them were held in Europe – about 60 per cent. If this figure indicates that Europe is still the world's most important region for congresses, it must be borne in mind that 40 years ago, Europe was attracting closer to 80 per cent of all international congresses. What has happened to cause this drop?

The biggest single factor is the rise of long-haul destinations for business tourism, particularly in Asia. Meeting-planners are increasingly looking towards venues in countries such as Thailand, India and South Korea, which are able to offer competitive rates and the attraction of having an 'exotic' image which will appeal to delegates. This is likely to continue to be the source of Europe's greatest competition for business tourism in the years ahead as long-haul travel for business becomes more widespread.

Nevertheless Europe's importance as an established destination for congresses is indisputable. The situation becomes clearer with an examination of the world's principal congress cities as shown in Fig 6.2.

Paris is easily the world's top venue for this form of business tourism, and has maintained this position for the past ten years, since it took over the lead from London. London, on the other hand, has not yet fallen below second place for decades. With the top six cities for congresses in any year being European capitals, they clearly offer a successful formula. Their combination of

Fig 6.1 The main countries holding international congresses

Where did the International Congresses go? (countries)

1987		1988		1989		1990	
USA	776	USA	881	USA	973	USA	894
UK	701	UK	750	France	734	France	757
France	579	France	693	UK	700	UK	722
West Germany	449	West Germany	488	West Germany	505	Germany	505
Italy	331	Italy	392	Holland	367	Holland	385
Holland	305	Australia	340	Italy	344	Italy	332
Canada	283	Holland	333	Switzerland	292	Switzerland	318
Spain	274	Switzerland	305	Belgium	284	Belgium	303
Switzerland	267	Belgium	279	Spain	273	Spain	294
Belgium	262	Spain	276	Austria	199	Japan	266
Japan	178	Japan	190	Japan	195	Canada	230
Austria	165	Finland	188	Canada	189	Austria	219
Finland	141	Canada	186	Finland	161	Denmark	176
Denmark	119	Austria	172	Sweden	138	Finland	166
Brazil	116	Sweden	135	Denmark	134	Sweden	159
Australia	107	Denmark	131	Australia	124	Brazil	142
Thailand	99	Brazil	125	Brazil	121	Singapore	136
India	95	India	99	Singapore	111	Australia	127
Hungary	91	Norway	94	Israel	96	Norway	101
Sweden	85	Hungary	94	Czechoslovakia	92	Hungary	100
South Korea	75	South Korea	92	India	88	Czechoslovakia	93
Israel	74	Thailand	88	China	84	India	89
Norway	69	China	82	USSR	78	USSR	87
Czechoslovakia	69	Yugoslavia	80	Argentina	78	China	85
				Yugoslavia	74	Yugoslavia	76
				Hong Kong	74	Hong Kong	74

Where did the International Congresses go? (cities)

1987		1988		1989		1990	
Paris	356	Paris	324	Paris	388	Paris	361
London	265	London	268	London	261	London	268
Brussels	160	Madrid	169	Geneva	170	Brussels	194
Geneva	150	Brussels	159	Brussels	165	Vienna	177
Madrid	146	Geneva	152	West Berlin	160	Geneva	166
West Berlin	134	West Berlin	141	Madrid	139	Berlin	166
Amsterdam	93	Rome	122	Vienna	120	Madrid	151
Rome	97	Sydney	119	Washington	120	Singapore	136
Vancouver	91	Singapore	109	Singapore	111	Amsterdam	108
Singapore	91	Washington	97	Rome	108	Washington	101
Vienna	88	Vienna	91	Amsterdam	101	Strasbourg	100
Strasbourg	88	New York	88	Strasbourg	82	Rome	91
Bangkok	83	Strasbourg	86	Hong Kong	74	New York	87
New York	79	Amsterdam	83	Stockholm	73	Copenhagen	85
Washington	66	Seoul	82	New York	72	The Hague	83
Tokyo	65	Tokyo	80	Copenhagen	70	Tokyo	81
Barcelona	64	Copenhagen	79	Tokyo	69	Stockholm	80
Copenhagen	62	Stockholm	78	Helsinki	62	Hong Kong	74
Helsinki	61	Bangkok	67	Buenos Aires	62	Barcelona	70
Budapest	61	Budapest	62	Munich	59	Budapest	69
Rio de Janeiro	61	Munich	61	Rio de Janeiro	59	Rio de Janeiro	68
Seoul	59	The Hague	60	Manila	55	Helsinki	67
Brighton	57	Hong Kong	60	The Hague	54	Seoul	60
Montreal	52	Helsinki	60	Barcelona	54	Manila	58
Munich	52	Manila	60	Bangkok	52	Beijing	53
Hong Kong	52	Oslo	60	Budapest	51	Bangkok	51
		Barcelona	54	Jerusalem	51	Montreal	51
				Beijing	49	Buenos Aires	51
				New Delhi	49		

Statistics — Union of International Associations

Fig 6.2 The main cities for international congresses

a wide choice of conference facilities, together with abundant resources for cultural activities and entertainment, and comprehensive transport networks give European cities a considerable advantage in the fierce competition for congresses of this kind.

The UIA's figures reveal other interesting characteristics of this sector:

● September is the top month for these events, with May second. Not surprisingly, the winter months of December, January and February are the least popular months for congresses.

● Concerning the size of these meetings, 36 per cent have fewer than 100 participants, 29 per cent attract between 100 and 250 delegates, and 35 per cent have over 250. Included in this 35 per cent, are the eight per cent of international congresses which have over 1000 delegates – the biggest events of this kind.

● The length of these events is divided almost evenly three ways: one-third last three days;

one-third last four or five days; and one-third last over five days. It is rare for congresses to last over one week.

● According to the UIA, two-thirds of delegates choose to bring a spouse or another 'accompanying person' with them when attending a congress.

● Congress venues are booked far in advance. Given the vast amount of organising which goes into them, **lead times** – the period between deciding on a destination and the actual date of the congress – are very long. Fifty-nine per cent are decided on two years in advance; 18 per cent, three years in advance; 13 per cent four years; and ten per cent are being planned five years or even more before the date they will take place. This means that the venues for several hundred congresses which will not take place until the end of this decade have already been chosen and booked in Europe.

Although these figures represent only one

sector of the business tourism market, they provide useful indicators of a market for which reliable statistics are in very short supply. Moreover, it is widely assumed that when corporate meetings and local and national association meetings are also taken into account, the trends approximately follow those shown above, with Europe still attracting more of this business than the rest of the world put together, but facing increasing competition from newer destinations.

INCENTIVE TRAVEL

Incentive travel is the term used to describe short breaks and holidays given by companies to their employees, in acknowledgement of some special achievement or good results at work. It is a method used by companies to **motivate** their employees by rewarding, for example, sales staff who reach their sales targets or members of the workforce who achieve significant reductions in costs or absenteeism. As incentive travel 'packages' are often awarded by companies to particular groups of employees, who all go off to the same destination together, incentive travel can also help build a 'team spirit' among the staff.

Since incentive travel involves people travelling because of their work, it counts as business tourism. Although the elements of an incentive travel package resemble those of the classic package holiday – both include transport, accommodation, excursions and entertainment – the work-related nature of incentive travel packages distinguishes them from holidays chosen freely and without reference to the workplace.

With incentive travel, the different elements of the package are usually chosen to match the lifestyles and the aspirations of their staff who are participating. Elaborate banquets in historical properties, attendance at prestigious cultural or sporting events, visits to places of interest (often work-related) and excursions are all used to make the incentive trip memorable.

Generally speaking, figures on the volume and value of incentive travel are as unreliable as those for conference and meetings. Incentive travel is often lost in the general statistics for leisure or holiday tourism, particularly when incentive travel is undertaken by individuals, as opposed to groups. Similarly, that significant

proportion of the conference market which is incentive-orientated (rewarding certain employees by selecting them to attend a conference in an exotic destination) tends to get hidden in general business travel statistics.

The *European Incentive Travel Survey* conducted in 1990 by the Economist Intelligence Unit is a useful source of information and statistics on this form of business tourism. A detailed questionnaire completed by members of the travel trade, incentive travel buyers and incentive houses shows this sector of business travel to be one of the most promising of all. Combining data from a variety of sources and using some built-in assumptions, the survey estimates that, worldwide, incentive travel represents a US $17 billion business, and that during the 1990s, this market will grow at around 13 per cent per year, achieving a value of US $56 billion by the end of the decade. The survey estimates that, worldwide, around 11 million people currently travel on incentive travel award trips every year. This figure excludes spouses, so the actual number of people travelling for this purpose is probably about 17–18 million per year. One interesting observation concerning incentive travel specifically in Europe is that only 30 per cent of those travelling on incentives are accompanied by their spouses, compared with 70 per cent in the USA. For the travel industry, of course, the ideal would be for 100 per cent of incentive travellers to be accompanied.

Figure 6.3 shows the worldwide value of incentive travel, by the main origin markets. North America is clearly the key generating market, responsible for over half of total global demand. However, the survey points out the very substantial growth in demand for incentive

Fig 6.3 Estimated value of incentive travel by main origin market, 1990 ($ bn)

Generating market	Total	Domestic	Outside country of residence
North America	8.8	5.3	3.5
Europe	6.4	2.0	4.4
Rest of the world	1.7	1.0	0.7
Total	16.9	8.3	8.6

Source: Travel and Tourism Analyst, *published by the Economist Intelligence Unit, London 1990*

travel from European companies, particularly British and German, with Europe now accounting for just under 40 per cent of global demand. Figure 6.4 shows that Europe attracts a high volume of incentive travel from within its own boundaries (both domestic and intra-European).

The vast majority of incentive travel with Europe as a destination is undertaken by the Europeans themselves, with only about one-sixth coming from North America and the rest of the world. Reflecting the trend in business tourism as a whole in Europe, Paris and London were shown by the survey to be the top European destinations for incentive travel packages. Interestingly, however, Eastern Europe was perceived by the majority of the survey's respondents to be the region most likely to become more attractive in future, for incentive travel. Further research carried out by the Economist Intelligence Unit, since the survey, supports this prediction. It was found that the principal barriers to Eastern Europe hosting incentive travel movements – outdated infrastructure and poor ground handling arrangements – were being addressed for example, by investment in new airport terminals, and the setting up of specialised incentive divisions within national tourist organisations. Generally, Eastern Europe was felt to be rich in the kinds of attractions that many incentive groups are seeking, including:

- cities full of culture and heritage, often situated on prime rivers such as the Danube, Vistula and Vltava

- attractive scenery and tourist sites for excursions

- national cuisine and, in some cases, well-known national wines and beers

- folklore, customs, song and dance

- established spas and health resorts.

EXHIBITIONS AND TRADE FAIRS

The remaining major sector of business tourism is that of exhibitions and trade fairs, or trade shows, as they are sometimes known. These are usually large events, at which a range of products and/or services are brought together under one roof, to be displayed either to the general public or to invited specialists with a professional interest in whatever is on show. Exhibitions and trade fairs are essentially market places, where providers of goods and services have face-to-face contact with potential buyers. The most successful events are those where business is done, deals are struck between sellers and buyers, and orders are placed.

The Paris Air Show is an example of a trade show, where the latest aircraft, for both civilian and military use, are on show. While members of the public may go along just out of curiosity, there are also people there with a professional interest, with a view to purchasing aircraft for their company or their government. The tourism industry itself produces several major trade fairs in Europe. Every year in Berlin, the ITB travel trade fair is attended by some 30 000 visitors from the trade and about 100 000 members of the public. In Britain, one of the best-known examples of an annual exhibition is the Ideal Homes Exhibition, to which visitors, as well as exhibitors, travel in their thousands. In Europe, the number of trade shows and exhibitions has risen in a spectacular fashion since the end of the Second World War, in particular the number of international trade fairs, which draw exhibitors and visitors from all over the world. Now, a great many specialised trade shows for all kinds of businesses and industries take place in Europe throughout the year. They draw their visitors from the worlds of agriculture, food, textiles, health and hygiene, transport, communications, sports and leisure, fashion and many other fields.

It is their ability to stimulate travel for large

Fig 6.4 Volume of incentive travel by main origin market, 1990 (mn trips)

Generating market	Total	Domestic	Outside country of residence
North America	5.7	4.4	1.3
Europe	4.2	2.2	2.0
Rest of the world	1.4	1.0	0.4
Total	11.3	7.6	3.7

Source: Travel and Tourism Analyst, *published by the Economist Intelligence Unit, London 1990*

numbers of people which leads exhibitions and trade fairs to be considered a part of business tourism. When several hundred exhibitors descend upon a city to represent their company at a trade show, there is an immediate boost for the transport and accommodation services in that city. Similarly, those who are attending exhibitions with a view to buying some of what is on show also need to be transported and accommodated during the course of the event. All taken together, this adds up to a great deal of business for the tourism industry and for other businesses such as retailers and communication services in the cities where exhibitions and trade fairs are held. This explains why national governments are so eager to have their countries host these events, particularly when the events are international. This is a highly competitive field, with different countries vying with one another to attract these lucrative events. Len Lickorish of the Exhibition Industry Federation, which promotes the exhibition industry in Britain, writes:

'Although a leading pioneer in the (exhibitions) field, Britain has recently lagged behind in the competitive race. Germany and France support their exhibition trades massively, to the extent that they are four times as large as in Britain, and attract perhaps as many as ten times the number of foreign buyers and visitors.'

Nevertheless, even in Britain, exhibitions and trade fairs are big business. As always, statistics are inadequate, but an estimate from the British Tourist Authority puts spending by exhibitors and visitors to shows at over £750 million annually, with around 10 million visitors attending these events each year. Included in these figures are around 500 000 foreign visitors to Britain, whose spending accounts for nearly £100 million. Multiplying these figures ten-fold gives an impression of the volume of incoming tourism to France and Germany created by these events.

As well as being an important sector in their own right, exhibitions are often combined with conferences. The prospect of advertising their wares to several hundred or even a few thousand potential buyers assembled together for a few days under one roof, is very tempting for providers of relevant goods and services. For example, pharmaceutical companies welcome the opportunity to show their products to those attending medical conferences. From the conference organiser's point of view, adding an exhibition to a conference can be a useful way of offsetting the cost of the conference, as manufacturers are usually prepared to pay generously for the opportunity to exhibit their products to the very people most likely to buy them. The greater the number of delegates, the easier it is to sell exhibition space. For this reason, about 36 per cent of international associations have an exhibition at their annual meeting, thus helping to subsidise the event.

BUSINESS TOURISM VS LEISURE TOURISM

It is not always possible to distinguish business tourists from those travelling for leisure purposes. Both groups may use the same forms of transport and accommodation. They may also use the same entertainment and leisure facilities, as activities such as sightseeing, shopping and cultural outings are often added to business tourism programmes.

However, there are some important differences between business tourism and leisure tourism:

● Most business tourists do not themselves **choose** the destinations to which they travel. These are determined by the demands of the business to be done, or by the decisions of other people, such as the meeting-planners who decide in advance where an event will be held. However, those with the responsibility of choosing the venue for a conference, for example, will often choose somewhere which they think will appeal to those who will attend.

● Business tourism is largely confined to towns and cities. It is in **urban settings** that most business centres and conference facilities are found, together with the standard of hotels preferred by business tourists.

● Most business tourists do not themselves personally **pay** for the trip – their employers pay. This means first that business tourism is **less price sensitive** than leisure tourism: cost is less important in determining the choice of destination than it is in the decision where to go on holiday. Second, average spending per day per head is higher for business tourists: as they are not paying, they are more likely to use luxury hotels, first class travel, and taxis etc. *However*, the **self-employed** business traveller looks for value-for-money, and in times of economic recession, companies often become more cost-conscious and cut back on the extravagant spending of their employees.

● When compared with the average holiday, business trips are of **shorter** duration, but they are also more frequent. They are also more likely to take place between Monday and Friday, while the weekend is the preferred time for short breaks and other forms of leisure travel. Business tourism is also far less subject to **seasonal variation** than holidaymaking. Meetings, trade fairs and product launches take place throughout the year. If any variation exists, it is the tendency for these events to be least frequent at the traditional holiday times of the year.

● The **decision-timings** for business tourism are usually much shorter or much longer than those for holidays. An executive may suddenly have to fly to another country at only a few hours' notice, to deal with an unexpected crisis. On the other hand, large conferences, with thousands of delegates, must be organised years in advance.

There are other characteristics of business travellers which make them very good people to have as visitors. Those who travel for business purposes are often professional people, such as scientists, doctors or senior executives – i.e. influential people and decision-makers. To have them visit one's town, for a conference for example, is an ideal opportunity to make a good impression and to boost the town's image as a tourist destination or the ideal place to locate a factory or research laboratory etc. For this reason, free tours of the town or region are often offered to delegates, in the hope of attracting them back either with their families as leisure tourists, or bringing some other kind of business activity there.

Finally, the impact of business tourists on the physical environment is very minor. Public transport is favoured, so car parking does not present a problem with the residents. And business tourists, spending most of their time indoors, are the most discreetly invisible of visitors!

FACILITIES AND SERVICES

Some of the above characteristics of business tourism explain why it is a sector of the tourism industry which destinations are very keen to develop for themselves. All over Europe, cities from Inverness to Istanbul are making great efforts to attract these visitors who, as well as being very high-spending, are also happy to come when hotels and other facilities most need them – during the week and out-of-season.

With the whole world competing to host events which will bring in business tourists, how does a single destination, be it a country or an individual town or city, work to attract business tourism? What facilities and services are required in order to succeed in this particular tourism market?

Infrastructure

Clearly, a destination must possess the basic infrastructure which enables meeting and exhibitions to be accommodated there. The growth of **conference centres** in particular has been very marked in Europe in recent years. Geoffrey Smith, Marketing Director of the European Federation of Conference Towns, writes:

'In Europe, every year is the Year of Conventions. New facilities rise on every side, and inaugurations happen with impressive regularity. Every town in Europe would, it seems like to be a meeting place, a conference Mecca. New conference centres are continually planned; we are pleased that their architects are more prone now to consultation with the meeting planners and suppliers who will use them . . . It is also true that many of the large buildings emerging from their scaffolding all over Europe this past decade are used for many things other than conferences. Music, sports, exhibitions, rallies – few community activities can't be handled in a convention centre . . . It looks as though public investment in multi-purpose centres will continue.'

Parallel with the construction of new conferences centres in cities all over Europe, the past few decades have seen the conversion of many fine historic buildings, to make them suitable for accommodating large meetings. Europe's palaces, castles, opera houses and elegant public buildings are increasingly being used for these purposes. Examples of this trend abound all over the continent. Among the more

Fig 6.5 The new International Conference Centre, Birmingham, opened in April 1991

unusual include the Bishop's Palace in Antwerp, parts of which will be restored in 1993 when that city becomes the European City of Culture, to enable it to host congresses and business meetings; Malta's Mediterranean Conference Centre, housed in a former hospital, which combines gracious historic architecture with modern meeting facilities – a popular combination for meeting planners; while, in Stockholm, a highly successful venue is Norra Latin, a renovated historic school building in the central part of the city.

While conference centres are usually conveniently situated in city centres, the vast surface area required by **exhibition centres** means that they are most often placed out-of-town, where rents are cheaper. Many European cities have found that halls for exhibitions and trade fairs are best sited between the city itself and its airport, for ease of communication for those arriving by air.

Airport and rail termini constitute another aspect of the infrastructure required for business tourism. Participants must be able to travel with ease to their destination, so safe, fast, and efficient transport is vitally important. Quick transfers between termini and the venue are also necessary, whether by taxi, car hire or coach.

Finally, a wide range of **accommodation and entertainment facilities** is necessary, to house and amuse participants when they are not in attendance at the main event. First class hotel accommodation is indispensible, since this is the level which most executives are used to. However, many conferences delegates have more modest tastes or more modest budgets, and use less luxurious forms of accommodation such as budget hotels or university halls of residence. The wider the range of accommodation on offer at a destination, the more flexible it can be in what it proposes to its business tourism customers. Entertainment in the form of excursions, night-life, and leisure activities are an essential ingredient in a destination's business tourism 'mix'. For incentive travel in particular, these elements are vitally important; but even conference delegates, trade fair exhibitors and those attending business meetings need to have something to do in their leisure time away from work.

BUSINESS TOURISM SPECIALISTS

Apart from the physical infrastructure, destinations with a desire to succeed in the business tourism sector need to be able to offer the skills of a great number of people with experience in bringing together all of the above elements and taking responsibility for the countless number of detailed arrangements which go into the organisation of a large event. Most managers have neither the time, the contacts, or the local knowledge required personally to undertake the organisation of a conference in a distant city, for their company or association. For this reason, the detailed planning and supervision of business tourism events is usually a matter for trained specialists in the field.

For example, the vast amount of planning and organisation required to put together and supervise an incentive trip means that most companies use outside specialists to carry out this work on their behalf. Such specialists, known as **incentive travel houses**, undertake the organisation of the whole operation, from designing the package and fixing a budget, to overseeing the various elements and accompanying the incentive travellers, to providing a final report for the company, with feedback questionnaires from the participants.

When it comes to conferences, the conference organiser's helping hand comes in the form of the **ground operator**. Ground operators are usually incoming tour operators who specialise in making the detailed arrangements on-the-spot, from the transfer of delegates from airport to hotel, to the organisation of social events and excursions to fill the accompanying persons' time. These are people who know the destination thoroughly, who can make interesting suggestions to make the event a memorable one, and who can get things done. They tend to be

the people who take on much of the basic, everyday details, taking much of the stress away from the conference organiser.

For associations or companies which lack the resources to employ a full-time conference or exhibitions organiser on their own payroll, there are a number of specialist companies in every country who will take on the entire task. Often known as **destination management companies**, these specialists will organise the entire event – sending out invitations, arranging publicity, inviting the press, booking accommodation and tours, and generally working with ground operators on-the-spot to create a successful event for their client.

PROMOTION IN EUROPE

With so much competition between countries and even between cities in the same country, for business tourism, who are the people who are there to promote destinations as a whole, as opposed to individual conference centres, exhibition halls, hotels etc? Who is there to persuade companies and associations to hold their events in Sweden, or in Barcelona, for example?

National tourism organisations all over Europe have long since recognised the value of business tourism, and it is now rare to find one which does not already have its own business tourism department. Such departments exist specifically to produce publicity material about the country's assets as a business tourism destination, and to give impartial advice and assistance to those seeking to hold an exhibition or congress or to send their staff there as an incentive reward.

If a conference organiser decides that his or her association or company is to hold its conference in a particular country, the business travel department of that country's tourism organisation will be able to supply contacts of suitable venues or the names of destination management companies and ground operators who will be able to help.

Often, these departments call themselves **convention bureaux**, to distinguish themselves from the rest of the organisation which deals with leisure tourism. Convention bureaux also exist at the level of individual towns or cities, which they promote as business tourism destinations. They produce publicity materials aimed at conference organisers, they help hotels and conference centres bid for events, and they generally coordinate all the elements leading up to the decision to hold the event in that destination.

CASE STUDY
THE WORK OF THE CONVENTION BUREAU OF IRELAND

The Convention Bureau of Ireland (CBI) is responsible for coordinating the marketing of Ireland as a centre for conferences and business meetings. Created by Bord Fáilte, the Irish Tourist Board, its membership is composed of the main public and private sector organisations which are involved in promoting and servicing conferences, business meetings and incentive travel in Ireland. Its members include Aer Lingus, the Incoming Tour Operators' Association, the Irish Hotels Federation, Ryanair, Regional Tourism Associations and the University of Dublin. In their brochure shown in Fig 6.6, the CBI lists the services they provide.

In their publicity material for conference organisers, the CBI points out the advantages of Ireland as a business tourism destination.

An Irish welcome for your conference

What makes Ireland special as a conference venue is the warmth of the welcome you will receive. We Irish will be glad to see you, and will work with you to make your conference a memorable event in the history of your organisation.

In the world of international conferences, the Irish are recognised as the experts. We have a long track-record of success in staging sophisticated conferences and business meetings of all kinds. We have the experience, we have the facilities, we have the backdrop of an exceptionally beautiful country that is rich in culture and heritage.

But most of all, we have our tradition as a people who go out of our way to make the visitor feel at home. From the moment your delegates arrive in Ireland to the moment they bid us a reluctant farewell, they will be favoured guests. Conference visitors are particularly important to us in Ireland, and the resources of our country will unite to

How we can help

The Convention Bureau offers a full and impartial consultancy service, so that all the accumulated experience of successful conferences and business meetings can be put at the disposal of anyone bringing this business to Ireland. Specifically, we can:

- *Advise* on how to bid for the meeting, including the mobilisation of support for the proposal so that it can be presented as a national invitation.

- *Help* in the preparing of proposals.

- *Support* inspection visits to Ireland by convention organisers.

- *Advise* on the organisation of the event, whether it is a conference with several thousand delegates or a business gathering of only a few people.

- *Act as a bridge* to suppliers of convention services. In particular, we can help with hotel accommodation, and with logistical matters — transport, translation, sight-seeing, etc.

- *Help* arrange special entertainments.

- *Help* arrange Government involvement and entertainment, where appropriate.

Fig 6.6 Services provided by the Convention Bureau

make your event a highly memorable success.

Fáilte is the Gaelic word for welcome. Bring your conference to Ireland and experience what it means.

Next, 'The Irish Experience', gives a snapshot

description of that country's attractions for the business tourist:

'The Irish Experience – plenty to see, plenty to do'

Before, during and after the conference, Ireland offers a dazzling variety of things to do.

Sightseeing is a must for any Irish visit. The incomparable beauty of an unspoilt countryside is matched by an historical and archaeological heritage that reaches back seven millenia. You could spend months or even years exploring the beauties of Ireland, but even the few days of a pre- or post-conference tour is enough to get a taste of one of the world's great travel experiences.

For the active conference visitor, Ireland is a delight. We are a sporting nation, and whatever your favourite outdoor activity, you will surely find an opportunity to enjoy it – or to join as a spectator in one of our national games. Golf, tennis, horse-riding and sailing are particularly popular in Ireland.

Exploring Ireland's rich culture and traditions will be another stimulating bonus for your conference delegates.

Ireland's rich heritage is both highly interesting and readily accessible. You have only to enter one of our pubs to experience the wit and the command of language that have made the Irish masters of literature down through the centuries. Our theatrical tradition is vibrantly alive, as is our love of music that produces world-class performers in everything from folk to rock and pop.

Irish arts and crafts are another source of excitement, providing the visitor with the choice of a wide range of purchases and an insight into the special character of Ireland.

Finally, Ireland's accessibility from the rest of the world is emphasised:

Ireland – at the crossroads of the world

A major advantage of Ireland as a conference location is that we are easy to get to.

From North America, Ireland is the nearest European country (5 hours from New York). It is served by four airports, at Dublin, Shannon, Cork and Knock.

From Europe, Ireland is only a short distance away. Most of the major centres are within less than two hours' flying time. Dublin has direct air connections to over 20 European cities, and direct car-ferry connections to three European ports.

From the UK, there are direct connections from 19 airports to no fewer than nine airports in Ireland – Dublin, Shannon, Cork, Galway, Waterford, Knock, Kerry, Sligo, and Carrickfin (County Donegal). There are many daily connections by car-ferry from UK ports to Dublin, Dun Laoghaire and Rosslare.

From elsewhere in the world, Ireland is easily reached by direct flights from such gateways of London, Paris, Amsterdam, Frankfurt and Zurich. London, less than an hour away, is linked to Dublin by over 50 flights a day.

CASE STUDY

THE EUROPEAN FEDERATION OF CONFERENCE TOWNS

On the European level, business tourism promotion for the entire continent is the responsibility of the European Federation of Conference Towns. Based in Brussels, the EFCT brings together the main business tourism cities of Europe, and works to maintain high standards in every aspect of European conference activity, and to achieve wider recognition of the vital importance of business tourism. It has seven main objectives:

● to act as a focal point, making it as easy as possible for meeting-planners to arrange events in Europe

● to make information on European business tourism destinations and facilities widely available

● to assist meeting-planners to find the city or town, anywhere in Europe, that meets their particular requirements

● to support its own members internationally

● to collaborate with international authorities, associations and other institutions

● to undertake specialised training in aspects of conference work

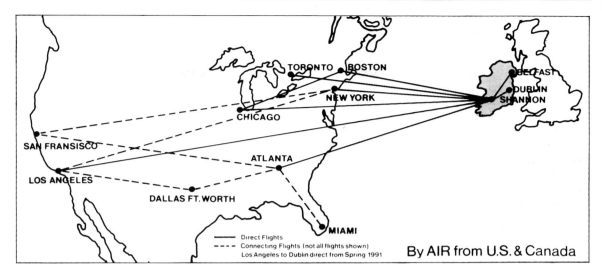

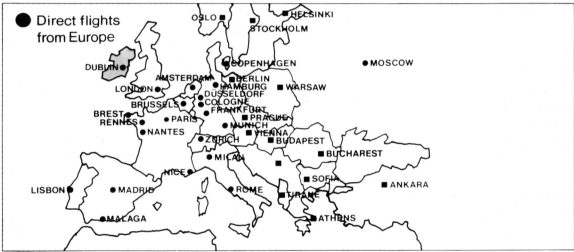

Fig 6.7 Direct flights to Ireland

• to act as a spokesperson on behalf of the European conference industry.

The EFCT, which was founded in 1964, has over 70 members from a total of 22 countries in Western and Eastern Europe. To be eligible for membership, a town must satisfy certain strict criteria:

• it must have conference facilities for at least 300 delegates, with proper equipment and good services

• it must have good quality hotel accommodation for at least 300 delegates

• it must be capable of providing adequate transportation for delegates

• it must have available a team of specialists in conference handling

• it must be experienced in handling a number of international congresses in recent years

• freedom of travelling to and from the member's country must be assured.

The EFCT's main publication aimed at meeting-planners, entitled *Your Convention in Europe*, lists basic information on each member town. It is financed by the advertisements which members buy, to help tempt the meeting-planners. Figure 6.8 shows the page on Vienna (Wien).

A personal contact is given, to whom the meeting-planner may apply for further information. But by using the symbols shown in Fig 6.9, readers should be able to decide if Vienna is a suitable destination for the size of convention they are planning.

Every year, the EFCT also publishes its *Report on Europe*, an annual survey of the European conference scene, giving a report from each country on the state of its business tourism market for that year. The introduction to its *Report of Europe '90*, written at the height of the Gulf crisis, makes gloomy reading. It describes the devastating impact of the Gulf war on Europe's meetings industry. However, 1990 had begun on a note of optimism and progress:

'Our survey indicates that (1990) was a good year, and responsible, professional operators, whether facility owners, services, or planners, were busy, effective and profitable.

More centres opened, and more hoteliers recognised meetings as an essential growth area – not just something to fill the bad months. Several chains appointed Conference Directors to take responsibility for an entire conference project and provide meeting planners with the help they have demanded for years.

Convention bureaux appeared in many towns, reflecting increased awareness among local governments of the essential nature of conferences, and the awareness that delegates are the most rewarding of all visitors.

Meeting-planners were more educated about the market, eager to get more for their money, aware that most things are negotiable, and more demanding than ever.'

CASE STUDY

MARKETING BRITAIN AS A BUSINESS DESTINATION

Workshops are used to conduct business in the realm of business tourism as well as leisure tourism. They bring together those with something to sell and those looking for something to buy. The buyers in this case were those people in large associations who are responsible for choosing conference venues. Conference planners are known to like to 'shop around' and evaluate a number of venues, before deciding on the most suitable for their event. This characteristic prompted the organising of a very specialised business tourism reception and workshop in Paris in 1988.

The British Conference and Exhibition Centres Export Council (BCECEC)

Those with something to sell, on this occasion, were the members of the BCECEC. The BCECEC represents the nine largest, purpose-built conference centres in Britain:

The Scottish Exhibition and Conference Centre, Glasgow
St David's Hall, Cardiff
The Bournemouth International Centre
The National Exhibition Centre, Birmingham
The Brighton Centre
The Harrogate International Conference and Exhibition Centre
The Royal Centre and Conference Hall, Nottingham
Wembley Conference Centre, London
The Barbican Centre, London

BCECEC's principal aim is to market overseas the facilities and services offered by these conference centres, in order to attract major conferences, congresses and exhibitions to Britain. Incoming tourism's technical standing as an *export* for the destination country explains why the BCECEC is termed an 'export council'. The other members of the BCECEC are the British Tourist Authority and British Airways, both of whom have, in their own way, a considerable interest in attracting business visitors to Britain.

Background to the workshop

In October 1988, the members of BCECEC were flown to Paris by British Airways to attend an important marketing mission, organised in the form of a workshop.

Paris was chosen as the venue for the workshop, as there is a high concentration of international associations which have their headquarters offices in that city – over 1000 out of 6000–7000 worldwide. International

Wien Österreich

Fremdenverkehrsverband für Wien
Kongressbüro
Kinderspitalgasse 5
A-1095 Wien
Tel. (43-222) 431608
Telex 1-34653
Fax: (43-222) 433292
Leopold E. Saul, Manager Kongressbüro

✈	1 600 000
→	Schwechat/19 km/31
🚌	33
H	A1, A2, A4, A20, A21, A22

Facilities		C	E
Austria Center Vienna	14	4200	8205
Hofburg	21	1500	4600
Stadthalle	6	11000	8600
Palais Schwarzenberg	8	250	500
Palais Auersperg	10	300	400
Palais Ferstl	5	400	900
Palais Pallavicini	13	250	440
Kongresshaus	5	690	600
Messepalaet	2	1320	2700
Künstlerhaus	3	300	600
Konzerthaus	3	1840	1200
segelände	3	400	unbegrenzt
Sofiensäle	4	1100	1200
Oberlaa	1	2730	1000

Hotels	⌂	☐	C	B
*****	14	3123	1250	—
****	66	6336	500	380
***	61	3675	—	—
**	39	1180	—	—

Fig 6.8 A page taken from EFCT's publication *Your Convention Europe*, advertising Vienna

Our member towns	Nos villes membres	Unsere Mitgliedstädte
The following pages show the overall facilities of our member towns. It is easy to get much more information about any of them by filling in the Enquiry Form on page 79. You can be sure that all the usual equipment, such as simultaneous interpretation, various forms of projection, and a variety of other useful services is available in every EFCT venue.	Dans les pages suivantes vous trouverez la présentation globale de nos villes membres. Des informations plus détaillées peuvent être demandées à l'aide du bulletin de commande à la page 79. Il va de soi que les centres de congrès de la FEVC disposent tous des installations usuelles pour la traduction simultanée, les diverses projections, etc.	Auf den folgenden Seiten finden Sie die Angaben über das Gesamtangebot unserer Mitgliedstädte. Nähere Informationen können mit dem Bestellschein auf Seite 79 angefordert werden. Selbstverständlich verfügen alle Kongresszentren der EVK über die üblichen Einrichtungen und Hilfsmittel wie z.B. für Simultan-Übersetzung, Projektionen, usw.
⌂ No. of hotels	⌂ Nombre d'hôtels	⌂ Zahl der Hotels
☐ No. of meeting halls (Conference Centres) No. of bedrooms (Hotels)	☐ Nombre de salles (Centres de congrès) Nombre de chambres (hôtels)	☐ Zahl der Konferenzräume (Kongresszentren) Zimmerzahl (Hotels)
C Maximum capacity	C Capacité maximale	C Maximal-Kapazität
B Maximum banquet capacity	B Capacité maximale pour banquets	B Maximal-Kapazität für Bankette
E Exhibition space in sqm	E Surface maximale d'exposition en m²	E Maximal-Ausstellungsfläche in m²
✹ City population	✹ Population urbaine	✹ Einwohnerzahl
✈ Airport name/Distance to city centre/no of international airlines	✈ Aéroport/distance du centre de ville/ Nombre de lignes aériennes internationales	✈ Flughafen/Distanz zum Stadtzentrum/Zahl der internationalen Fluglinien
⚓ Sea-port/no of departures weekly	⚓ Port maritime/Départs par semaine	⚓ Seehafen/Abfahrten pro Woche
🚂 No of international trains daily	🚂 Nombre de trains internationaux par jour	🚂 Zahl der internationalen Züge pro Tag
H Highways	H Autoroutes	H Autobahnen
***** De luxe hotel	***** Hôtels de luxe	***** Hotels der Luxusklasse
**** First class hotels	**** Hôtels de 1er rang	**** Hotels erster Klasse
*** Standard class hotels	*** Hôtels classe standard	*** Hotels der Standard-Klasse
** Tourist class hotels	** Hôtels classe touriste	** Touristenklasse

Fig 6.9 The key to symbols used in Fig 6.8

associations were the target market for the workshop, as these are the type of organisations which hold the major annual congresses which the BCECEC members are well equipped to host.

Using mailing lists compiled by the BTA, invitations to attend the workshop were sent out to key contacts working for associations known to stage meetings for 400–plus candidates. In the event, acceptances to attend were double the number expected, demonstrating the effectiveness of the contacts mailing lists. Much of the BTA's research in this respect goes into the pattern of decision-taking. It may be one person, a committee, or a ballot of all members who select an association's next conference venue. The success of such events as business travel workshops depends on inviting those in the position of making the decision.

The evening before the event was used to hold a meeting of the BCECEC, since all of its members were present. Plans were finalised for the council's forthcoming marketing missions to the USA and Scandinavia – all financed by the BCECEC's £40 000 budget, of which a quarter is provided by the BTA.

The running of the workshop

The St James's Club, a small chateau-hotel near the Bois de Boulogne, owned by the British hotel group, Norfolk Capital, was the venue for the event. Business for the day was conducted in French, the first language of most of the guests. Since not all members of the council spoke fluent French, staff from the BTA's Paris office were on hand to act as interpreters. Around 50 guests were present, representing associations ranging from the International Federation of Advertising Clubs to the International Civil Airport Association.

The event started with a presentation outlining the day's programme, given by an executive of the BTA Paris office, followed by a general introduction to Britain's advantages for conference planners – good communications, modern hotels, traditional country houses, as well as purpose-built exhibition and conference centres.

Next, the Marketing Manager of the Bournemouth International Centre gave a thumbnail sketch of the different facilities on offer at each of the nine conference centres, and personally introduced each of those representing those centres at the event, as well as the British Airways representative. This was followed by the screening of a short video entitled *La Grande-Bretagne Parle Affaires*, the French version of the BCECEC's promotional video, *Britain's Talking Business*, which features the nine conference centres.

Over lunch, and during the early part of the afternoon, the serious business of the day was conducted, as individual BCECEC members and guests discussed, person to person, what the former were looking for in conference venues and what the latter had to offer. Contacts were forged, notes taken, and agreements made to exchange more detailed information, or to meet again, at future dates.

After the guests left (each with a free copy of the video, together with an information pack, giving technical details of the centres), there was a debriefing session of BCECEC members, during which everyone contributed information which they had picked up from the guests: size of conference, next date, special requests, and so on. This pooling of information enabled any member to follow up, and possibly make a bid for, any forthcoming conference to be held by any of the guests – not only those to whom he or she had spoken.

Conclusion

The BCECEC Paris workshop was the first of its kind held by the council, and it was generally agreed by all the members to have been very successful. Prior to this event, in order to try to attract conferences, members had had to rely on individual mail-shots, a much less effective marketing method. The workshop had provided the opportunity for BCECEC members and potential customers to get together and discuss business face-to-face, giving Britain itself a head start over other countries trying to attract major congresses.

The cooperation with the British Tourist Authority and British Airways gave the workshop an impact which individual conference centres working alone would not be able to create. Consequently, this kind of joint-scheme marketing has been used regularly by the BCECEC since 1988 to bring important international conferences to Britain.

CONCLUSION

The business tourism market for Europe is a buoyant one, in the three main sectors, meetings, incentive travel, and exhibitions and trade fairs. Nevertheless, the Gulf War showed how unpredictable events can upset the entire market, and how quickly people can opt to conduct their business from home rather than risk a trip abroad in troubled times. The tourism industry was reminded at the time of the options to business travel. Video conference services, for example, can bring together business people from different continents much more safely and much more cheaply. A two-hour video connection between London and New York, for example, cost about £2400 using a public video conferencing room leased from British Telecom. Six people can take part. By contrast, just one round trip business class airfare on British Airways from New York to London is £2112. Add to this the cost of a night in a hotel and the time lost travelling, and the advantages of opting for high technology instead of business travel become obvious.

However, business tourism in all of its forms concerns much more than simple dialogue. The need to meet face-to-face and to relax together as well as do business together is a very human one, and the general signs are that people will continue to travel to meet those with similar interests, business or otherwise, to their own.

Furthermore, there are certain indications that business tourism within Europe is set for a period of growth. Ongoing political and economic changes in Europe, connected particularly with the advent of the Single European Market, will inevitably create demand for extensive intra-European business travel. The expected rush of takeovers following the single internal market legislation, described in Chapter 2, will create new multi-national companies in Europe, with a corresponding increase in the volume of international business meetings.

It is also likely that over the next decade, East European countries will emerge as generators of demand for business travel, as their own economic activity steps up and they look further afield for new trading partners. They will also grow as destinations for business tourism as they are already equipping themselves with the necessary infrastructure and skills.

ASSIGNMENTS

1 The International Rotary Association Conference. The International Rotary Association's members are representatives of Rotary Clubs from over 50 different countries around the world. The Association has decided to hold its annual five-day conference in Britain, in 1995.

2000 delegates are expected to attend, with about 60 per cent being accompanied by their spouses.

The conference will include an exhibition on the theme of charity work undertaken by the different Rotary Clubs. This will require about 1500 square metres.

Some of the delegates are elderly, and, therefore, walking distances should be kept to a minimum.

The spouses will require a separate room for their own meetings, but they will also want to have a programme of other activities, such as visiting places of interest in the region.

For the five days in question, conference centres in Bournemouth, Harrogate, Glasgow and Cardiff have availability. As the Association's meeting-planner, you have to choose the venue.

On the basis of the information given in Fig 6.10, which one would you recommend? Give as many reasons as you can for your choice, including your reasons for rejecting each of the other three. How would you arrange the various elements of the conference in your chosen venue?

2 Incentive travel in Monaco. The newspaper article in Fig 6.11, published in the *Financial Times*, describes business tourism developments in Monaco.

As the manager of a major incentive travel house eager to break into the Monaco market for this form of business tourism, you have to draft two letters. One will be mailed out to the hoteliers of Monaco, and the other will be a mailing to the managing directors of large businesses in your own country.

In the first you have to convince the hoteliers of the *advantages* to their businesses of having incentive travel participants as guests, in order to interest them in this market. In the second, you have to convince the managing directors of the value of incentive travel as a reward for well-achieving employees. Also, say why Monaco would be an ideal destination for incentives, giving an example of a possible five-day incentive travel itinerary.

Keep both letters as business-like as possible, but use language which is most likely to persuade the readers of these letters.

Fig 6.10 (a) Bournemouth International Centre; (b) St David's Hall, Cardiff; (c) Scottish Exhibition and Conference Centre, Glasgow; (d) Harrogate International Centre

BOURNEMOUTH INTERNATIONAL CENTRE
CENTRE INTERNATIONAL DE BOURNEMOUTH   Exeter Road, Bournemouth BH2 5BH

Bournemouth International Centre Exterior View
Centre International de Bournemouth Vue de l'Extérieur

CAPACITIES	AREA (SQ M)	THEATRE STYLE	CLASSROOM STYLE
Windsor Hall	2,000	3,900	900
Tregonwell Hall	900	1,200	360

CAPACITE	SUPERFICIE (m²)	STYLE THEATRE	STYLE SALLE DE CLASSE
Windsor Hall	2.000	3.900	900
Tregonwell Hall	900	1.200	360

BIC
Modern and purpose-built, the Bournmouth International Centre offers superb, sophisticated facilities for conferences and/or exhibitions. Both main halls are fully air-conditioned, with amplification to conference standards, and offer facilities for simultaneous interpretation and projection.

ANCILLARY ACCOMMODATION
There is a variety of meeting rooms and catering areas in the BIC for seminars, break-out sessions, committee meetings, registration, poster displays, conference offices, VIP receptions and lunches.
The BIC is centrally situated on the seafront and close to all amenities. There is on-site car parking for 710 cars and 16 coaches/lorries.

HOTEL ACCOMMODATION
Bournemouth has a wide range of hotel accommodation, ranging from five-star luxurious to the simple guesthouse, with a total of 35,000 beds. Many of the main hotels are within a few minutes walk of the BIC and there is a local accommodation agency who will handle all reservations.

INTERNATIONAL CONNECTIONS
Excellent motorway links with London's Heathrow and Gatwick Airports (90 and 120 minutes' by coach), and the continental ferryports of Portsmouth and Weymouth (40 minutes by coach). The local Bournemouth International Airport also has European flights. Central London is only 80 minutes by train.

BOURNEMOUTH PAVILION
The Pavilion, three minutes walk across the Gardens, offers superb facilities for banquets, civic receptions and gala occasions.

CENTRE INTERNATIONAL DE BOURNEMOUTH
Moderne et construit spécialement, le Centre International de Bournemouth propose des installations superbes pour conférences, congrès et/ou expositions. Les deux principales salles sont climatisées, équipées d'un matériel d'amplification répondant aux normes établies pour les congrès et permettant l'interprétation simultanée et la projection.

SALLES ANCILLAIRES
Le centre offre diverses salles de réunion avec possibilité de restauration pour colloques, séances secondaires, réunions de comité, immatriculation, exposition d'affiches, bureaux de congrès, salles d'accueil pour personnalités de marque et déjeuners.
Le Centre International de Bournemouth est situé près du centre ville, au bord de la mer, et tout près des magasins, etc. . . . Il y a un parking sur place pour 710 voitures et 16 autocars/camions.

CHAMBRES D'HOTEL
Bournemouth possède des hôtels de toutes catégories, depuis les grands hôtels de luxe à cinq étoiles jusqu'aux petites pensions. En tout, 35.000 lits. Bon nombre des grands hôtels sont à quelques minutes à pied du Centre International. Une agence locale peut, s'occuper de toutes les réservations sur demande.

LIAISONS INTERNATIONALES
Excellentes liaisons par autoroute avec les aéroports de Londres Heathrow et Gatwick (90 et 120 minutes en autocar) et les ports à ferries de Portsmouth et Weymouth (40 minutes en autocar). L'aéroport international de Bournemouth a des liaisons avec le continent. Le centre de Londres n'est qu'à 80 minutes en train.

PAVILLON DE BOURNEMOUTH
Le Pavillon (trois minutes à pied, à travers les Jardins) est superbement équipé pour les banquets, les réceptions civiques et les grands galas.

Windsor Hall

Windsor Hall

ST DAVID'S HALL, CARDIFF, WALES

Please note many areas in St David's hall are of irregular shape and have a variation in ceiling height. In general minimum measurements are shown.

ST DAVID'S HALL, CARDIFF, PAYS DE GALLES

Venue	CAPACITIES						DIMENSIONS			ACCESS	
	Theatre	Classroom	Boardroom	Reception	Banquet	Dinner Dance	Width	Length	Height	Vehicle Access	Disabled Access
Auditorium	2000	—	—	—	—	—	Semi Circular			—	✔
St. Asaph Room	75	35	30	100	60	—	23' (7m)	38' (11.5m)	9' (2.75m)	—	✔
Green Room	60	30	30	85	—	—	26' (7m)	35' (10.5m)	9' (2.75m)	—	—
VIP Room	20	12	14	20	14	—	16' 6" (5.4m)	18' 3" (6.0m)	9' (2.75m)	—	✔
Celebrity Restaurant	—	—	—	155	140	150	Irregular Shape	8.6' 8"		—	✔
Level 2 Foyer Lounge	—	—	—	270	—	150	Irregular Shape	8'		—	✔
Level 3 Foyer Lounge	—	. —	—	400	270	350	Irregular Shape	8'		—	✔
Level 4 Foyer Lounge	—	—	—	100	—	100	Irregular Shape	8'		—	✔
Level 5 Foyer Lounge	200	50	35	300	150	250	Irregular Shape	8'		—	✔
7 x Dressing Rooms	Suitable for small syndicate/office use ranging from a capacity of 5–25 people						—	—	—	—	—
7 x Changing Rooms							—	—	—	—	—

TECHNICAL FACILITIES
St David's Hall, the most televised Concert/Conference Hall in the U.K., has unrivalled technical facilities including a permanent BBC studio for full radio and TV coverage. It also houses a full Conference Co-ordination Division.

MEETING AREAS
The main Auditorium seats up to 2000; a selection of smaller meeting and display areas is also available.

CATERING
St David's Hall offers a full in-house catering service including a restaurant and facilities for VIP receptions.

HOTEL ACCOMMODATION
Numerous quality 4 star hotels are situated within minutes walk of St David's Hall; a good range of 2 and 3 star accommodation is also available. Most have parking facilities for residents and are conveniently located for walking access to the conference centre, shopping facilities and places of entertainment.

TRAVEL
Cardiff Wales Airport: regular Amsterdam connections; Cardiff–Paris flights planned for 1989. London Heathrow and Gatwick Airports easily accessible by road and rail.
Main Line Rail Station: high speed connections to all key centres in U.K. London less than 2 hours away.
Motorway Links: M4 Motorway (from London); nearby City centre car-parking.

INSTALLATIONS TECHNIQUES
Le Hall de St David, la salle de concert et de congrès la plus télévisée de Grande-Bretagne, propose des services techniques inégalés, notamment un studio permanent de la BBC pour toutes les émissions de radio et de télévision. Il possède aussi une division Coordination Congrès au complet.

LIEUX DE RÉUNION
La salle principale peut recevoir jusqu'à 2.000 personnes assises. Il y a aussi d'autres lieux de réunion et de présentation de dimensions plus modestes.

RESTAURANTS
Le Hall de St David offre un service complet de restauration, notamment un restaurant et des salles de réception pour personnalités de marque.

CHAMBRES D'HÔTEL
Il y a de nombreux hôtels de qualité quatre étoiles à quelques minutes de marche du Hall-. Il y a aussi de nombreux hôtels à 2 et 3 étoiles. La plupart de ces établissements ont des parkings pour les résidents et se trouvent à proximité du centre des congrès, des magasins et des salles de spectacles qui peuvent s'atteindre à pied.

VOYAGES
Aéroport Cardiff-Pays-de-Galles: liaisons régulières avec Amsterdam. Des vols Cardiff – Paris sont prévus pour 1989. Les aéroports de Londres Heathrow et Gatwick sont aisément accessibles par la route et le rail.
Gare de chemin de fer: liaisons rapides avec tous les grands centres de Grande-Bretagne. Londres est à moins de 2 heures.
Liaison routière: Autoroute M4 (de Londres). Parkings près du centre de la ville.

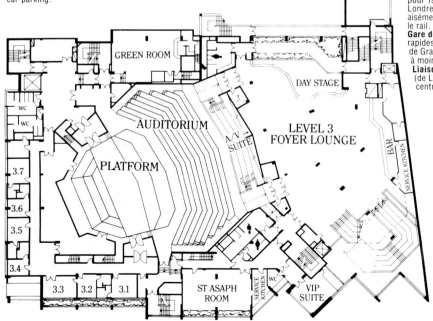

(b)

Centre écossais d'expositions et de conférences

General Information

Scottish Exhibition & Conference Centre (SECC) is a purpose built venue providing 19000 sq metres of exhibition space. The Centre consists of 5 halls and provides accommodation for exhibitions, conferences and spectator events.

5 Flexible Halls

The Centre has five halls and can accommodate up to 10000 conference delegates:

Hall 1: Principal conference auditorium with seating 2000 people. 1570m^2.
Hall 2: 775m^2.
Hall 3: 2315m^2.
Hall 4: The Centre's largest hall with delegate capacity of 10000 people 10065m^2.
Hall 5: 4105m^2:
Bovis
Suite: Breakout room with seating theatre style for 250 people.

Facilities and Access

In addition to 5 halls, the Centre offers car parking for 3200 vehicles, has its own heliport and railway station, 4 restaurants, 5 bars, bank, shop, car hire and business centre.

Forum Hotel Glasgow

On site accommodation comprising 285 bedrooms. The Forum provides 14 conference rooms (with delegate capacity of up to 1200 people), banqueting facilities, restaurants, etc. These rooms complement the 4 breakout rooms already in the Centre.

Contact:
Scottish Exhibition & Conference Centre, Glasgow G3 8YW.
Tel: 041-248 3000

Informations générales

Le Centre écossais d'expositions et de conférences (SECC) est spécialement construit, comprenant 1900 metres carrés de halls climatisés. Les 5 halls sont disponibles pour des expositions, conventions et spectacles.

5 Halls à fonctions multiples

Le Centre offre 5 halls et peut recevoir jusqu'a à 10000 délégués.

Hall 1: Salle principale de conférences avec sièges pour 2000 personnes 1570m^2.
Hall 2: 775m^2.
Hall 3: 2315m^2.
Hall 4: La plus grande salle du Centre qui peut recevoir 10000 délégués 10065m^2.
Hall 5: 4105m^2.
Bovis
Suite: Salle de réunion avec sièges style théâtre pour 250 personnes.

Facilités et Accès

Le centre offre également parkings pour 3200 voitures, gare de chemin de fer, héliport, 4 restaurants, 5 bars, banque, magasin, centre de commerce et location de voiture.

Hôtel Forum

Situé à côté du Centre, l'hôtel offre 285 chambres, 14 salles de réunion (pouvant recevoir jusqu'à 1200 délégués), salles de banquets, restaurants, etc.

S'addresser à:
Scottish Exhibition & Conference Centre, Glasgow G3 8YW.
Tel: 041-248 3000

(c)

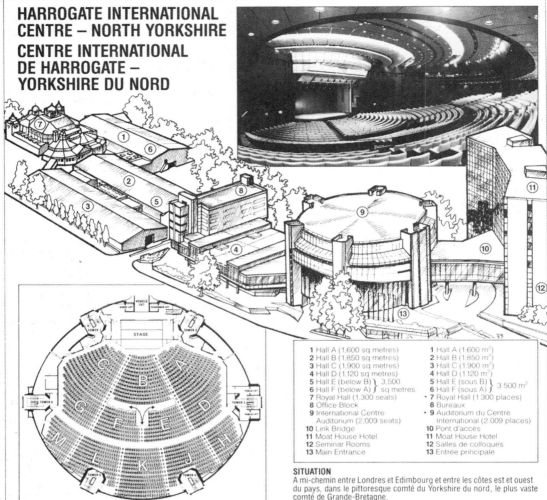

HARROGATE INTERNATIONAL CENTRE – NORTH YORKSHIRE
CENTRE INTERNATIONAL DE HARROGATE – YORKSHIRE DU NORD

Main Auditorium   *Principal auditorium Français*

1 Hall A (1,600 sq metres)	1 Hall A (1.600 m²)
2 Hall B (1,850 sq metres)	2 Hall B (1.850 m²)
3 Hall C (1,900 sq metres)	3 Hall C (1.900 m²)
4 Hall D (1,120 sq metres)	4 Hall D (1.120 m²)
5 Hall E (below B) } 3,500	5 Hall E (sous B) } 3.500 m²
6 Hall F (below A) } sq metres	6 Hall F (sous A) }
7 Royal Hall (1.300 seats)	7 Royal Hall (1.300 places)
8 Office Block	8 Bureaux
9 International Centre Auditorium (2,009 seats)	9 Auditorium du Centre International (2.009 places)
10 Link Bridge	10 Pont d'accès
11 Moat House Hotel	11 Moat House Hotel
12 Seminar Rooms	12 Salles de colloques
13 Main Entrance	13 Entrée principale

LOCATION
Halfway between London/Edinburgh and East/West coasts in picturesque North Yorkshire – England's largest county.

ACCESS
Air – Manchester International Airport (60 mins drive), Leeds/Bradford Airport (direct links with London Heathrow etc) (20 mins drive).
Sea – N.S.F. from Europort to Hull (90 mins drive).
Road – Motorways M1, M62 & A1 (15 mins drive).
Rail – InterCity service Kings Cross/Harrogate and numerous links via Leeds and York.

CONFERENCE FACILITIES
International Centre – 2,000 seats, air-conditioned, V.I.P. suites, etc.

EXHIBITION FACILITIES
Over 10,000 square metres in six interlinked halls.

BANQUETS
For up to 1,300 in dual purpose Hall D (see plan).

ACCOMMODATION
Plentiful from large to small with a warm welcome.

AMENITIES
Restaurants, tea rooms, golf, swimming, theatre, cinema, nightclubs, wine bars, specialist shopping, antique markets, parks and gardens, history and heritage, natural beauty and traditional Turkish Baths!

SITUATION
A mi-chemin entre Londres et Edimbourg et entre les côtes est et ouest du pays, dans le pittoresque comté du Yorkshire du nord, le plus vaste comté de Grande-Bretagne.

ACCÈS
Par avion: Aéroport de Manchester International (60 minutes en voiture du Centre). Aéroport Leeds/Bradford (Liaisons directes avec Londres Heathrow, etc. . . .) (20 minutes du Centre en voiture).
Par bateau: Ferries Mer du Nord de l'Europort de Hull (90 minutes en voiture).
En voiture: Autoroutes M1, M62 et A1 (15 minutes en voiture).
Par train: Service Intercity Kings Cross/Harrogate et nombreuses lignes via Leeds et York.

CONGRÈS ET CONFÉRENCES
Centre International: 2.000 places, climatisation, salles pour personnalités de marque, etc. . . .

EXPOSITIONS
Plus de 10.000 mètres carrés, dans six salles communicantes.

BANQUETS
Pour un maximum de 1.300 personnes, dans le hall D (voir plan) à double fonction.

CHAMBRES D'HÔTEL
Nombreuses, dans des établissements grands et petits. Accueil chaleureux.

ATRACTIONS
Restaurants, salons de thé, golf, natation, théâtres, cinémas, boîtes de nuit, 'wine bars', shopping spécial, marchés d'antiquités, parcs et jardins, histoire et héritage, beauté du paysage et bains turcs traditionnels!

(d)

Conferences, trade fairs gain ground

MONACO is intent on maintaining the image it has built since the establishment of Monte Carlo as a top-of-the-range tourist destination in the second half of the 19th century.

This has meant adapting to changes in people's habits since then. For example, the high season in Monaco is now the summer, not the winter, and the principality has to cast its net further afield than the pages of Debrett or the Almanach de Gotha.

But Monaco preserves a reputation as a place where the very wealthy can stroll around in their diamonds and furs, without being robbed or being trampled by hordes of tourists.

"I would say that safety, cleanliness and decorum, in that order, are the three main charms of Monaco," says one long-term resident.

The principality's tourism statistics present a slightly different picture.

Occupancy of the principality's 2,400 hotel rooms, which averaged 68 per cent in the first half of the 1980s, plunged to 55 per cent in 1986.

It has since recovered somewhat, to reach averages of 61.5 per cent in 1988 and 61.6 per cent last year.

Even in the peak summer months, Monaco's hotels are far from bursting point.

Last year, occupancy reached 67 per cent in June, 64 per cent in July and 73 per cent in August.

To counter this, Monaco has an active policy of seeking to draw new visitors and to spread their visits more evenly throughout the year.

This has been done both by the development of business tourism – through conferences and incentive travel – and by the creation of special attractions – such as ballets and operas, auctions, Formula One car races and tennis tournaments, or charity balls and social galas.

"We have two elements to help us regularise the occupancy of hotels: congresses and the creation of events," says Mr Gilles Noghès, managing director of the Monaco Government Tourist and Convention Authority.

Room occupancy is in fact highest in May (77 per cent) and September (81 per cent) when special events and conferences combine with the summer season to fill up the principality.

The development of Monaco as a congress centre began as early as the 1960s, but did not take off until the opening of the 600-room Loews Hotel on the seafront in 1975 – at the time the largest hotel on the Côte d'Azur – and the inauguration of the Centre de Congrés-Auditorium in 1978.

Congresses now account for around 30 per cent of Monaco's tourism.

The list includes a few professional organisations, but the principality attracts mostly company conferences and product launches with up to 1,000 participants.

Mr Noghès is confident, however, that Monaco will be able to extend its appeal in the future when the new Centre Culturel et des Expositions, under construction on the Avenue Princesse Grace, near the Larvotto beach, opens at the end of 1994 or the beginning of 1995.

The increase in top class hotel capacity includes the 200-room Abela in Fontvieille and the 170-room Metropole

The centre will boast a 1,200-seat auditorium and a 900-seat amphitheatre, as well as six smaller halls. Most importantly, it will offer 4,800 square metres of exhibition space.

"The centre will help us to develop our business tourism, and in particular trade fairs.

"The present Congress Centre has hosted a lot of trade conferences, but it does not have the space for big exhibitions," Mr Noghès explains.

"By tradition, and by its hotel rooms, Monaco is at the top of the range.

"Over 80 per cent of our rooms are in the four-star or five-star luxury category. We have to seek this top-of-the-range image as much for congresses as for leisure tourism," he adds.

The creation and promotion of special events is the other way Monaco boosts tourism when visitors might not otherwise think of coming.

"We have to compromise. We might like to have our events in flat periods, but we also have to arrange them in periods when people are available," says Mr Raoul Biancheri, chairman and chief executive of the Société des Bains de Mer (SBM), the leading operator of casinos and hotels, which sponsors many of Monaco's best-known events in its halls, theatres and sports arenas.

Some events have been established on the calendar for years. The Grand Prix will be raced for the 48th time on May 27, and the 58th Monte Carlo Rally was run this year.

More recent additions to the Monaco calendar are the Fireworks Festival, now 25 years old, and the Circus Festival, 15 years old. The Tennis Open is younger still.

"The events serve two functions – to fill the hotels, and to provide publicity for the principality and for the hotels. The Bal de la Rose is an event for Monaco and for the SBM. I can't say that all our events make money. Some break even, others cost us a bit," Mr Biancheri explains.

Monaco has also made considerable efforts to simplify access for hurried travellers – an important consideration, since the average length of stay has fallen sharply to around three nights.

The heliport, on the seafront in Fontvieille, plays an important role. More than 110,000 passengers used the service to and from Nice airport last year. The journey takes seven minutes and, for a single traveller, it is cheaper than a taxi.

More leisurely means of access, however, are also being promoted. Mr Noghès is keen to develop Monaco as a centre for luxury cruises, with vessels like the Norwegian-registered Sea Goddess I and II, or the Bahamian sailing yachts Wind Spirit and Wind Star operating from the principality. He also hopes the Orient Express will be able to stop in Monaco.

If Monaco's hoteliers are concerned about their room occupancy rates, they appear paradoxically calm about the increase in hotel capacity.

This includes the 200-room Abela in Fontvieille, and the 170-room Metropole, which opened in January only a stone's throw away from the Casino, in a position to directly compete with the Hotel de Paris or the Hermitage.

Mr Nabil Boustany, who spent eight years and $120m rebuilding the Metropole, feels that there will be no problem of excess capacity, even when the new 400 room hotel to be built on the Larvotto peninsula opens around 1994.

"I had expected to be in the red for one or two years before we started to break even. In fact, we are breaking even already, and have not had a single month in the red," he says.

Mr Boustany had originally hoped to build his luxury hotel in Ashrafieh, in his native Beirut – possibly an even more beautiful site than Monaco, but ravaged by war.

Instead, he has lavished every attention on building a splendid marble palace in Monte Carlo, often overruling his partners, Conrad International, a subsidiary of the Hilton Hotel group, to equip it in keeping with his taste.

"They wanted me to put stainless steel cutlery in the brasserie. I refused and bought Christofle instead, and I bought Limoges china, not Far Eastern," he says.

Mr Boustany says the Metropole has already begun to win a share of the conference trade, and he sees no reason why it should not achieve 70 to 80 per cent occupancy next year.

Mr Biancheri of the SBM also believes that Monaco can continue to extend its clientele, possibly among wealthy Japanese who in the past have gone to Europe, usually on tours.

"It is not a question of finding thousands of new clients, just a few dozen in each country," he says.

Besides the 245,000 visitors who spent the night in Monaco last year, the principality also receives around 3m day trippers. With them the problem is inversed: so that the Government has to find ways of managing the flows so as to prevent saturation.

"The Government attaches considerable importance to giving a good welcome to day trippers, to improving the movement of tour buses and channelling the flow of visitors. We have to find daily solutions so that there is no friction between day trippers and longer-stay visitors," Mr Noghès says.

Fig 6.11 (*Source:* Financial Times, *14 May 1990*)

TOURISM FOR ALL: SOCIAL TOURISM IN EUROPE

As tourism and leisure continue to play an increasingly important part in the life of the late 20th century, the inability to participate becomes more and more an isolating factor, which can undermine the morale and health of those excluded in this way. A number of factors make holiday-taking difficult or impossible for large numbers of people – low income, physical and mental handicaps, and family circumstances, for example. The non-participation of people thus affected represents not only a missed opportunity for them, but also a loss of clientele for the tourism industry.

The social tourism movement exists as an alternative route to participation in tourism for those who, by reason of their low level of income or other restrictions, are excluded from buying in the commercial sector of tourism – that sector to which social tourism might be seen as a counterpart and complement.

This chapter examines:
- The definition and history of social tourism
- Social tourism policy in Europe
- Social tourism facilities
- The EC and social tourism

DEFINITIONS

Of the many different definitions of social tourism, the two most commonly used are the following:

1 The definition used by the **European Commission**: 'Social tourism, sometimes known as popular tourism is, in certain countries, organised by associations, cooperatives and trades unions, and is designed to make travel more easily available to as many people as possible, particularly those from the most disadvantaged sections of the population (families, young people, the handicapped, those in retirement).

2 According to the **International Bureau of Social Tourism** (BITS), social tourism is the name given to all of those activities which represent access to tourism for those from the least financially secure levels of society, this access being made possible or facilitated by certain well-defined **social measures**.

Other terms have been used to represent this phenomenon, but 'social tourism' is the one adopted by the EC, since it has the advantage of being capable of being translated literally into all the languages of the Community. Within the EC, the term tends to be most in use in those countries where social tourism provision is most widely established. These countries are Belgium France, Greece, Italy, Portugal and Spain.

On the other hand, the term 'social tourism' is less commonly used in Denmark, Germany, Luxembourg, the Netherlands, the United Kingdom and Ireland, where no particular national policy for it exists. Nevertheless, these countries are served by a wide range of initiatives, many taken by private associations and charities, which makes it reasonable to regard them as being active in the domain of social tourism.

THE HISTORY OF SOCIAL TOURISM

Until this century, tourism in Europe was an activity reserved for a privileged few, the small elite of people with the time and money to travel for their own pleasure and education. An important step towards opening up this activity to the wider population came during the 1930s, when annual paid holidays were introduced for the first time in the industrialised countries of Europe and beyond. It was this initiative which first created the demand for travel and holiday facilities for ordinary working people. For the vast majority, going away on holiday was still an impossibility, even with paid holidays. The tourism industry which existed at that time was geared towards providing luxury services for the wealthy traveller, not for the masses on severely limited budgets. For the latter, the necessary transport and accommodation facilities simply did not exist. Those who were able to take advantage of their newly won right to paid holidays simply went on day-trips, or stayed with relatives.

Any moves by European governments to bring tourism more within the reach of their ordinary citizens were halted by the outbreak of the Second World War. However, the impetus towards the greater democratisation of tourism was not forgotten; if anything, this cause was strengthened by the general democratising impact of the war itself in Europe. After the war, the need for a break away from work and everyday life became more pressing too, as industrialisation advanced and, with it, increasing urbanisation in many countries.

Consequently, in many European countries, the 1940s and 1950s witnessed a great explosion of activity designed to make tourism more accessible to all. This activity set the basic pattern for providing assistance to help people go on holiday, which is still followed in Europe today. It focused not only on those who had to stay at home due to lack of financial resources (such as workers on low wages, old-age pensioners), but also those who had difficulties taking a holiday, for practical reasons (such as handicapped people, or families with young children, who were often refused accommodation in hotels 30 years ago).

The pattern which emerged involved two complementary partners:

1 Action by the **state** itself as well as by local authorities to promote the provision of social tourism. This took two forms:

(*a*) financial assistance given directly to the families or individuals in need (in some countries, in the form of holiday 'vouchers' which could be used towards the cost of a holiday); or

(*b*) grants given to organisations to enable them to construct special holiday accommodation and facilities and to make it available at an affordable price.

This method of financing social tourism is still used today. In France, Belgium and Germany, the state provides assistance directly to individuals *and* to organisations to help them construct accommodation. But in Greece, for example, the state assists individuals only, while in countries such as Italy, only finance for investment in facilities is available.

In most cases, the state's motivation for subsidising social tourism was two-fold: to enable more people to take a holiday; and, to breathe economic life back into regions of the country which were in decline – often rural areas or mountain zones. A frequent condition of receiving grants for the construction of social tourism accommodation was that it should be situated in regions which were depopulating or which had been earmarked for economic assistance. In this way, social tourism was used as a tool to stimulate the economy of certain regions, by creating employment for local people and attracting the spending of the users of the social tourism facilities.

2 The growth of the **social tourism movement** itself. This was a movement composed of co-operative groups, self-help organisations, trades unions and other associations (youth groups, churches etc) who worked to create opportunities for their own members to go away on holiday. These organisations acted either as not-for-profit tour operators, negotiating favourable transport and accommodation rates for their members; or as managing agents for the social tourism accommodation which they either owned or rented.

It was this combination of public financial assistance plus the efforts of the social tourism movement itself which accounted for much of the rise in the rate of holiday taking in most European countries after the Second World War. The Eastern Bloc countries with centrally planned economies were a special case. In the absence of any private enterprise, *all* tourism was controlled by the state, with holidays often being offered by the state to high-achieving workers and their families. Practically all domestic tourism in countries such as Poland and Hungary, therefore, might be considered social tourism, since it was centrally controlled and made available to the population at affordable prices. This system continued until recently, with state-owned spa resorts and rest homes being an important component in many Eastern Bloc countries' domestic tourism. One difference is that this form of tourism is no longer restricted to those who work hardest, but is offered to families more generally.

By 1950, there were so many national and regional organisations working to provide holidays and travel for disadvantaged groups that two international bodies were created to help them communicate with each other. The International Federation of Popular Travel Organisations, based in Helsinki, coordinated the work undertaken by social tourism organisations in different countries; and the Federation of International Youth Hostel Organisations in Copenhagen promoted international travel for young people.

The first international forum dealing exclusively with the development of social tourism was the **International Bureau of Social Tourism** (BITS), created in 1963, for organisations active in this field. Its membership includes social tourism organisations from over 25 countries, mainly European, but also from Latin America and Africa. Based in Brussels, the BITS Secretariat still exercises a coordinating role, organises conferences, and publishes studies on issues affecting social tourism on an international basis.

SOCIAL TOURISM IN EUROPE TODAY

The provision of social tourism, like the rate of participation in tourism generally, is unevenly spread over Europe. It differs from country to country, according to various factors. Provision is most widespread in those countries which have:

1 an explicit **national policy** concerning tourism for disadvantaged groups in society; and

2 certain **well-defined measures** to enable these groups to take holidays and short breaks.

The presence or absence of a national Ministry of Tourism is an important factor, since those countries with a tourism ministry or tourism secretariat tend to be those most likely to have a national policy for social tourism. Of these, some even have a service specialising in social tourism within the ministry – as is the case with Spain, Portugal, Belgium, France, and, to a certain extent, Italy. These countries not only have the best-developed policies for social tourism, with specific legislation on this issue, but also the best-developed facilities.

Other factors explaining the uneven distribution of social tourism provision over Europe include:

1 National attitudes. In some countries, the organising of one's holidays is felt to be a matter only for the private individuals concerned, and not something which requires the intervention of the state or other public authorities (except perhaps in the most extreme cases of poverty).

2 Economic priorities. Despite the fact that tourism in general is being increasingly recognised by different countries as a powerful economic force and creator of employment, the extent to which it is actively encouraged by governments (through, for example the provision of social tourism structures) depends on the degree to which other, more pressing, needs exist. For example, the need to finance priorities such as social security cover, pensions, or unemployment benefits limits the scope of certain countries (Ireland and Portugal etc) to subsidise social tourism programmes.

3 The existence of organisations which can assume responsibility for the provision of social tourism services. Social tourism is most prevalent in those countries which have a wide range of organisations which act as the state's partners, managing facilities or organising holidays for their members, and so on. Voluntary, not-for-profit organisations exist in all countries, but in some, their involvement in social tourism is limited, often because the law prevents them from certain activities, such as the organisation of holidays, for example. The degree to which trades unions are present and influential in a country and their financial 'muscle' is also a factor, since in general these organisations are traditional providers of social tourism services for their members.

Britain presents a special case worthy of mention here. With its history of government welfare provision and its traditional trade union heritage, it is perhaps surprising that Britain did not develop the same systems of state-subsidised social tourism as many countries in continental Europe. Hence no separate social tourism sector as such, with its own specific facilities, exists. Although specially constructed social tourism accommodation for families on low budgets is not available, there has long been a tradition in Britain of inexpensive holiday accommodation such as bed & breakfast establishments and Butlins-style holiday camps, which for a long time have been uniquely British institutions. These may in part explain why social tourism provision in Britain takes such a different form to that found in other European countries.

There is also no centralised system of financial assistance for the specific purpose of taking a holiday. Local authority social security departments have discretionary powers to help those most in need to take a holiday, and they exercise this function in collaboration with a host of charitable and voluntary bodies and the commercial sector of tourism.

With so many different types of organisations involved in helping those with special needs to take holidays and short breaks, the role of the **Holiday Care Service** is a vital one. This organisation, established as a recognised charity by the English Tourist Board in 1981 is Britain's central source of holiday information for people whose age, disability, or other personal or family circumstances affect their choice of holiday. It speaks directly to the travel and tourism industry as a catalyst, encouraging and advising transport, accommodation and attractions operators on the development of appropriate provision for these groups. The Holiday Care Service's emphasis is on integration and accessibility, as is seen in the extract from their recent report, 'Tourism for All', shown in Fig 7.1.

CASE STUDY
SOCIAL TOURISM POLICY IN DENMARK

Approximately 65 per cent of Danes go away on holiday every year, with approximately 45 per cent of this number taking a holiday overseas. This rate of holiday taking is one of the highest in Europe, and can be partly explained by the relatively high standard of living of the population. The importance attached by the Danes to culture, the defence of the environment and outdoor activities is an important factor in their choice of holiday activities.

Tourism policy in Denmark

Since no Ministry of Tourism exists in Denmark (only a National Tourism Office), there is no government service specialising in social tourism. There are, however, several sources of finance for the subsidising of tourism and leisure facilities.

Within the Danish Ministry of Labour, there is an institution, the **Arbedsmarkedets Ferie Fond**, which finances holidays, predominantly for members of trades unions and their families. It gives help in the form of loans and grants, towards the purchasing of land for the construction of holiday centres and holiday homes.

Most of the financial assistance from the Arbejdmarkedets Ferie Fond goes to the organisation, Dansk Folke-Ferie, which is mentioned later in this case study. Another source of support for tourism and leisure is the Danish Sports Lottery. Funds from this lottery go towards financing the organisation, **Friluftsradet**, the coordinating council of outdoor associations. This council brings together various sporting associations, political and religious organisations, as well as camping and caravanning bodies.

Finally, local authorities contribute, by giving grants to retired people to assist them with their holiday expenses.

Social tourism organisations

Dansk Folke-Ferie (Danish Peoples' Holidays) is the principal social tourism organisation in

ACCOMMODATION

Accommodation is one of the most important components of a holiday. We were impressed with the efforts that have been made to cater for people with disabilities. The London Tara hotel pioneered the way in the hotel sector by providing specially adapted rooms for disabled people; as did Trusthouse Forte in the budget category through Travelodges, where at least one room is designed to accommodate a guest using a wheelchair. In the self-catering sector, the National Trust has set very high standards with its adapted cottages, and Country Holidays' inspection programmes contain a detailed appraisal of accessibility. Center Parcs has an admirable record on accessibility to most facilities, with excellent adapted chalets. Haggerston Castle Holiday Centre near Berwick has fully accessible caravans which could serve as a model for that sector.

Some holidays are offered, at little or no cost, to the Family Holiday Association for low income families referred to them by welfare agencies.

Some problems, however, were brought to our attention.

Many accommodation operators said they would like to do more for people with special needs, but claimed to have found difficulty in getting good information on what to do and for whom. We found that often hoteliers had tried hard to put in facilities suitable for disabled people, but had not received adequate advice - for example, an en-suite bathroom with a doorway wide enough for a wheelchair was still inaccessible because the positioning of the washbasin prevented the door from opening fully.

Other operators said that it would have been helpful if would-be guests could have been more specific about their particular needs when booking: they would then have been able to offer better service, and any misunderstandings could have been avoided.

The most commonly mentioned problem for consumers concerned a lack of reliable or sufficiently detailed information. "The hotel said it was suitable for disabled people but when we got there it wasn't. There were steps down to the dining room, and the doorway to the en-suite bathroom wasn't wide enough for the wheelchair"; or from a one parent family "The brochure said the chalet slept four; when we got there it had two double beds, which was quite unsuitable for our particular needs".

Another growing concern is the needs of single people. A significant number of older people, many of whom have lost their partner, wish to occupy a room on their own. The trend in accommodation provision is firmly away from single rooms to twin-bedded or double rooms, with the result that people on their own are often faced with paying for a double room or a 'single room supplement'.

Fig 7.1 An extract from Holiday Care Service's report, *Tourism for All*

Denmark. This cooperative organisation runs 11 holiday villages in Denmark, and others in Norway, Italy, Spain, Portugal and Malta. These account for a total of 12 000 beds, and amount to an annual turnover of 300 million Danish kroner. Due to the financial assistance it receives from the Arbejdsmarkedets Ferie Fond and the trade unions, the prices charged by Dansk Folke-Ferie are about 25 per cent lower than those charged by commercial business for similar services.

Those using the holiday villages are practically all trade union members. However, trade union membership generally in Denmark is at a very high level, so the villages are, in practice, open to virtually all working people.

Fig 7.2 Gilleleje Holiday Village run by Dansk Folke-Ferie (*Reproduced by kind permission of the Danish Tourist Board*)

Dansk Folke-Ferie is also very active in the organisation of trips overseas, and has close links with other cooperative structures in Sweden, Finland, Norway and Iceland, and exchange visits are regularly arranged with these countries.

Young people and families

Several organisations exist to help families and children who experience difficulty in taking a holiday. 'Landsforeningen Ungdomsringen' are young people's clubs which organise sports and leisure activities, but which also have accommodation for families. The overall capacity of this accommodation is about 14 000 beds, including two centres in Copenhagen, with around 800 beds in total.

'Kongskilde Friluftsgard' is an education centre of 86 beds, used as subsidised accommodation for young people and families during the summer. This centre, which is financially supported by Copenhagen City Council, is used primarily for people interested in activities related to nature and the environment.

Retired people

The organisation most active in arranging holiday trips for this group is 'Pensionnisternes Sanvirke', which brings together most of Denmark's pensioners' clubs and works through tour operators to negotiate special packages for

them. Another organisation, EGV-Ferie specialises in arranging low-cost holidays for retired people living alone.

Handicapped people

Danish associations for the handicapped, such as 'Dansk Blindesamfund', for the blind, or 'Landsforeningen af Vanfore', for handicapped people in general, organise a number of holidays for their members, although this is only one of the services they provide among many.

FACILITIES AND SERVICES

What kind of facilities are open to clients of social tourism? And how do these differ from facilities owned and operated by the purely commercial sector?

CASE STUDY
SOCIAL TOURISM FACILITIES IN BELGIUM

Belgium possesses an extensive network of social tourism facilities, and every kind of social tourism accommodation to be found in the rest of Europe is represented there. The facilities may be divided, in terms of their clientele, into the following sectors:

- family holidays;
- young people's holidays;
- senior citizens' holidays; and
- holidays for the handicapped.

Family holidays

This is by far the most developed sector in Belgium, consisting for the main part of a major network of **holiday villages** or **holiday centres**. In Belgium, these are concentrated mainly in the Ardennes mountains and on the coast. Most have a capacity of between 200 and 1000 guests. Some consist of a single multi-storey building containing family accommodation, for example apartments, studio flats, etc, and the public rooms for eating, entertainment, reception. Others consist of separate bungalows or chalets grouped around a central, public building.

The standard of accommodation in these centres is high, with all modern comforts and rooms with private facilities (WC, showers, etc), linen, and sometimes a fully equipped kitchen and lounge area. The general facilities in these centres are designed with the needs of the whole family in mind, and often include a laundrette, multi-purpose activity rooms, bar, restaurant, TV room, and a medical care room. Often situated close to natural attractions, such as forests or coastlines, Belgian holiday villages and centres usually occupy a large extent of land, with facilities for sports. Organised activities are often laid on, but these are not compulsory.

For several years now, Belgian holiday villages, like many of their equivalents else-where in Europe, have been opening themselves up to a wider clientele than simply the family. In the effort to extend their period of opening and their profitability, they have been used out-of-season for senior citizens, schools' nature trips, seminars and conferences, and weekend breaks of all kinds.

In Belgium, most of the holiday villages and centres are owned and run by not-for-profit associations, the most influential being the Christian Trade Union movement, the Socialist Trade Union movement and the Catholic Mutualist movement. Between them, these three associations offer accommodation consisting of almost 24 000 beds.

Young people's holidays

In Belgium, as in most European countries, social tourism facilities for young people are generally distinguished from those intended for families by several factors: less emphasis on comfort and peace and quiet; more emphasis on activities and contact between the guests.

Accommodation organised along social tourism lines for young people in Belgium consists of three main types: **gîtes**; **youth hostels**; and **holiday camps and colonies**. Gîte accommmo-dation consists often of old houses or castles which have been restored and equipped to receive small groups. Rooms contain from two to ten beds, and washing and cooking facilities are usually communal. Gîtes are let out to small groups, who take care of their own cooking, cleaning, entertainment and so on. Often no member of staff is present, and responsibility for the group lies with the group leader. During the Belgian school holidays, stays in gîtes last between five and ten days, on average. As is the

case with the holiday villages, the gîtes in Belgium and in other countries are in the process of trying to diversify their clientele, by offering their accommodation to school parties, and, increasingly, the not-so-young – ramblers' groups, for example.

Youth hostels in Belgium form part of an international network of accommodation aimed primarily, but not exclusively, at young people. Basic accommodation in rooms with a minimum of ten beds is offered to a clientele which is essentially on the move, rarely passing more than two nights in the same youth hostel. Belgium's youth hostel guest numbers fell in the 1960s, with the trend towards more individual-ism and taking holidays further afield. Now, they are making efforts to attract a wider clientele, and there has been a marked increase in recent years in the proportion of their guests composed of families. Belgian youth hostels offer around 2300 beds in total.

Packaged breaks (transport plus accommo-dation) in holiday camps and colonies are organised for children and teenagers, usually by recognised youth groups. Often these follow a particular theme or activity, such as potholing or archaeological exploration. In many cases, the activities are led by volunteers who lend their services in return for board and lodging only. Holiday colonies offer breaks in either purpose-built accommodation or in large houses which have been converted for this purpose. In Belgium, these colonies are used mostly by children between the ages of 8 and 12 years. Holiday camps do not use commercial camping sites, but land on which the organisers have obtained permission to pitch their tents, for example attached to a farm or common ground. As is the case with the colonies, the group is responsible for providing for all its own needs.

All social tourism accommodation provision for young people in Belgium, including youth hostels, amounts to a total of 24 000 beds. This, added to the 24 000 beds for social tourism family holidays, exceeds by far the total number of hotel beds in Belgium, estimated at around 32 000.

Senior citizens' holidays

Holidays and short breaks for this age group in Belgium are organised by a range of organis-ations which work with senior citizens –

pensioners' rights groups, welfare organisations, etc. Retired Belgians benefit from a special annual holiday payment awarded by the state, just as working people do. However, there is no specific tourism infrastructure in Belgium for this age group. Holiday villages are often used out-of-season, with appropriate entertainment laid on. Often, the choice of holiday village or holiday centre is determined by the particular ideology of the organisers: for example, a priest will send his retired parishioners to a Christian centre, while a local authority with a socialist majority will choose a socialist centre.

Holidays for handicapped people

Several Belgian not-for-profit associations and welfare organisations arrange trips and holidays for this group: weekends in Belgian holiday resorts, or longer breaks by the sea, in the Ardennes, or, increasingly, abroad. Accommodation is often in hotels or holiday centres which have facilities for those with handicaps. The preferred trend is to use facilities of this kind, rather than to build special, segregated accommodation designed for handicapped people only. Once more, out-of-season travel is favoured, because of the lower costs and because this group is more likely to receive a better welcome and better treatment which staff have more time to devote to their needs.

With its various facilities and services, what are the characteristics of social tourism which distinguish it from the commercial sector?

This question would have been easier to answer 30 years ago, when social tourism had an identity more clearly differentiated from that of the products on offer by the commercial sector. Changes in public taste have influenced social tourism as well as the commercial sector, in many cases eroding the differences between the two. Nevertheless, the original philosophy and practices have survived, albeit in a modified form in many cases, and these continue to give social tourism its distinctive characteristics. The three most important of these are:

1 **Communal facilities**. In the holiday villages, centres, etc, many of the facilities are of a communal nature – dining rooms, television rooms, and dormitory bedrooms for example.

Activities and entertainment, too, tend to be designed for groups of guests. Originally, this emphasis on the communal as opposed to the individual had two functions: keeping costs down, and creating a feeling of group solidarity among the guests. More recently, this emphasis has decreased, as social tourism facilities have responded to the wishes of guests in search of more privacy and independence. Thus, there is a growing tendency to equip rooms in holiday centres with individual cooking facilities for example.

2 **Activities**. Most social tourism holidays and breaks offer access to a range of activities and entertainment, led by an organiser or *animateur*. Although this is now also a feature of certain commercial tourism packages, the difference lies in the fact that in social tourism, these activities are included as an essential part of the package and no extra charge is made for them.

3 **Sensitivity to their locality**. Representing early models of 'responsible tourism' (*see* Chapter 8), social tourism facilities have always been characterised as being respectful of the local environment, both natural and human. Accommodation is built to be in harmony with the surroundings, using local materials and architectural styles. An effort is usually made to integrate the visitors with those living locally, through visits to local craftsmen, for example; and care is taken to ensure that the resident community reaps benefits from the influx of visitors, in the form of employment, business for local shops, etc.

Generally, the commercial sector has been quick to adopt many of the working methods and features of social tourism. In many ways, the associations which provided subsidised holidays for their members in the early days of social tourism were pioneers in their own right, introducing into the tourism industry many structures which are now taken for granted in the commercial sector, but which, 40 years ago were practically unknown. This innovating role of social tourism associations is underlined by the French authors Pasqualini and Jacquot, who, in their book, *Tourismes*, give three examples of this:

1 **Holiday centres and villages**. The holiday villages set up by the early social tourism

associations in Europe were the forerunners of the now highly successful 'club' formula for holidays, epitomised by the French company, Club Méditerranée. 'Club Med' itself started its existence as a not-for-profit social tourism organisation.

2 Direct sell. Social tourism associations were the first to use this method of selling holidays to the public. In countries such as France, legislation meant that, as associations and not tour operators, they were unable to use the travel agency network to sell their products. The associations were, therefore, obliged to set up their own outlets in order to sell their holidays and travel programmes.

Fig 7.3 The cover of Club Mediterranée's summer brochure (*Reproduced by kind permission of Club Mediterranée*)

3 Activities. The provision of organised activities for guests also finds its origin in the social tourism movement. Now a familiar feature of the holiday centre and 'club' type holiday, organised activities were first offered as an essential element in the earliest holiday villages, where they had a socio-cultural role – for example, discussion groups, workers' education classes and so on. Later, sports and other leisure activities were added, often led by an *animateur*.

THE EC AND THE SOCIAL TOURISM MOVEMENT

As soon as the Tourism Directorate (*see* p 24) was created within the European Commission, separate pressure groups were created by the various sectors of the tourism industry – the hotels and catering sector, travel trade, airline companies, the railways etc – to lobby this department on their behalf. The pressure groups keep the Tourism Directorate informed of their own activities and of any particular problems they are facing. In this way, the different sectors are able to look after their own interests by making sure that, through the Commission, the European Parliament listens to them and takes their views into account when devising new laws.

CECOTOS

CECOTOS (Comité Européen de Coordination du Tourisme Social) is a Europe-wide organisation, created in 1984 at the instigation of the International Office for Social Tourism (BITS – Bureau International du Tourisme Social) and the International Union of Cooperative and Associative Tourism (UITCA – Union Internationale du Tourisme Coopératif et Associatif). This organisation acts in the interests of the social tourism movement in Europe, and is the umbrella organisation for the cooperatives, associations and mutual aid societies which work in the tourism sector, especially those which are active in the area of social tourism.

Its objectives are:

● to represent the general and specific interests of social tourism in dealings with the institutions of the European Community

• to inform its members of tourism-related initiatives taken by EC institutions

• to contribute towards the development of a Community-wide policy on tourism, and on social tourism in particular

• to facilitate links with other European bodies with similar interests represented at Community level

• to encourage the exchange of information, personnel and services between its member organisations and to encourage their joint activities, as necessary.

It was through the efforts of CECOTOS that in 1986, an influential report sent to the Council of Ministers cited social tourism as an element of European tourism which deserved to be encouraged by the Community. Also, it was due to CECOTOS' lobbying that social tourism's contribution to bringing economic and social activity to isolated areas was included as an item in a major report on Regional Development presented to the European Parliament the following year.

In 1987, the Commission asked CECOTOS to produce a report on social tourism in the 12 Community member countries. Later that year, it was published. As well as describing the situation regarding social tourism in each member country, it makes a number of recommendations for action by the EC, including the following:

1 To achieve a better use of social tourism accommodation.

(*a*) In many EC countries, holidays are concentrated into a very short time of the year, due to all schools being on holiday simultaneously *and/or* businesses closing down and giving all of their employees holidays at the same time. As well as the tourism industry in general, the social tourism sector in particular is badly affected by this concentration of holidays, since its clientele is essentially a family one. The report urges the Commission to set in action a range of measures to encourage schools and businesses throughout the Community to stagger their holiday periods.

(*b*) A number of actions to promote and develop social tourism within the EC are recommended. These include: the publication of information on the social tourism activities available in each country, as well as details of grants etc available

to the participants; the removal of barriers which prevent the inhabitants of one EC country from using the social tourism facilities of another country; and the including of the social tourism sector's products in EC tourism promotion campaigns aimed at wider markets beyond Europe itself.

2 To set up a Community-wide programme for social tourism.

(*a*) The establishing of a European stamp of quality for social tourism facilities, with a guaranteed standard of comfort, entertainment etc, for facilities awarded this stamp.

(*b*) The launching of a number of pilot bi-national or multinational holiday villages in special development zones of Europe, to facilitate cultural exchanges between guests.

3 To organise the sharing of information in the field of social tourism.

(*a*) The creation of multinational groups of advisers to help associations creating new social tourism operations.

(*b*) The creation of training programmes specifically for social tourism professionals.

(*c*) The organising of exchanges for social tourism professionals from different countries.

Many of these themes were reiterated a few years later, in May 1990, at The Second European Conference on Social and Youth Tourism, held in Rome. There, Raymond Stélandre, the General Secretary of the BITS, described the importance of social tourism as a means of integrating the different nationalities within the EC. Regarding a Europe-wide social tourism network, he presented three objectives for the years ahead:

1 To establish a Europe-wide holiday voucher scheme. The holiday voucher schemes of countries such as France and Switzerland have been effective in bringing new sections of the population, notably the less affluent, into the market for tourism. The BITS objective would be to replicate these schemes in all European countries, and for the holiday vouchers to be valid for use in any country in Europe.

2 To open up holiday villages to a pan-European clientele. Each country's existing social tourism holiday villages and holiday centres should henceforth make positive efforts to attract a clientele from other European countries in addition to their own. Future facilities of this kind should be developed on the basis of international cooperation, following the model of the Franco-Belgian Eurovillage at Cap d'Agde in the south of France, which draws its clientele from France, Belgium, Italy, Switzerland and Germany.

3 To develop a tourism training programme which includes the social tourism sector. To prepare the next generation of tourism professionals in Europe, a system of first-class training in tourism should be set in place. The essential core of this training programme should include the study of the aims, objectives and characteristics of the social tourism sector.

THE TASK AHEAD

The EC survey, *Europeans and their Holidays*, gives an indication of the challenge still faced by the Social Tourism movement in Europe after more than 50 years of working to achieve 'tourism for all'.

Respondents' answers to the question 'How many holiday trips (each lasting four days or more) did you make this year?' suggest that, in total, 44 per cent of the population of all Community countries took no holiday trips at all during the year of the survey. If this figure seems inordinately high, a more detailed question reveals a more accurate picture of those members of the EC population who are excluded from taking holidays, for whatever reason: respondents who said that they had not gone away were then asked if they had gone on holiday the previous year *and* if they planned to take a holiday the year following the survey. Those replying in the negative to both these questions might be considered as 'those who habitually stay at home', the survey's own category for them.

A breakdown of the responses, country by country, are given in Fig 7.4.

About half of those who did not go away during the year of the survey fall into the category of those who habitually stay at home – roughly 21 per cent of the EC's total population of 53 million people.

Figure 7.4 also reveals important differences between the holiday taking habits of individual EC countries. The greatest differences from one country to another are to be found in the two extreme groups: those who habitually stay at home (16 per cent in the Netherlands, 49 per cent in Portugal) and those who go away more than once (7 per cent in Portugal, 27 per cent in France).

The economic factor is clearly of major importance in determining whether people take a holiday or not. As a general rule, the proportion of a country's population taking a holiday tends to rise in line with its general standard of living. (Although one notable exception is Belgium, which has a high standard of living but a very low percentage of its population taking a holiday.)

Responses to more detailed questions concerning people's reasons for not taking a holiday reveal the main obstacles, and how these obstacles differ from country to country. One hundred people from each country who did not take a holiday were asked why they had not gone anywhere. The table in Fig 7.5 gives their responses.

Denmark, Belgium and Italy are the countries where the largest proportions of those who did not go away said that they preferred to stay at home. Portugal, Ireland and Greece are those where lack of finance was mentioned most often.

The survey concluded that of all the variables influencing people's decision to take a holiday or not, socio-occupational status and the level of family income have the greatest influence on holidaymaking patterns. Over the Community as a whole, 75 per cent of families in the top income group for their country took a holiday, while only 36 per cent in the bottom income group did so.

These figures reveal just how much remains to be done before the 'tourism for all' objective is finally reached and the population of Europe as a whole has genuine opportunity of access to tourism – an activity no longer confined to a small elite, but still distributed unevenly and inequitably throughout the continent's population.

CONCLUSION

Not all Europeans have shared in the post-war tourism boom, but the social tourism movement has played a major role in bringing holidays and short-breaks within the reach of those either lacking the means to purchase these commodities in the open market or having special needs.

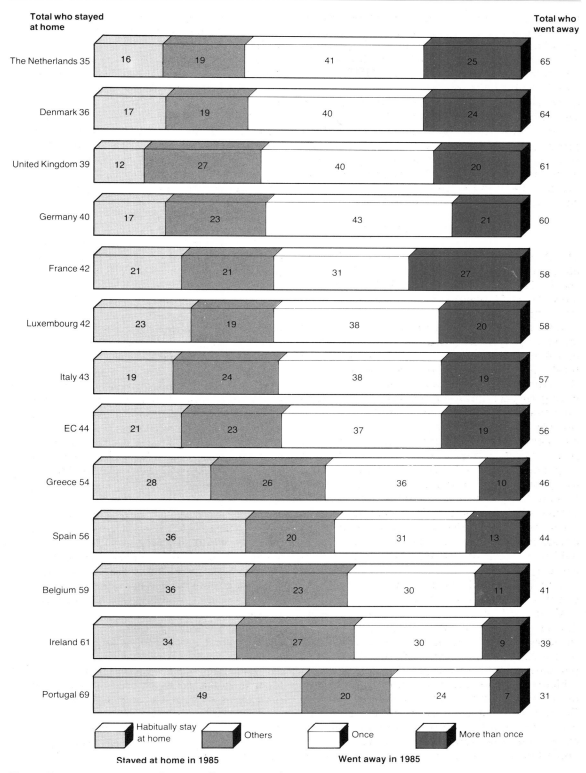

Total who stayed at home

The Netherlands 35	16	19	41	25	65
Denmark 36	17	19	40	24	64
United Kingdom 39	12	27	40	20	61
Germany 40	17	23	43	21	60
France 42	21	21	31	27	58
Luxembourg 42	23	19	38	20	58
Italy 43	19	24	38	19	57
EC 44	21	23	37	19	56
Greece 54	28	26	36	10	46
Spain 56	36	20	31	13	44
Belgium 59	36	23	30	11	41
Ireland 61	34	27	30	9	39
Portugal 69	49	20	24	7	31

Total who went away

Habitually stay at home   Others   Once   More than once

Stayed at home in 1985   Went away in 1985

Fig 7.4 The response to the EC survey, *Europeans and their Holidays*

Fig 7.5 Reasons for not going away on holiday

(a) I preferred to stay at home
(b) I was not able to get away from work
(c) I couldn't afford it
(d) Special reasons (health, moving house, family, etc)
(e) Worry about safety, terrorists, etc
(f) Other reasons

	(a)%	(b)%	(c)%	(d)%	(e)%	(f)%
Belgium	32	7	40	14	*	4
Denmark	38	8	23	16	*	16
Germany	27	12	41	29	1	3
Greece	12	24	55	35	*	*
Spain	14	22	50	15	*	9
France	22	23	44	25	1	2
Ireland	14	10	61	10	1	6
Italy	30	22	31	21	2	2
Luxembourg	23	16	20	31	*	10
Netherlands	22	9	32	27	1	14
Portugal	12	19	67	14	1	2
United Kingdom	14	6	50	21	1	16
All EC	22	16	44	22	1	6

* less than 0.5%

(With some respondents giving more than one answer, the total for each country generally exceeds 100%)
(*Source:* Europeans and their Holidays)

Changes in society as a whole have been reflected in the changing characteristics of the social tourism movement: moves towards more emphasis on the freedom of the individual rather than the insistence on the solidarity of the group; and the movement operating in a more commercial environment, for example. It is upon the ability of the social tourism movement to continue to move with the times, while preserving its fundamental philosophy, that its future depends.

ASSIGNMENTS

1 Social versus commercial tourism. Divided evenly into two groups representing (**1**) the social tourism sector; and (**2**) the commercial sector of tourism, the class should debate the following points:

(a) Is it fair that tourism companies operating in the commercial sector have to compete with social tourism organisations which can keep their costs down because they are subsidised by the government? Or would the tourism industry as a whole *and* the consumer benefit more if the buying and selling of holidays was left entirely to free-market principles?

(b) Does the existence of the two sectors mean that there is a risk of a two-tier system of holiday provision – one for the rich and one for the poor?

(c) Are there better possible ways of governments helping the disadvantaged take a holiday, than the existing arrangements which exist for social tourism support?

2 Tourism facilities for handicapped people. Physical handicap is a major feature in preventing people from going on holiday or on day trips. Choose a tourism business which you can study in some depth – a hotel, tourist attraction or transport company, for example – and investigate it from the point of view of facilities for the handicapped. Write a report giving details of the special facilities which the business already offers for handicapped people, in terms of access, special measures for the blind or hard of hearing etc. Also include in the report any proposals you could make to the management of the business for measures which would enable them to attract more custom from tourists with physical handicaps.

SMALL IS BEAUTIFUL: RESPONSIBLE TOURISM IN EUROPE

The 1980s will be remembered as the decade in which the market for tourism finally matured. It was during those years that tentative, small-scale experiments in new kinds of tourism gave birth to a host of alternatives to the conventional mass tourism which had dominated the market in Europe during the 1960s and 1970s.

This chapter examines:
- The impact of conventional tourism
- The rise of responsible tourism
- Responsible tourism products in Europe
- European responsible tourism organisations

THE IMPACT OF CONVENTIONAL TOURISM

During the 1960s and 1970s, the mass travel market in Europe was dominated by the standard package holiday to the main Mediterranean resorts. These were the principal destinations for the new travelling public who were, for the most part, experiencing foreign travel for the first time.

The classic two-week package to a resort in Spain, Italy, Greece or, for the more adventurous, Yugoslavia suited the market well in many ways: it was offered at a price which matched the limited budgets of the clientele. The package formula provided a high degree of security for tourists unaccustomed to overseas travel – having chosen a product from a brochure, paid for it, and arrived at the airport, they were then safely in the care of the tour operator for the duration of the holiday. To further reduce tourists' anxiety at finding themselves on unfamiliar ground, destinations offered many features easily recognisable to their visitors, for example, familiar food and entertainment, menus in the tourists' languages, and even, in some cases, pricing goods in the tourists' own currencies. Finally, there was the added security which came with travelling overseas *en masse*, with dozens of one's compatriots.

Although the package holiday appeared to suit the market well, there emerged, during those first two decades of mass travel, a growing body of conclusive evidence which showed that this form of tourism created problems of many kinds for those destinations which received tourists in vast numbers.

THE HARMFUL FEATURES OF CONVENTIONAL MASS TOURISM

Most of the criticisms of mass tourism centre on its **negative impact** on the destinations and those living at the destinations, the 'host communities'. Yet, the impact of an industry as immense as the tourism industry is far from clear-cut and simple. An examination of tourism's different impacts on destinations shows a complex interaction of benefits as well as damage to the destinations.

Economic impact

The economic benefits brought by tourism represent the single most common reason for governments encouraging its development. Tourists' spending can be an important source of foreign currency. Jobs are generated not only in the facilities directly servicing tourists, but also in local shops and other businesses which benefit from an enlarged market for their products and services.

However, destinations can find that a significant share of the revenue generated by tourism does not stay in the country, but 'leaks' away, back to the multinational hotels and agencies which control much of the mass holiday market. Servicing the needs of tourists can involve the expensive importation of luxury goods and materials to build and equip hotels, airports, etc, all of which diminish the profits from tourism. Often too, the wealth created by tourism benefits only a small area of a country, or a local elite.

Cultural impact

Tourism can help a country discover or rediscover its national identity and heritage. Customs may be revived and monuments restored and protected, for example, because of tourists' interest. New markets are created for indigenous arts and crafts, and there are new audiences for song, dance and other performing arts. All of this can give a country or a community new pride in its culture.

However, a destination's culture can be exploited to the extent that it becomes divorced from the inhabitants' everyday life, and is degraded and devalued in the process. Traditions and lifestyles can become fossilised if they are over-adapted to suit visitors' needs.

Environmental impact

When the interests of tourism promoters and conservationists coincide, there can be many benefits for destinations: areas of outstanding natural beauty are often protected from other forms of development because of their potential for attracting tourists. Towns and cities can be made more attractive, such as through building renovation and preservation schemes or the planting of trees and flowers, to increase their visual appeal for visitors.

However, Europe abounds in examples of places where the natural and built environment has been degraded or destroyed by uncontrolled tourist development. In those areas where tourism is highly concentrated in particular, the industry has brought with it a measure of pollution which affects the land, sea, and air. The fragile ecosystems of the Alpine ski-slopes are suffering soil erosion, land-slips and landslides. Some parts of the Mediterranean holiday playground experience severe sewage and waste disposal problems every summer, as well as the depletion of key items of fauna and flora.

Social impact

Tourism development can be accompanied by an improvement in the educational infrastructure of a country or region, with improved training opportunities to equip the host population with the skills they need to work in tourism. Also, the arrival of tourists can signal the end of a restricting insularity for isolated communities, with the added stimulation and new perspectives which contact with other cultures can bring.

However tourism can also bring social imbalance and racial tensions in its wake. Traditionally, tourist-host population contact has been founded on **inequality**. The tourist is perceived as wealthy, leisured and in a position of superiority over the inhabitants, whose role is to serve. The constant presence of vast numbers of demanding tourists from wealthier countries can create an unhealthy mixture of resentment, envy and dissatisfaction, particularly among the young members of the host population.

THE RISE OF RESPONSIBLE TOURISM

During the 1980s, the domination of the market by the standard sun, sea and sand package was increasingly challenged by the growth of a tourism trend which sought to minimise these negative features of mass tourism.

In that decade, tourism terminology expanded to include certain new expressions used to describe those forms of tourism which were held to typify this trend: **alternative** tourism, responsible tourism, **discreet** tourism, **green** tourism, **ecotourism**, **sustainable** tourism, and, in German, *sanfter Tourismus* ('soft tourism').

These terms themselves give some indication of the essential differences between conventional mass tourism and the current movement which is presented as an alternative to it. The terms all differ slightly in their emphasis, and to some extent are used interchangeably. 'Green' tourism clearly focuses on activities which benefit, or at least do not damage, the natural environment. 'Alternative' or 'discreet' tourism have been defined by the writer and lecturer, Anthony Travis, as

'those forms of tourism which seek to give the tourist an experience of host cultures, host environments and compatible activities, in ways which respect the values, nature and integrity of both hosts and guests. Such tourism cannot be mass tourism, as hosts should not be outnumbered by guests, and it should be conducted in ways which encourage non-exploitative contact between the hosts and guests.'

'Sustainable' tourism involves forms of tourism which, because they do not destroy the host physical environment, may last for a long time, with proportionately greater economic benefits. It evokes the image of a long-term goal – the ability to reconcile and sustain the three elements of tourism's 'eternal triangle': host areas, holidaymakers, and tourism operators. Bernard Lane of the University of Bristol's Rural Tourism Development Project sums up the basic attributes of sustainable tourism as follows:

'For the host area, it should provide carefully planned economic growth which provides satisfying jobs without dominating the local economy. It must not abuse the environment, and must be architecturally respectable. Decision-making should be local, and land speculation avoided. Traditional values and societies should be maintained . . . The benefits of tourism should be diffused through many communities, not concentrated on a narrow coastal strip or scenic valley. There have to be limits to growth; that growth should be gradual and organic.

For the holidaymaker, it should provide a good value, harmonious and satisfying holiday experience. The experience must respect the intelligence of both the visitor and the host, and not patronise. Host and holidaymaker should be on equal terms. The successful sustainable tourism operation will develop brand loyalty and repeat visits; the visitor will gain in-depth understanding and knowledge of the area, its landscape and peoples. The tourist will become concerned.

For the operator, sustained brand loyalty will bring its own rewards in long-term economic success. Responsibility will be a key to this reward. Responsibility entails accepting and building up the role of go-between, explaining the need for the long-term ecological care of the tourism resource (scenery, place, people, fauna, flora) to both host area and visitor. This is essentially an educative role.'

'Responsible' is perhaps the best general term to distinguish these kinds of tourism from mass tourism. The essential difference between the two forms stems from the fact that responsible tourism products are designed with a high degree of concern for the impact they have on the physical environment and the inhabitants of the destination. Responsible tourism seeks to ensure that residents at a destination directly benefit from visitors, or at least escape any disadvantages from their presence.

How is this achieved in practice? There are certain features common to responsible tourism products. These products tend to favour:

- the use of facilities which are owned and managed by those living at the destination

- small-scale enterprises

- direct contact between hosts and guests, emphasising mutual understanding and equality between them

- environmentally friendly developments

- authenticity

- activities which draw on the destination's special attractions.

Holiday products demonstrating some or all of these features, were increasingly in demand during the 1980s and into the 1990s, by consumers in search of an alternative to the standard mass tourism package. Yet, concern for tourism's impact on the physical and human environment of destinations is only part of the explanation for these recent changes in holiday tastes of many Europeans; and even this concern itself has to be set in the wider context of trends affecting Western society as a whole, which includes:

- the expansion in general ecological and sociological awareness of the 1980s

- the growing concern for personal health and fitness

- the growth in consumer sophistication *and* the

general increase in disposable income available for spending on holidays and short breaks

● the greater confidence of consumers who had grown accustomed to travel abroad and felt that they could cope with the challenge of more independent travel.

The combination of these trends led to the demand for more responsible tourism products from a public which had outgrown or become wary of the holidays offered by the large, traditional tour operators. Very quickly, this gap in the market was filled by small, specialist companies offering a new breed of package holiday. These packages feature to a greater or lesser extent the characteristics of responsible tourism as described above: many are small-scale enterprises, catering for groups of a limited size, using locally owned and/or managed services and accommodation, in authentic settings. Environmental awareness is also a feature of many of these holidays. While most of the responsible tourism companies emphasise that their products have no negative impacts on the natural setting of the destination, some even claim that the tourist products they offer can have a beneficial effect on the environment.

However, it would be a mistake to think in terms of the public now having to choose between two rigidly opposed types of tourism, either opting on the one hand for a traditional package which has a totally pernicious impact on the destination, or on the other hand choosing a holiday which is a model of responsible tourism, bringing nothing but genuine advantages to the host population and their environment. In fact, responsible tourism in its purest form is an ideal, one end of a spectrum of holiday 'styles', with the mass-tourism package holiday at the other end. Most tourist products now lie on the spectrum between these two extremes. Nor does the current trend represent a wholesale instant transfer of tourist activity from one pole of this spectrum to the other, but rather a gradual weighting in favour of holidays which display more of the characteristics of responsible tourism.

RESPONSIBLE TOURISM PRODUCTS

Sensing this move towards looking for something more responsible and more adventurous than flying to a Mediterranean destination for a standard two-week package holiday, tour operators have responded in various ways. Many long-established tour operators have simply repackaged their existing products as 'ecotours' – such is the case with many outdoor-orientated tours and safaris, for example. At best, this approach is misleading; at worst, the 'last-chance-to-see' attitude only hastens the disappearance of those species and habitats in question.

On the other hand, there has been an upsurge in new, genuinely responsible, tourist products. Katie Wood draws attention to some of these in *The Good Tourist*:

Conservation holidays are holidays where the emphasis is not only on enjoying nature, but giving something back to it as well. Many tour operators are now working with governments and conservation groups to protect the environment through the products they offer. Conservation holidaymakers are usually in search of more than simple traditional holiday fun. They are more likely to spend their time restoring Yugoslavian churches, reclaiming topsoil in Wales, or working alongside professional naturalists to protect wildlife habitats in National Parks. Despite the hard work and food and accommodation which is often fairly basic, these holidays have seen a rapid growth in popularity in recent years. Young and old find that conservation holidays offer a rewarding and educational experience, going far beyond the usual tourist clichés and providing a much deeper sense of place and culture. *Earthwatch* is a not-for-profit organisation which opened its European office in Oxford, England, in 1990. Its mission is to match field scientists in need of manpower and money with members of the public willing to help. Its services are in great demand, since scientific funding is drying up at a time when ecological problems are multiplying. For between $500 and $1000, Earthwatch arranges for participants to join a range of environmental and conservation projects for periods of two or three weeks: tracking pilot whales in the Canary Islands to help determine how the animals are faring now that they are no longer hunted; helping to excavate new revelations about Stone Age settlements from underneath vineyards and Romanesque churches in the Auvergne region of France; or exploring Majorcan sanctuaries that hold clues to monitoring the effects of sea level rise.

Wildlife/ecological holidays: increasing environmental awareness has led to an expanding market for holidays for those who wish to know more about the natural world. Travel for the purposes of viewing the fauna and flora of specific regions is not new, for example birdwatching and safari holidays are well-

Fig 8.1 Dr Martin Sharp's project studying glaciers in Switzerland, to assist in the understanding of global warming and the future of the world's water supply (*Reproduced by kind permission of Earthwatch*)

established in many parts of the world. What is different is that the emphasis is moving away from widespread hunting and shooting holidays towards the more responsible observation, viewing and study of wildlife. The best tour operators in this sector are sensitive to the increasing pressure on fragile and relatively undisturbed habitats, as well as to the problems of introducing tourists into 'non-tourist' areas. *Walser Viaggi* is an Italian tour operator offering nature tours in the Piemonte region of northern Italy. Their tours, devised by the Vercelli Province Parks Department aim 'to show the discerning visitor something of the natural and cultural heritage of this diverse region'. The itinerary takes in Vercelli, Parco Lame del Sesia, Parco della Burcina, Valsesia, Lake Orta and Sacro Monte. Guests speakers and interpreters present the flora and fauna to the visitors.

Alternative holidays: this fast-growing sector of the market is aimed at people looking for holidays offering 'something different'. It covers a wide range of non-mainstream holidays, usually based around some activity. Under this heading come holidays with an educational or discovery theme, those based on hobbies and pastimes, and those designed to introduce tourists to the inhabitants at a destination. Since most of the tour operators in this sector are small companies catering for small groups, these holidays are usually on a scale which is compatible with responsible tourism. Cycling holidays in the Netherlands; international study breaks at a Danish Adult Education College; self-discovery weeks in Buddhist retreats from Wales to the mountains of South-East Spain; naturist holidays on the French Mediterranean coast; homestays with British families; and First World War battlefield tours of Belgium, France and Italy: the list of alternative holidays is long, and growing, as more and more people seek something more 'off-beat', as their main, or more often, *second* holiday.

CASE STUDY

DIFFERENT SHADES OF GREEN – TWO TOUR OPERATORS

Cox and Kings is a good example of a tour operator showing concern for the physical environment in the products they offer. Their **Environmental Journeys** programme typifies the approach of tour operators catering for the growing market of those who are concerned about the environment and keen to see it preserved.

Their programme includes three different kinds of trips, all escorted by guest lecturers who are specialists in the field concerned: **botanical study tours**, such as to Crete, to observe the island's rich spring flora; **wildlife study tours**, such as to Newfoundland, to see its whales, seals and numerous seabirds; and **naturalist photography tours** of areas such as Zambia's Luangwa Valley National Park. Cox and Kings' philosophy of 'responsible and constructive tour operating' is illustrated in Fig 8.2, which is taken from their brochure.

With its admirable donations to conservation programmes, its limiting of the size of its groups, and its concern to substitute tourism as an alternative source of income for local people, Cox and Kings' Environmental Journeys programme shows many of the characteristics of responsible tourism. On the other hand, certain elements of responsible tourism in its 'purest' form are absent from the programme: for

Fig 8.2 The trenches where the Battle of the Somme was fought in 1916. Tours are taken to the sites of battlefields all over the world. (*Reproduced by kind permission of Major and Mrs Holt's Battlefield Tours, Sandwich, Kent*)

example, as the clients are accommodated exclusively in hotels, interaction with the indigenous populations at the destinations may be limited to their dealings with members of the hotels' staff only. Nevertheless, Cox and Kings is clearly at the responsible end of the tour operators' spectrum.

The British tour operator, Sally Holidays, is the sister company of Sally Ferries. This company offers 'The freedom of independent travel with the value of package holidays' in their brochure and invites readers to 'discover the *real* France, Belgium, Holland, Germany, Switzerland, Austria and Italy'. The extracts taken from the introduction to their brochure, shown in Fig 8.4, give an indication of how Sally Holidays emphasise that their products are different from the classic package holiday.

Sally Holidays offer 'tailor-made holidays', a phrase which is increasingly common in tour operators' brochures. Customers put together their own itinerary from the list of accommodation and travel options on offer in the brochure. This is how Sally Holidays describe their tailor-made holidays formula:

'We have designed our holidays for the **independent traveller**, enabling you to choose the holiday that you want – rather than having to compromise on a package. If you would like to mix a week on the Italian Lakes with a stay in a farmhouse in Tuscany, then we can arrange it, together with overnight stops en route. Perhaps you would rather take a tour of our country chateaux and hotels? Just let us know how many nights in each, and away you go. A touring holiday in Germany or France? The freedom of the open road yet with the security of knowing you have a room to stay at the end of the day? Our 'Go As You Please' programme gives you that. In fact, any and all of the holidays in this brochure can be tailor-made to suit you'.

While Cox and Kings emphasise the 'green' qualities of their products, Sally Holidays draw

ENVIRONMENTAL JOURNEYS

Environmental Journey's is the culmination of Cox & Kings' commitment and dedication to responsible and constructive tour operating.

Its development lay in the simple recognition that environmentally - concerned tourism was perhaps the most powerful force available to preserve and continue to observe some of the world's most threatened, yet beautiful, areas.

DONATION TO CONSERVATION

All travellers on Environmental Journeys wildlife programmes will be contributing to the conservation of fragile habitats and species. Cox & Kings will buy one acre of rainforest in Belize for every client booking on a wildlife holiday to ensure it remains in its undisturbed and natural state. For each client travelling on one of our whale-watching holidays in Baja California, the Galapagos Islands or Alaska, Cox & Kings will provide one week's sponsorship to Fernando Trujilo, a research associate for the Whale & Dolphin Conservation Society, who has been conducting field studies on the Amazon river dolphins since 1987. The money donated will provide an ongoing public education programme advising protection of these threatened dolphins in the eco-system.

WHY YOU SHOULD TRAVEL ON ENVIRONMENTAL JOURNEYS

Environmental Journeys is essentially the development of our long-standing Special Interest programme. Many of these tours are the result of previous projects with specialist societies and many are popular tours from past brochures. Others are new and exciting ventures, the product of the enthusiasm and love of our guest lecturers for particular and unusual destinations.

Environmental Journeys allow those who share our passion for the natural world to combine active appreciation with beneficial and long-term support. Our work has, over the years provided tangible benefits for the areas visited and has perpetuated and heightened the case for active conservation. Cox & Kings are U.K.'s official tour operators for the programme for Belize and are the exclusive operators for BBC Wildlife Magazine's series of tours. Cox & Kings work regularly with the Whale & Dolphin Conservation Society and have promoted the protection of the mountain gorillas of Rwanda. Most recently, a whale-watching holiday was donated to the winner of Time Magazine's competition for the most creative environmental advertisement.

OUR OBJECTIVE

Our ideal has been achieved by researching and developing programmes with those committed and involved in the field of conservation. Eminent naturalists whose work is dedicated to this cause accompany our tours and are involved from the initial planning stages. Their concern and ours is that the money spent on these tours is productively used and contributes towards the long-term preservation of these areas. Local agents are selected with considerable care and only those that meet our demands are used. Cox & Kings are also bonded by ABTA which ensures that the stringent demands on quality as detailed in the Tour Operators Code of Conduct are adhered to. Group size on all tours is strictly limited to maintain our high standards of personal service and to avoid the damaging impact large numbers have upon fragile environments.

Without revenue from foreign visitors, local people are no longer able or willing to sustain a living from the land as it is. The destruction of these areas for ranching, timber or other lucrative purposes is an unfortunate reality that can hopefully be avoided by the provision of an alternative source of income.

Environmental Journeys seeks to counteract the destruction that is taking place in fragile ecosystems worldwide. The presence of responsible tourism is increasingly encouraging governments to preserve their unique wildlife sanctuaries and has made the indigenous population aware that personal benefit can be derived from conservation.

OUR PROGRAMME

We believe that the tours selected here are the best of their kind available anywhere. A vast spectrum of diverse and unusual habitats are included from the lush rainforests of Central and South America to the remote wilderness of Alaska and the arid Atacama of northern Chile. The fauna we will encounter is equally extreme, from the great whale to the tiny hummingbird. Closer to home we enjoy an abundance of colourful flora with alpine specialities, Mediterranean and island species.

How to capture the spectacular and unique moments of a wildlife tour on film without disturbing the fragile surroundings is a question we are frequently asked. In response to this, we have specially designed a series of naturalist photography tours, taking us to the most stunning locales: tropical rainforests and remote islands; snow-capped mountains soaring above vast shimmering lakes; glaciers and fjords and wild arid plains. Accompanied by experts, advice will be given on the special techniques required to retain the essence of your holiday forever.

Our philosophy is ultimately quite simple: conservation and long-term environmental consideration must be an integral part of responsible tour operation. The foreseeable demise of these delicate and irreplaceable areas may in this way be avoided. Everything that Cox & Kings can do, from investment, to the use of recycled paper, we are committed to do.

We invite you to join us on an Environmental Journey — enjoy the most memorable and rewarding holiday available and help us to ensure that the areas visited may be appreciated for many generations to come.

Fig 8.3 An extract from Cox and Kings' brochure

The **FREEDOM** of Independent Travel...

If you have travelled abroad before, you will enjoy our "unpackaged" approach to holidays. We do all the **hard** work - book the ferry crossings, en route hotels, accommodation and insurance - but leave you **free** to enjoy your holiday **your** way. With your own car you can go as **you** please, en route and at your holiday destination.

Nobody Makes It **EASIER**
If you've "done" package holidays, and now want to experience the **real** pleasures of Europe, or you are a family that wants "**freedom-without-tears**", then Sally Holidays is for you. We make it easy en route with our stopover programme- and easy when you get to your holiday destination with maps, instructions and local information. We can sort out personal and car breakdown insurance, so there are no worries to spoil your fun.
So if you are going to Europe this summer, make sure you go the better way, the easier way with Sally Holidays.

A BETTER CHOICE
Hotels, Chateaux, Auberges, Pensions
Whatever your style of accommodation, you'll find we've got something for you. From luxurious chateaux in the Loire Valley and the chic elegance of hotels on the Cote d'Azur to rural inns in France and characterful pensions in Austria. If you want pampering, we've chosen a superb range!

GREATER VALUE
Cottages, Farmhouses, Villas
If getting-away-from-it-all is your idea of a holiday, then try one of our carefully selected country cottages in the heart of France. Or perhaps living on the farm is what appeals to your children: try an Austrian farmhouse, and join in. Then there are our Tuscan villas, up in the hills, but close to the sites as well as the coast.

MORE ACTIVE FUN
Holiday Parks, Venture Holidays, Apartments
Be active-and get more out of your holiday! Keep the kids entertained, and you can relax more. That's why the new-age holiday parks are proving so popular, even with families who hate the idea of "Hi-Di-Hi". You can be as active as you wish, and use your car to explore the region. Many of our apartments also have pools and add-on activities, but if you **really** want an active holiday with a difference, see Page 11 for our Alpine Venture.

TAILOR MADE HOLIDAYS
We have designed our holidays for the **independent traveller**, enabling you to choose the holiday that you want- rather than having to compromise on a package. If you would like to mix a week on the Italian Lakes with a stay in a Farmhouse in Tuscany, then we can arrange it, together with overnight stops en route. Perhaps you would rather take a tour of our Country Chateaux and hotels? Just let us know how many nights in each, and away you go. A touring holiday in Germany or France? The freedom of the open road yet with the security of knowing you have a room to stay at the end of the day? Our Go As You Please programme gives you that. In fact, any and all of the holidays in this brochure can be tailor made to suit you.
To work out the price of your own tailor made holiday just take the price of the holiday for the first main centre, and add on the extra nights or weeks accommodation as shown. En route stopovers are costed at the extra nights price. Add it all together, and you have the package cost. Ask your travel agent to call our Tailor Made department and we will make all the reservations for you - it could not be simpler. All we ask is that for **holidays with more than three accommodation centres**, you send us, or pass to your travel agent, a booking form, and the correct deposit before a reservation is made.

Fig 8.4 An extract from Sally Holidays' brochure

on another facet of changing holiday tastes, by stressing the flexibility and independent aspect of theirs. They can also claim to help support the local economy of their destinations by using family-owned and run hotels, and, for their self-catering holidays, farmhouses and cottages owned by local people. (Nevertheless, some of the accommodation mentioned in their brochure falls well short of the responsible tourism ideal – offering multinational hotel chains, modernistic resorts, etc.)

CASE STUDY

THE BENAMONARDA COOPERATIVE

Background

Up in the Serrania de Ronda mountains, the Andalusian village of Jubrique (population 1000) is the setting for a bold experiment in responsible tourism. There, a workers' cooperative runs an imaginative tourism business which contrasts strongly with the mass tourism of nearby Málaga.

A flavour of the kinds of holiday on offer there is given in this extract from their brochure:

Jubrique is one of the white villages of the Serrania de Ronda, a rugged upland area famous for its hospitality, natural beauty, and rich cultural heritage. Our picturesque little village, with its whitewashed houses and maze of narrow alleys, lies in the luxuriant Genal valley, an ideal place not only to relax amid splendid scenery and become familiar with the ancient mountain traditions, but also to discover the new tendencies of Andalusia today.

Accommodation and meals. You will stay in comfortable village houses and enjoy the delicious regional dishes prepared by your host family or served at typical village inns. On excursions, you will lodge in comfortable, friendly hotels or guest houses.

Excursions. We feature visits to the region's most interesting sites: *Ronda* – a natural fortress town, with a bustling market and elegant old quarters suspended over a gorge. *The white villages* – the villages of Andalusia are rightly famous for their harmonious architecture of narrow streets of whitewashed houses with red-tiled roofs. *Pileta cave* – a cave with fantastic galleries decorated by prehistoric paintings. *Acinipo* – a well-preserved Roman theatre in an outstanding site.

Activity holidays. A wide range of activities are available to visitors to Jubrique. These include:

● mule-trekking. Leisurely rides following the ancient tracks of the Andalusian muleteers through the enchanting mountain scenery of the Sierra Bermeja.

● Birds of Western Andalusia. Watch some of the most important colonies in Europe, such as the majestic raptors of the Sierrade Grazalema, or the waders of the Marismas del Odiel.

● Spanish language teaching. All levels, with Andalusian studies, seminars, films and theatre workshops.

● Rural crafts. Courses in leatherwork, wicker, pottery and harness-making.

● Walks for the whole family. A series of short, easy itineraries for the Easter holidays, on paths crossing fragrant Mediterranean woods and valleys studded with spring flowers.

The idea to form the Benamonarda Cooperative arose out of casual contacts between the inhabitants of Jubrique and two foreign visitors to the region in 1984. For three years, the idea was elaborated as more people, both in Spain and abroad, became involved, and in 1987, the cooperative was formed, the 'Sociedad Cooperativa Andaluza de Activadades Turistico-culturales Benamonarda'. It was finally founded by: ten Andalusians (five working members from Jubrique itself: a nature guide, an ecologist, a historian, a teacher and a youth animator); three mayors (from Jubrique and two neighbouring villages) and two village councillors from Jubrique; a Belgian hispanist and a British natural scientist.

Aims

The principal aims of the cooperative are to develop the region and to promote responsible tourism there. Therefore, the cooperative's objective is *not* to make money for its members (profits, if any, are used to improve the infrastructure of the region), but: **to reduce emigration** by providing direct and indirect employment for local people; and **to introduce a number of visitors** to a genuine **Andalusian** mountain area with its traditional village life and unspoilt scenery.

Clientele

Benamonarda's customers are from a wide range, from all over Europe, and from a broad spectrum of social backgrounds. The only stipulation made by the cooperative in their publicity is that visitors should be prepared to merge into a new environment while on holiday, rather than impose their own on Jubrique. The aim of attracting this type of visitor is achieved through the information given in their publicity material. This emphasises the mountain traditions and the local welcome rather than the 'standard of service', and the quality of the leisure activities rather than a luxurious infrastructure. Their publicity is also selective, distributed all over Europe, but mainly in

Britain, France, Belgium, Luxembourg, Switzerland, Italy, Germany and Spain, through:

- Spanish Tourist Offices in Spain and abroad;
- Youth information centres and educational institutions;
- magazine articles;
- mailing lists from previous years;
- recommendations of past visitors;
- advertisements in walking, nature, ecological, hispanist magazines and newspapers;
- alternative travel agencies; and
- travel fairs.

According to the cooperative, the cost of their publicity is a cause for concern. It currently amounts to about 25 per cent of the price of their programmes, which they regard as too high a proportion. It is partly a question of scale: a small stand at a travel fair, for example, costs about half or one third that of a large company, which will sell some 20 times as many holidays during the same fair.

Benamonarda operates eight months a year, over which period it welcomes some 150 visitors. The average group of visitors is of between three and eight people, depending on the programme and the season. The groups are international, with a predominance of Belgian and British visitors. More than half of them have some previous knowledge of Spanish.

Infrastructure

The infrastructure of the cooperative itself is minimal. Much use is made of the local facilities of Jubrique village, in particular its sports centre, swimming pool, library, and adult education centre with television and video facilities.

Visitors fit in with the normal village life. They are accommodated with local families, they have their meals at the village inn, they participate in village festivals and special events and they visit the local craftspeople. The cooperative has supplemented the local infrastructure by purchasing equipment such as two long wheelbase four-wheel-drive vehicles, teaching materials for the Spanish courses and camping material.

Benefits to the village life and surroundings

There are a number of economic benefits to those dealing directly or indirectly with the visitors – host families, the innkeeper, bar owners, local craftspeople, as well as local shopkeepers and tradespeople. On the employment side, visitors create temporary work for teachers, riding instructors and guides in the Natural Parks, and for extra staff to work in the inns and bars of the village.

However, the main benefit is felt to lie elsewhere, in the realm of psychology. The fact that outsiders come and appreciate the local customs and environment, and share the life of the villagers can revalue in local people's eyes their own traditions. One important result of this is the counterbalancing of the feeling, common among the local youth in particular, that 'real life' lies elsewhere, in the cities or on the coast, for example.

How successful is Benamonarda?

The local people

A potential obstacle to the setting-up of the project had been the problems in recruiting host families. It was very difficult to get the local people interested, for two reasons. First, 'bed and breakfast' is very unusual in Spain and villagers were not clear about what would be expected of them; and second, the only contact local people had had with tourists had been on the nearby Costa del Sol, and these experiences had not always been favourable. However, after two 'pioneers' had put up the first tourists in their homes and enjoyed doing so, the accommodation problem was soon resolved as new families rushed to volunteer. Fortunately for the cooperative, the village people in general are very open. They do not make much distinction between a 'foreigner' from the next village and one from abroad, and are happy to introduce visitors to the local way of life.

The visitors

As the tourists are few, of various nationalities, and most of them eager to learn the local customs and language, they mix easily with the villagers and often remain in contact with them after their holiday or course. According to the responses to a customer questionnaire, about 95 per cent of the visitors are enthusiastic about their opportunity for contact with the local people, the natural environment and new activities. The others suffer a culture shock, which, although they find interesting, they would not repeat if it could be avoided. *All* find their holiday or course 'good value' and 'better value' than they expected, as more activities are provided than they thought, and meals and accommodation are very much better than they had imagined. So far, about 18 per cent of visitors have returned to Jubrique and/or sent friends and relatives.

The Benamonarda cooperative itself

Benamonarda's weakest point is its own economic survival. The cooperative tries to maintain fair, democratic prices and individual attention to a very small group of visitors, and at the same time provide support to local small businesses and families. Most members of Benamonarda, therefore, often work without being paid, to assure its survival. Their experience underlines the difficulties of the sustainable approach to tourism and its precarious nature. One of the founders has estimated that for the cooperative's activities to be secure and truly viable, an increase of 30 per cent in the number of yearly visitors would be necessary, particularly in the spring period. Meanwhile, their aim remains the same: to benefit local people and to run a small-scale, economically viable tourism business.

RESPONSIBLE TOURISM ORGANISATIONS

During the 1980s, a network of groups promoting responsible tourism was established in Europe and beyond. These groups work on a range of activities, providing and collecting information for discerning tourists, running conferences, encouraging research into tourism's impact, mounting exhibitions, and producing educational materials.

One of the foremost European groups in this field is **Tourismus mit Einsicht** (tourism with insight), a German-based consortium of agencies working in the fields of tourism, environment and development. It was formed specifically to present an alternative viewpoint at Berlin's annual International Travel fair, the ITB. For example at the 1991 ITB, Tourismus mit Einsicht mounted a major exhibition on the theme of responsible tourism, and organised a series of lectures and debates. The main debate, Courage, Wit and Resistance, focused on initiatives in the Alps, from campaigns against thoughtless tourism development schemes, to 'green' tourism projects.

One feature common to many of these groups is the production of a manifesto, setting out guidelines and advice for tourists. Figure 8.5 shows an extract from the Tourismus mit Einsicht manifesto which gives the host population's points of view regarding responsible tourism.

More often, groups supporting responsible tourism give advice and guidelines for those planning a trip or buying a package tour.

Another such group is CART (the Centre for the Advancement of Responsible Travel), a Christian organisation set up to 'raise the standards of international tourism'. When purchasing a holiday, CART recommends that people ask themselves the following five questions:

1 Does the tour operator or travel agent demonstrate a cultural and environmental sensitivity to your destination? How are the local people and the culture you are to visit, portrayed in advertising brochures or orientation materials (guidebooks, etc)?

2 Who benefits from the cost of your trip? Which sectors of the host country benefit? What percentage of your money stays in the country you visit rather than 'leaking out' to the transnational travel industry, the hotel chains and airlines?

3 Is a realistic picture of the host country presented to you, or just a 'packaged' version for tourists?

4 Will you, on your visit, use the kinds of accommodation and transportation used by the members of the local society?

5 Does your travel plan allow adequate opportunities for meeting with local people? Does the pacing of your trip provide time for you to create or accept opportunities for interacting with local people?

We, the responsible host population

1. We need tourism for our economy: it creates jobs and brings income. We know, however, that it also represents a danger to our culture and our environment. We therefore want to supervise and control its development so that our country may be preserved as a viable economic, social and natural environment.

2. By independent decision making in tourist development we mean that the host population should decide on and participate in all matters relevant to the development of their region: tourist development by, with and for the local population. We encourage many forms of community participation in decision making, without neglecting the interests of minorities.

3. The tourist development we aim for is economically productive, socially responsible and environment-conscious. We are prepared to cease pursuing further development where it leads to an intolerable burden for our population and environment. We want to avoid the pitfalls of economic imperatives.

4. We determine the tourism development targets in our areas in a binding way, limiting them to what is desirable and not what is feasible. We adhere to this policy and are prepared to put up with the bottlenecks that may arise from doing so.

5. We want to keep control over our land. We pursue an active planning and land use policy. We limit our new construction by carefully considered zoning policies. We decline to sell land to non-locals. We promote and encourage the utilization of the existing buildings and infrastructure.

6. Our infrastructural development policies are based on restraint. We are therefore careful in building new or extending the existing infrastructure (especially roads, parking lots, airports, water supply and sewage systems) and tourist transport facilities (aerial cableways, ski-lifts) and strictly observe the set developmet targets.

7. We want to protect nature and the landscape effectively. In addition to careful land management and conservative infrastructural development, we create large nature reserves in order to preserve particularly valuable ecosystems. We ensure the participation of environmentalists and nature conservation experts in all planning and construction activities.

8. We want to counter the danger of one-sided economic development and over-dependence on the tourist trade. We support the strengthening of agriculture and small-scale trade as well as their partnership with tourism. We strive for a qualitative improvement of jobs in tourism. We also continually explore all possibilities for the creation of new jobs outside the tourist trade.

9. One of our principles in tourist development is to observe and foster the natural and cultural characteristics of our region. We expect our guests to be prepared to accept this principle. We want our local culture to remain independent and alive. We protect and promote our architecture, our handicrafts, our art, our language, our customs and our cuisine.

10. We shall provide information for all concerned: the local population, the tourist trade, politicians and tourists, and try to win their support for socially responsible and environmentally conscious behaviour. We shall use all tourism marketing tool and general information channels to promote our concept.

© by Working group "Tourism with insight and understanding"

Fig 8.5 An extract from a brochure published by *Tourismus mit Einsicht*

The Swiss organisation **Arbeitskreis Tourismus und Entwicklung** (Working Group for Tourism and Development) offers consumers the following list of points to watch when travelling:

● **Indigenous hotels.** In many countries, there are hotels, guest houses and pensions belonging to the indigenous people and run according to the style of the country. In these, you can experience the uniqueness of your host country. National Tourist Offices will give you information.

● **National foods.** National foods are part of the culture of every land. Local food is more interesting and more tasty than the menus of the international hotels whose ingredients must often be imported. Buying indigenous food and drink saves foreign exchange and strengthens the local economy.

● **Local transportation.** Local transport opportunities abound: buses, trains, taxis etc. These are usually inexpensive. Their use fosters contact with indigenous people and allows you to see cities and the countryside in an authentic, everyday manner.

● **Getting to know the people.** Hospitality is a central feature of the peoples of many countries. Traditionally such people are polite and generous. Too often, their hospitality is abused by tourists from the world's materially richer countries.

● **Facade for tourists.** Travel brochures often depict only the tourist sights of the country, thus reinforcing the stereotyped tourist image of its culture. Questions need to be asked (tactfully) about the current reality in that country: working and living conditions, wages and prices, the political system, language, customs, religions, the school system, and the place of women. The accuracy of the answers to these questions depends on the knowledge of your tour guide. *Local* guides usually know more about their own country.

● **Handicrafts/souvenirs.** Ostensibly handi-crafted souvenirs may often be made in Hong Kong, Taiwan, etc. Enquire about local handicrafts: they provide an authentic souvenir, and the money paid for them, if spent at a local community outlet, is much more likely to go to the people who actually made them. (Beware: local businessmen exploiting their own people as well as tourists can be a problem.)

Finally, **Greenpeace International**, although not an organisation dealing uniquely with environmental problems caused by tourism, recognises that tourists themselves have a role to play in protecting the natural resources of the areas they visit. Their leaflet 'Let's Save the Mediterranean' draws attention to the major problems of that region – untreated sewage being discharged into the sea; oil pollution; industrial dumping and pesticides; and over-exploitation of the fishing resources:

What can you do?

100 million tourists visit the Mediterranean every year. You may be one of them.

● Before you depart for the Mediterranean, write to the embassy of the country you intend to visit and tell them that you will respect their environment and ask them what they are doing to protect the Mediterranean.

● If you witness any environmentally destruc-tive activity, such as dumping, etc, please write a report, with photos if possible, and send it to your local Greenpeace office.

● If you are witness to a kill of an endangered species such as marine turtles, cetaceans, monk seals etc, denounce it to the nearest police station. Explain quietly, rationally and respect-fully your reasons for opposing this activity to the people involved – they may not have access to the education and information that you enjoy. Write a report and send it to your local Greenpeace office.

● Beware of forest fires. Do not camp in polluted areas. Do not discard cigarettes, matches or glass.

● Do not dump litter in rivers, the sea or in the countryside.

● Respect the life and culture of the local inhabitants. If you have an opportunity, share your concern for the environment with them.

● Do not buy coral goods: red coral is disappearing in the Mediterranean.

● Do not buy or eat turtle products.

● If you are diving, do not practise underwater fishing.

CONCLUSION

Responsible tourism was the inevitable result of the maturing of the holiday market combined with various trends in society as a whole. Its effect upon the tourism industry is only beginning to be felt, partly through the arrival of specific 'responsible' tourism products, but also more widely, through the growing obligation on the part of all tour operators to take into account their clients' sensitivity to the impact their activity has on the environment and the host population.

The responsible approach to tourism is a move towards greater quality – quality of product, for an increasingly discerning clientele, and quality of life for those living at the destination. The widespread recognised benefits of this movement mean that it is a trend which no operator in the tourism industry can afford to ignore in future.

ASSIGNMENTS

1 Green credentials. In December 1990, a new initiative was launched in Britain to provide an opportunity for tourism industry and conservation interests to work together. **Green Flag International** is a showcase where travel companies are able to display their environmental credentials.

The organisation sells special Green Flag packs at £5 each, to members of the public looking for 'green' guidelines when buying holidays. The pack gives short environmental profiles of the companies which have joined the scheme, giving such 'green credentials' as the fact that one company sponsors conservation projects, while another uses recycled-paper for its brochures, and so on.

One tour operator states in the pack, 'Through Green Flag, we can seize the opportunity to begin to impose a conservation discipline on ourselves, and in turn on the host countries receiving our clients'.

(*a*) Using your own ideas and the pointers given to potential tourists by the various responsible tourism groups, make a checklist of ten responsible tourism credentials to look out for when choosing a tour operator's products. (Use of indigenous accommodation, contact with local people, small groups, etc.) The checklist of ten items should be arranged in order of importance.

(*b*) Obtain a wide selection of tour operators' holiday brochures. (Remember that it is wasteful to use current brochures which could still be used to sell holidays. Try to make an arrangement with a travel agent, for example, who will supply you with out-of-date ones for this purpose.) Using your green credentials checklist, go through each brochure looking for the kind of responsible tourism features you have identified.

(*c*) Draw a grid, with your ten credentials along one axis and the tour operators along the other.

Complete the grid, marking in which credentials are displayed by which tour operators.

2 Discussion: a small answer to a big problem? The passage below is an extract from a report written by tourism lecturer, Brian Wheeler, expressing serious doubt over the ability of responsible tourism to satisfy the global demand for tourism products in any *quantitative* sense.

At the destination, control of the volume of tourism is seen as paramount by many of those concerned with tourism's negative impacts. Everywhere one is beginning to read of soft, green tourism development, sensitively planned to ensure that tourist numbers are limited to sensible levels. The need for an appropriate scale and rate of development, invariably small and slow, is usually stressed to ensure the development is both environmentally and culturally 'friendly'. I see Sustainable Tourism as an integral part of the desire for small scale, controlled tourism. However, though the notion of small scale development is laudable, it does not tackle the large scale problem of volume. The overall problem of tourism is that it is 'big', yet Sustainable Tourism is essentially 'small'. If all tourist destinations could carefully calculate their appropriate tourist numbers below these limits and if all the tourists were indeed 'sensitive travellers', then – even then, the tourist problem as a whole would not be solved as the effective demand for tourist destinations at a macro level would far outstrip the supply. At best, it is a micro solution to what is essentially a macro problem.

Is he right? As a group exercise, discuss whether small-scale responsible tourism can ever become the dominant form of tourism in the world. Or does sheer volume of demand mean that, in the future, as now, mass tourism will continue to be the only realistic option open to the vast majority of holidaymakers? With the rise of responsible tourism, is there a real danger of a new *elitism* emerging, with one form of tourism for the 'discerning traveller' and another for the 'masses'?

C H A P T E R   9

EUROPEAN RURAL TOURISM

Although far from new in Europe, rural tourism is widely regarded as being well-placed to benefit from the changes in holiday tastes and habits currently affecting the tourism industry. One reason for the optimism over this sector's future is its tendency to be characterised by many of the features described in Chapter 8 as being typical of the kind of 'responsible' tourism products now coming into vogue. However, rural tourism, closely connected as it is with Europe's agricultural sector, has been caught up in the fundamental changes affecting that sector in recent years. As a result, the chances of survival of the farming and rural populations of Europe increasingly depend upon country-dwellers' willingness to share their countryside with this new wave of high-spending, but demanding visitors.

This chapter examines:
- The definition of rural tourism
- The history of rural tourism in Europe
- Rural tourism accommodation
- The role of the EC in the development of rural tourism

DEFINITION

Rural tourism is generally regarded as including a wide variety of tourist accommodation, activities, events, festivities, sports and recreation, all being developed in an area characterised as being rural. However, when it comes to an exact definition of rural tourism, usable over Europe as a whole, numerous problems present themselves.

'Rural tourism is a concept which includes all tourist activity in rural areas'.

This statement might be regarded as uncontroversial. However, what is meant by 'rural areas'? In Germany, the Netherlands, Belgium, Luxembourg and France, the equivalent of the term 'rural areas' is used to denote areas which may be distinguished from towns, the coast and mountain areas. In Italy, the term denotes areas which are neither towns nor the coast, and therefore 'rural areas' there include mountainous regions. In Ireland and Britain, rural areas are practically synonymous

with the notion of 'countryside', as opposed to towns of any size. In Spain, Portugal and Greece, there is a tendency to equate rural areas with those parts of the country used for agricultural production.

The concept of rural areas, therefore, does not have the same meaning in all European countries. The main consequences of this problem arise in connection with any attempt to measure, for example, the economic and social impact of tourism development in rural areas. The absence of any Europe-wide agreement on the concept of rural areas makes comparisons between different countries difficult, and global statements in this sector extremely limited in value.

Even if this geographical question did not arise, the definition might be rejected on other grounds. Increasingly, the term 'rural tourism' implies the presence of those features which qualify tourism products as being 'responsible'. Therefore, for example, a guided tour of a car factory in a rural setting, or a day spent at a vast theme park buried deep in the countryside would not represent rural tourism in the sense in which the term is now used. Taking up this point, the British writer, Bernard Lane, Director of the University of Bristol Rural Tourism Development Project, asks, 'Does rural tourism have special intrinsic qualities, or is it simply tourism in a rural location? What are the features which rural tourism must possess in order to be truly rural?' His list includes: closeness to nature, absence of crowds, quietness and a non-mechanised environment . . . personal contact – the antithesis of urban anonymity . . . a sense of continuity and stability, of long and living history . . . the possibility of getting to know an area and its people well. Local control, by manor house, farm, business or council, and, for the rural community, retention of individual identity, are also features of genuine rural tourism.

An alternative definition avoiding the geographical problem might be:

Rural tourism is a concept which covers tourist activity devised and managed by local people, and based on the strengths of the natural and human environment.

This wider definition is one which might be accepted almost universally, distinguishing, as it does, rural tourism from tourism activity in coastal resorts, cities, and winter sports resorts, where the sheer numbers of visitors and the nature of their activities preclude any meaningful exchange between tourists and the local populations which make up the human environment. The one weakness of this definition appears on the economic level, since rural tourism occasionally includes the involvement of outside organisations, such as accommodation built by outside investors, for example.

In the absence of any agreed definition of rural tourism throughout the EC and beyond, the term **green tourism** is widely used, as a colour-coded means of distinguishing this form of tourism from **white tourism** (winter sports), **blue tourism** (holidays by the sea), and **tourism of lights** (city tourism). In this way, green tourism may be defined as tourist activity practised in the countryside, but also in lightly populated regions (too lightly populated to qualify as tourism of lights), on those parts of the coast where tourism is not highly developed, as well as in mountainous zones not given over to winter sports. In all of these locations, green tourism is characterised by the desire, on the part of visitors, to integrate themselves with the natural and human environment, and the firm involvement of the local populations in the provision of services for tourists.

Agritourism is a much narrower concept, referring to the different forms of tourism directly related to agrarian activities and/or buildings with an agrarian function. This particular form of rural tourism is, therefore, run by farmers, usually as a secondary activity, with farming remaining their principal occupation and source of income. Often, a distinction is made between agritourism and the term **farm tourism** or its equivalent, which is used to refer simply to the use of former farmhouses as tourist accommodation – as rented holiday cottages, health clubs, etc. This is not agritourism in the strictest sense, since such farmhouses have usually lost their agrarian function, or are no longer owned by active farmers. Despite its loss of any direct relationship with the agrarian sector, farm tourism is an important form of rural tourism, which makes a considerable contribution to the local economy wherever it takes place.

HISTORICAL CONTEXT

Tourism in the countryside has a long history in Europe. For as long as people have travelled, there has been a tradition of those living in rural areas providing accommodation and catering for visitors. The European countryside has long been criss-crossed by various ancient 'routes', along which travellers have passed, on their way to a variety of destinations. For example, there were the many trade routes for those conveying products such as salt, silk, wine or amber; there were those routes followed by those on pilgrimages or crusades – to Santiago de Compostela, Mont-Saint-Michel, or Jerusalem, for example; or the routes to health resorts such as the Roman thermae or spas.

Because of the means of transport available at the time, these journeys involved the slow crossing of many rural areas, in which travellers had to find board and lodging, and satisfy other material needs. Those passing through came with their own habits and customs, and often spoke a language different to that of their hosts. The misunderstandings and tensions between those with vastly different lifestyles which these encounters brought about have always been features of rural tourism which, through time, may have been minimised, but not altogether eliminated.

In the era of modern tourism, much of the rise of rural tourism in Europe is linked to the great wave of urbanisation which took place, leading up to and following the Second World War. In this period, new patterns of industrialisation and farm mechanisation led to a vast population shift away from rural areas into Europe's fast-expanding towns and cities. In France alone, between 1945 and the present day, some six million people moved off the land, and agriculture's share of the active population dropped from 35 per cent in 1939 to eight per cent now.

As holidays became available to the vast majority of working people, a substantial proportion of the early rural tourism clientele was composed of these new city-dwellers returning to their 'own' countryside to visit those they had left behind there. Visitors were most often accommodated by friends and family, and leisure activities were in most cases limited to helping on the farm or catching up with village gossip. Where a rural tourism 'industry' existed as such, standards of comfort and the provision of services tended to be modest. In many countries, rural tourism came to be synonymous with 'cheap tourism', an economical alternative for those who could not afford to follow the annual mass migrations to the beaches.

From the 1970s, rural tourism in Europe increasingly felt the impact of important changes in consumers' attitudes and demands, resulting in an accelerating pace of change in the rural tourism product itself. The move away from mass tourism, with the rise of individualism; changes in preferences for the type of holiday setting, as concern over the environment led holidaymakers to seek alternatives to seaside destinations; growing interest in sports, health, and sightseeing; the search for authentic, small-scale destinations: all of these were favourable to the development of rural tourism. Changes in attitudes were paralleled by changes in patterns of holiday-taking by Europeans, leading to shorter holidays being taken more often during the year and the development of short-breaks.

RURAL TOURISM IN EUROPE TODAY

By the mid-1980s, rural tourism was already a clear beneficiary of these trends, with an average of 25 per cent of the populations of EC countries taking their main holiday in the countryside, and 23 per cent taking it in mountain areas. Figure 9.1 shows the proportions, country by country, for preference types of main holiday destinations.

The countryside and mountain areas have especially grown in popularity in most countries as destinations for second holidays and short-breaks, as shown in Fig 9.2.

Fig 9.1 Types of holiday destination (main holiday)

	Countryside %	Mountains %	Cities %	Seaside %
Belgium	25	19	5	55
Denmark	35	14	40	42
Spain	27	19	27	53
France	29	27	18	51
Greece	8	11	20	70
Ireland	27	8	37	46
Italy	11	24	19	58
Luxembourg	19	29	17	62
Netherlands	39	32	21	36
Portugal	29	8	24	62
Germany	34	30	15	44
UK	29	13	19	58
EC Average	25	23	19	52

The totals reading across the lines come to more than 100, since some holidaymakers stayed at more than one type of location.

Source: Europeans and their Holidays, *Commission of the European Communities.*

Fig 9.2 Types of holiday destination (other holidays) for countries where at least 20% of the total population takes more than one holiday

	Countryside %	Mountains %	Cities %	Seaside %
France	29	33	22	28
Netherlands	49	26	24	19
Denmark	34	13	36	27
Britain	38	8	25	36
Italy	13	33	21	37
Germany	30	29	33	15

Source: Europeans and their Holidays, *Commission of the European Communities.*

However, changes in attitudes and holiday taking patterns have been accompanied by changes affecting the *quality* of holidays sought by those choosing rural tourism. The rough-and-ready amateurism and basic standards of the early years of rural tourism, which led it to be associated with 'cheap' tourism, are less and less prevalent, as operators become convinced of the need to respond to the new demands of the tourist. These demands are for high levels of comfort, service, and, above all, a supply of activities to keep the holidaymakers entertained and active during their stay in the countryside. Perhaps the greatest fear of city-dwellers, regarding the countryside, is that of being bored. They do not seek from the countryside the same kinds of stimulation which cities offer, but they do expect to find a sufficient number of interests and activities available to keep them fully entertained during their stay.

Consequently, operators in European rural tourism have come to recognise that accommodation in itself is no longer sufficient to satisfy the demands of their clientele. Farm tours, nature studies, cycling and walking tours, cultural activities, craft courses, health-related activities, and a wide range of water and land-based sports help attract customers into the European countryside. These are now as vital a part of the rural tourism product as the various forms of accommodation associated with rural areas. Facilities are as important as accommodation, and the greatest rural tourism successes have been seen where the two have been planned together.

If there have been a number of changes in the attitudes of the clientele, there have also been changes in the attitude of the commercial sector towards rural tourism. Traditionally the commercial sector of the tourism industry has held great reservations concerning rural tourism, regarding it as being largely composed of small-scale businesses, which are difficult to control in terms of management, and as not being competitive with the commercial tourist infra-structure. In the past, rural tourism was almost considered to be anti-commercial, taking into account the often low standards of facilities and comfort, and the lack of professionalism and organisational structures which once prevailed.

Now, tour operators are increasingly reappraising their attitudes towards this sector, and more and more rural tourism products are finding their way into tour operators' brochures. Without losing their essential characteristics, activity holidays using rural accommodation are now on offer, even from some of Europe's large tour operators, who sign contracts with individual operators (chalet owners, rural hotelkeepers, farmers etc), with the operators retaining their independence.

Finally, as well as seeing changes in the attitudes of the clientele and tour operators, rural tourism is now also being regarded differently by those living in the countryside itself. At a time when Europe's agricultural production is going through great upheavals, with farmers being encouraged by the EC to produce less and less, and when the continuing drift of young people into towns and cities is threatening to turn many rural areas into deserted zones and ghost-villages, rural tourism is coming to be regarded as part of the solution to these problems. However modest the profits from their rural tourism businesses, those living in rural areas have come to realise that these can be just enough to enable them to cope with Europe's current farming problems, to maintain their farm or even to stay on living in the countryside. The income from rural tourism can be just sufficient to keep local shops going, to prevent people from moving to the cities in search of work, or to maintain farm buildings in a reasonable state.

Thus, the development of rural tourism throughout Europe has come to be seen as having a valuable *social* function in providing rural areas with an additional means of strengthening their economic structures to the point where life in the countryside remains viable and comfortable for those born there. It is rural tourism's social function, above all, which has prompted the measures undertaken by the European Commission to stimulate this sector. These measures are described later in this chapter, after an examination of an essential part of the core product of rural tourism, the accommodation stock.

RURAL TOURISM ACCOMMODATION

Rural tourism uses almost every type of accommodation found in Europe. However, due to the general lack of precision and agreement over the definition of rural areas and rural tourism itself, statistics on the supply of tourist accommodation situated in the countryside are extremely rare. Nevertheless, over Europe as a whole, there exist certain types of tourist accommodation which are essentially rural in character as well as location. These are described as follows in the report *Rural Tourism in the 12 Member States of the EC*:

Rural hotels

In Europe, rural hotels are generally small to medium-size hotels, typically family-run. Such hotels are often classed in the lowest categories, where there is a classification system, such as one-star and two-star hotels, hostels or family pensions. In many countries, small rural hotels have long constituted a sector which has grown accustomed to facing the problems of small isolated businesses without the benefits of scale from which the large hotel chains benefit. Nevertheless, in certain countries, there have been imaginative developments to help the rural hotel sector.

In France, 1949 saw the first initiative taken in Europe to preserve the rural heritage through the revitalisation of the rural hotel sector. Small hotels in the French countryside were invited to join a new movement based on strict adherence to a charter which guaranteed their clients certain standards. The result was the voluntary hotel chains, **Logis de France** and **Auberges de France** for small rural one-star and two-star hotels with restaurants. In order to belong to either chain, hotels must agree to various conditions, including the provision of a personal welcome for clients and the offering of services reflecting aspects of their rural location, for example, regional and local dishes on their restaurant menus. With over 6000 hotels as members, the Logis and Auberges de France movement now constitutes Europe's biggest voluntary hotel chain.

In Ireland, the **Village Inns Hotels** movement has played a similar part in attracting clients to rural hotels of character. This voluntary chain consists of hotels selected, according to their publicity material, 'for the essential role which they play in the life of the village in which they are placed. The villagers gather there to have a drink, to joke together in a typically Irish way, and, when the atmosphere is right, to play and listen to good Irish music. Each of these hotels

is family-run.' Clients are guaranteed home-cooking in a comfortable setting reflecting the authentic atmosphere of Irish villages. Growing rapidly in international popularity, Village Inns Hotels are now marketed in New York, London and Frankfurt.

Not all rural hotels in Europe are of the humble family-business type, however. Prestige establishments, although much less numerous, also have an important part to play in attracting visitors to the countryside, and these are found in almost every country, often grouped together in voluntary chains: **Paradores** in Spain, **Relais et Châteaux** in France, and **Manor House Hotels** in Ireland are among the many examples of deluxe rural hotels based on Europe's plentiful supply of castles, palaces and stately homes.

A growing trend is for individual and chain-affiliated rural hotels to specialise in the services they provide, offering clients a particular activity as well as accommodation. Hotels with private hunting grounds, fishing facilities or horseriding, for example, increasingly serve the needs of clients keen to learn or practise these activities. A good example is that of the French **Relais Saint-Pierre** group of country hotels, which offer clients full fishing facilities – specially reserved stretches of river, equipment for hire, mealtimes arranged to suit the times of fishing expeditions, and caught fish cooked and served for dinner, if required.

Voluntary chains have played an important part in increasing the standing and profitability of rural hotels, both modest and prestige, and this structure might well be repeated in other European countries in the years to come. Despite their success, however, for the moment, their clientele is essentially drawn from the inhabitants of the countries in which the chains exist, with, in most cases, only a small proportion of foreign visitors. Much remains to be done to promote existing and future rural tourism hotels throughout Europe as a whole, as well as beyond, by drawing attention to the existence of chains where they exist, and emphasising the special nature of what rural hotels offer – a rural setting, regional character, the possibility of taking part in country pursuits, etc.

Camping sites

The percentage of European holidaymakers who go on camping holidays is considerably high, as

Fig 9.3 Europeans who practise camping during their holidays	
Holidaymakers from	%
Belgium	17
Denmark	18
Spain	13
France	22
Greece	8
Ireland	9
Italy	12
Luxembourg	10
Netherlands	31
Portugal	19
Germany	10
UK	19
EC as a whole	16

Source: Europeans and their Holidays, *Commission of the European Communities.*

shown in Fig 9.3. At a time when coastal campsites in many parts of Europe are becoming increasingly congested, and concern is mounting over the environmental impact of the concentration – both in time and space – of vast numbers of campers in these locations, rural campsites may have the potential to form part of the solution to these problems.

Rural campsites exist in every European country, but are often characterised by standards inferior to those generally found in campsites situated by the sea. Nevertheless, in cases where owners have deliberately used the rural setting to enhance and develop their campsites, there have been some spectacular successes. Increasingly, it has become clear to rural campsite owners that their best hope of attracting clients is not by imitating the sites found by the sea, but by playing on the particular strengths and attractions of the countryside around them. In recent years, two lessons have been learnt:

1 Clients are drawn to sites which offer a **high degree of comfort**. Upgrading of rural campsite facilities is, therefore, a sound policy for Europe as a whole.

2 The **rural nature** of such sites must be regarded as a strength, not a weakness. The possibility of fitting into the countryside, experiencing the natural environment at first hand, and taking part in sporting activities should all be strongly emphasised in all promotional material.

Privately let accommodation

Staying as a paying guest of country people, whether in their own homes or in independent dwellings close by, is undoubtedly the strongest marketing image for rural tourism throughout Europe. Those offering such accommodation may be divided into farmers and non-farmers. The case of farmers is dealt with under the heading 'Agritourism' (*see* below).

Although it is simple to state with some confidence that privately let accommodation is extremely widespread throughout the rural areas of Europe, and that it plays a crucial role in attracting visitors to the countryside, putting a figure on the quantity of such accommodation is another matter. The number of private individuals who offer accommodation in their own homes or on their own land is almost impossible to estimate, since in most European countries, this kind of activity almost entirely escapes regulation. The explanation is that the majority of country-dwellers who receive paying guests, do so without the prior permission or knowledge of the authorities, in order to avoid paying taxes on the income they make from this activity.

However, no doubt exists as to the value of privately let accommodation in preserving and enhancing the rural architectural heritage of Europe. Indeed, in many countries, the existence of such accommodation is actively encouraged by public bodies concerned with this heritage. Italy, Portugal, Luxembourg and France provide many examples of moves taken by conservation bodies to encourage the use of country buildings as tourist accommodation.

Independently rented accommodation

In certain countries, there is a terminological distinction made between privately let, furnished accommodation found in holiday resorts by the sea, and in cities, for example, and furnished accommodation which is essentially rural in character. In Denmark, 'chalets' represent the most widespread form of rural tourism accommodation, and are subject to strict forms of control as to their classification and use. In Belgium and France, there exists the distinction between the 'gîte', and other forms of privately let furnished tourist accommodation, the gîte being characterised by its rural nature and the personal welcome given to

Fig 9.4 A gîte in the Vendée (Western Loire), France
(*Reproduced by kind permission of Gîtes de France*)

holidaymakers. Similarly, in Portugal, there is a special category of accommodation which denotes those furnished houses which show examples of regional architectural styles in rural areas.

Wherever the distinction between essentially rural furnished holiday accommodation and other furnished holiday accommodation has been made official and labelled in some way, the proportion of clients opting for the former has risen, sometimes dramatically. Successes have been greatest in cases where, as with the regulations applying to French gîtes, labelling has been accompanied by a guaranteeing of certain standards. Rural tourism stands directly to benefit from such measures. For this reason, pressure is increasing, from the EC in particular, for tourism promotion organisations to develop systems which clearly identify rural tourism accommodation of character, and which impose minimum standards, giving the client confidence in selecting in this market.

Rooms rented in the occupier's home

Although bed and breakfast accommodation is widely regarded as a purely British phenomenon, renting a room in a private individual's house – with or without breakfast provided by the occupier – exists in some form in most European countries, and is particularly widespread in rural areas. The regulations which apply to the use of private homes for this purpose differ from country to country, with varying degrees of control by the authorities, as shown by the following examples. In Germany, no permission is required to open up business as 'zimmer frei', and the revenue from such businesses is only liable to tax if the number of beds used exceeds seven; while in Denmark, the use of rooms in private homes for tourist accommodation is permitted, but not encouraged, and is closely monitored by local tourist offices, who also forbid any prior reservation of these rooms. In France, the authorities discouraged this form of accommodation, until, at the time of the Winter

Olympics in Grenoble in 1968, it was finally authorised as a result of an acute accommodation shortage, and the 'chambre d'hôte' appeared; in Greece, where the practice is extremely widespread, householders renting out rooms should, in theory, notify the authorities, but this is only very rarely done; and in Ireland, rooms are offered under the labels, 'town houses' and 'country homes'. Strictly speaking, the occupier must notify the authorities, who arrange an inspection of the house, and then formulate an agreement, but in practice many householders do not go through this procedure.

The European Commission's report, 'Rural tourism in the 12 Member States of the EC' puts at over 300 000 the number of rooms offered in private homes in rural areas of Europe, not counting rooms rented out in farmhouses.

Agritourism accommodation

Accommodation offered by farmers includes furnished accommodation in independent buildings on the farm, bed and breakfast, and camping on the farmland. Bed and breakfast is the formula most commonly used in agritourism in most European countries, while camping on the farm is most important in the Netherlands and France, where it is limited to five and six tent pitches, respectively.

In Germany, France, Italy and the Netherlands, certain farms offer special activities with the accommodation, such as fishing, horseriding and nature studies; others offer accommodation for special groups, including handicapped people, children, and school parties.

EC ROLE IN DEVELOPING RURAL TOURISM

At the European level, widespread optimism exists as to rural tourism's potential for mitigating some of the harmful effects of the EC's agricultural policies, for protecting the heritage of the continent's rural areas, and for improving the overall tourism product.

However, there are problems to be overcome. Not every rural area or every farmer can expect to make a success out of tourism. Areas vary considerably in the assets they offer in terms of geographical location, natural tourism resources, the cultural profile of the area, etc. Also, developing, planning and marketing rural tourism in Europe is a major task, too great for local authorities or even national authorities to tackle by themselves. The task of organising Europe's rural tourism is made even more difficult by the dispersed nature of the operators, their numbers, and the scale of their activity. The professionalism which is required to penetrate a highly competitive tourism market is often lacking.

The current tendency of the tourism industry towards largeness of scale and the internationalisation of the tourism market makes it necessary to develop high-quality products, and to do this in a professional and marketing-based way. How can farmers or groups of farmers, or local communities which are lacking a tourism tradition be equipped to cope with this challenge to avoid going out of business or being swallowed up by some multinational project developer or tour operator?

The EC's main objective is to develop a tourist product which gives a direct imput to the earning of farmers, the livelihood of rural communities and the preservation of the rural heritage, with a minimum of leakage to external bodies. Their interventions in this sector are, therefore, designed to achieve these objectives by providing the assistance necessary to overcome the problems detailed above.

The justification given for the EC's growing intervention in this sector is that where local authorities are not equipped to start off the rural tourism development process in a sustainable way, where national authorities are placing their priorities in the development of large-scale tourism resorts, there is a role for European organisations to step in and take a leading role in the development of rural tourism. This is especially the case in peripheral regions and border areas, which are often out of focus in national tourism development policies.

EC measures for which rural tourism businesses qualify

1 Common Agricultural Policy

Community regulations designed to improve the efficiency of agricultural structures provide for a system of financial aid, which extends to investment in tourist and craft activities on farms. The scheme is based on the Commission's own definition of agritourism, which means that it applies only to farmers who derive at least 25 per cent of their total income from farming. Below this threshold, any tourism activity carried out on the farm is no longer considered part of farming and is, therefore, not eligible for aid under these regulations. As well as these general regulations applying to the whole Community, there are specific agritourism measures providing financial assistance to less favoured areas, including the west of Ireland, parts of Italy and certain Scottish islands.

2 Community regional policy

Because it most often takes place in those regions eligible for aid through the Community's Structural and Regional Development Funds (as described in Chapter 2), rural tourism has benefitted considerably from support from these two sources. For example, most of the Community support frameworks for its rural development objective provide for the possibility of measures to promote rural tourism and vocational training in the field of tourism. These include the financing of investment in tourist facilities, such as farm accommodation, and the development of natural parks or sports facilities (golf, skiing etc).

3 The LEADER initiative

In 1990, the Commission adopted a new Community initiative for rural development, entitled LEADER ('links between actions for the development of the rural economy'), under which the Community will encourage integrated rural development at local level. Through the LEADER initiative, a network of around 100 local rural development action groups will be established. Each group will be given the task of managing grants for the financing of the following measures within its own geographical area:

- providing information on all Community measures and finance likely to encourage rural development in the area
- vocational training and assistance for employment
- rural tourism
- small firms, craft enterprises and local services
- exploitation and marketing of local agricultural products.

ADDITIONAL COMMUNITY ACTION TO PROMOTE RURAL TOURISM

The above measures, including support from Common Agricultural Policy funds and Regional Development funds mean that most of the investment required for the provision of tourist facilities qualifies for some sort of Community assistance. However, although amenities for tourists in a rural environment are necessary, they are not on their own sufficient to accommodate on a lasting basis the growing demand for an integrated range of tourist products. Promotion and marketing efforts are also required, on a Europe-wide basis. This was among the conclusions of a study undertaken on behalf of the Commission in 1987. The report, 'Rural Tourism in the 12 Member States of the EC', makes seven propositions for the development of rural tourism in the EC:

1 **To arrive at a more precise definition of rural tourism**: a definition which could be agreed upon by all member states. As well as facilitating the collection of statistics on this sector of the tourism industry, a better definition of rural tourism would also make it easier to **sell** this product – following the principle that it is easier to sell something which is well-defined for the consumer. A common agreement on the content of rural tourism as a sector of activity would also make it easier to devise strategies to **develop** this sector across Europe, as tourism planners and other professionals in different member states would be working with the same precise definition of what was meant by 'rural tourism'.

2 **To clarify the notion of agritourism**, in the interests of better promoting this sector to the consumer. In certain member states, the sector of 'agritourism' is defined simply according to the profession of those operating in this sector. In these countries, anyone who owns a farm can open it up to tourists in search of 'agritourism'; but this includes owners of large, modern, mechanised farms which show little trace of rurality, and which often practise an intensive monoculture, totally devoid of the pastoral characteristics sought by tourists. Similarly, there are countries where the term 'agritourism' may be used only to denote those products

offered by farmers who derive less than half their total income from the tourism side of their business, the rest coming from their farming activities. If more than half their income comes from their tourist activities, then these farmers cannot claim to be operating authentic agritourism, although the farm itself and the welcome provided by the farmer and his family may be just what the visitor is seeking. These inconsistencies must be dealt with to ensure that the term 'agritourism' describes, and only describes, that kind of product and those services which prompt tourists to visit farms and the countryside.

3 To codify rural tourism products. Those operating in the field of rural tourism should arrive at a Community-wide agreement on a precise codification of rural tourism products on offer in the market. This is not to prescribe any uniformity or standardisation of these products, but to arrive at a common language which would meet two needs: that of comparing like with like in different member states, and that of better marketing rural tourism inside and beyond the EC.

4 To popularise the principal elements of rural tourism through the use of pictograms. It should be possible to invent a system of pictograms and symbols to represent the main elements of the rural tourism product – rural hotels, rural camping, country bed and breakfast, farm tourism etc. – in order to make these products immediately recognisable to clients.

5 To harmonise tourist road signposting. Since rural tourism is essentially practised by tourists using private cars, it is vital that country road signposting is effective in enabling them to reach their destinations, which are often far from main roads. In order to be effective, road signposting should be understood by all, therefore it is necessary that, across the Community, road signs and signals should be harmonised.

6 To promote centres of rural tourist attraction. Community aid should be made available to local authorities and local business people, to enable them to develop support structures which stimulate the production and the commercialisation of rural tourism services.

7 To encourage the Europe-wide cooperation of organisations involved in rural tourism. In each member state, there are organisations active in the field of rural tourism. In order to achieve the objectives contained in the first six propositions, these must collaborate at the European level. In this way, they would form an international network which would constitute, for the Community authorities, a body of competent and representative negotiators on rural tourism matters.

In response to these recommendations and to demands from the industry itself, the Commission announced in 1990 a series of measures aimed at creating and improving rural tourism products, to be implemented in conjunction with operators in the industry. The Community Action Programme, planned to run from 1991 until 1994 with a budget of ECU 5.8 million, has these three main objectives:

1 Helping to define rural tourism products. The Community will take action on two fronts:

(*a*) Providing more detailed information on the demand for rural tourism products: a EC-wide **survey** will be conducted with a view to pinpointing the characteristics and trends of the rural leisure market. The findings will be widely disseminated and used by operators in devising specific new rural tourism products, along the lines of theme-based tours (visiting vineyards, abbeys, etc.), transfrontier cultural and rural itineraries, health tourism, integrating the environment into rural tourism products, etc.

(*b*) Improving the ease with which rural tourism products may be identified by the consumer: part of the purpose of defining a rural tourism product is to improve access to that product. The possibility of using a **logo** as a quality label for European rural tourism products will be examined, in consultation with operators. If it is agreed that a logo is necessary and feasible, help will be given in designing it and promoting its use. The use of a logo as a quality label would help achieve the harmonisation of tourist accommodation in rural areas, category by category (hotels, campsites, furnished accommodation etc), and would be the first step towards devising a system of **symbols** providing tourists in Europe with better information on the local facilities available in rural areas. The Commission, in collaboration with experts from the various member states, would define the minimum components of the European quality label, including the minimum standards for each type of tourist accommodation.

2 Helping to create and develop rural tourism products. A series of measures will be implemented in all regions of the Community:

(*a*) To provide better information on, and access to, **Community aid schemes** in respect of rural tourism, including the availability of grants, a series of official texts on legal, tax, and financial matters relevant to the creation of rural tourism products for each member state will be produced, for use by operators and local authorities.

(*b*) To encourage **cooperation** between rural tourism businesses, the LEADER action groups will encourage seminars, exchanges of experts and study visits, to stimulate the exchange of experience and the transfer of practices from the areas they cover to other Community regions wishing to introduce rural tourism products. They will also encourage the establishment of regional networks sharing common projects linked to tourism in two or more member states, for example, spa-based holidays, Mediterranean networks offering integrated rural tourism packages, networks bringing together Celtic regions, such as Finistère and Cornwall, etc.

(*c*) To foster more dynamic **human resources** as a means of improving the management of rural tourism activities, a number of measures will be considered, designed to improve the skills and knowledge of those active in this sector, through rural tourism training programmes and exchange schemes.

3 Promoting access to the market in rural tourism products. The above measures relating to the supply of rural tourism products (definition, harmonisation, grants, etc) will be backed up by demand-side measures to encourage the use of the products that will have been created or improved:

(*a*) Customer information: in order to increase customer awareness of what is available, a number of guidebooks are planned: a European farmhouse-tourism guide was prepared as part of European Tourism Year, and this will be followed by a practical rural tourism manual giving details of all the main rural tourism organisations in Member States, from which tourists can obtain more detailed national guides. Other possibilities include European subject-related guidebooks (horse-riding, cultural tourism, etc).

(*b*) Marketing of rural tourism products at the European level: cooperation between rural tourism suppliers and promoters/sellers will be encouraged through several measures including the establishment of a European rural tourism section at tourism fairs, in order to increase awareness of what rural tourism has to offer and to promote the use of the European label.

(*c*) The creation of a European network for the distribution of rural tourism products: the Commission will provide assistance towards the setting up of a European computerised databank managed by the industry itself and covering the full range of products available, *and* assistance in bringing into service one or more computerised central reservation systems, enabling a large number of rural tourism products to be marketed at the European level.

CASE STUDY

RURAL TOURISM – THE ANSWER TO SPAIN'S PROBLEMS?

Spain is a world leader in the tourist industry and the main destination for European tourists travelling to the Mediterranean. According to the World Tourism Organisation, Spain is visited by around 35 million tourists a year, accounting for 9.1 per cent of world tourism and 3.6 per cent of total expenditure on tourism. Spain's hotels account for 5.2 per cent of world capacity, a figure which would be even higher if it were to include Spain's share of all available types of tourist accommodation (holiday apartments, campsites, etc).

Economically, tourism is very important for Spain. It accounts for nearly ten per cent of the country's gross national product, or 11.6 per cent if the construction industry is included. In Majorca, tourism accounts for 60 per cent of the gross national product, or 85 per cent including the construction industry.

However, despite its elevated position as a tourist destination, Spain experienced, in 1989, the start of a slowdown in its tourism growth, the first the country had registered since its rapid development as a top destination during the boom years of the 1960s. In all, 0.2 per cent fewer people visited Spain in 1989 than in 1988, and nights spent in Spanish hotels were 11 per cent down on the previous year's figures. There was a fall in numbers from practically all the main national markets: Germany (−1.7 per cent), France (−0.8 per cent), Britain (−3.9 per cent) and Belgium (−0.6 per cent). These were not compensated for by the increases registered in the number of tourists from Italy (+13.4 per cent), the Netherlands (+1.5 per cent), and Sweden (+1.6 per cent).

There is a heavy concentration of British and German nationalities among Spain's foreign tourists. Tourist destinations are highly concentrated too (the Balearic Islands, the Canary Islands, Catalonia, Andalusia and the area of Valencia), and the tourist influx is very seasonal, being largely concentrated into the summer months (*see* Fig 9.5). There were various causes for the slowdown:

• a decrease in the demand, due to favourable weather conditions in northern Europe, high mortgage rates in Britain, etc

• competitive package tours to new destinations such as Tunisia, Turkey, Morocco, Yugoslavia, and the Caribbean

• deterioration of Spain's tourist resorts (outmoded high-rise buildings, over-concentration, noisiness, pollution, etc).

The Spanish are reacting to this crisis partly by

looking to other markets: to the smaller European countries such as the Netherlands which could not compete with the buying power of the mighty British and German tour operators. They are also looking with interest at the emerging Eastern Europe market, guessing that this enormous potential market will not fuss over the standards of accommodation.

However, as far as the Western Europeans are concerned, there is no doubt that changing attitudes towards the quality of the holiday environment have played a part in persuading tourists to turn their backs on Spain.

Thirty years ago, places such as Benidorm, Lloret de Mar, and Torremolinos were picturesque, but poor, fishing villages. The mass tourism explosion changed these villages into sprawling coastal resorts, often built in a haphazard, unplanned way to satisfy what appeared to be an unstoppable demand from other Europeans. In the beginning, these resorts were well-suited to the needs of this new, undiscriminating market that was able, for the first time, to buy holidays abroad. High-rise developments with small rooms, thin walls and any basic design for exteriors were acceptable, as for most visitors, this was their first experience of a hotel. Tour operators advised hotels to Anglicise or Germanise the food and entertainment they offered.

Rising standards of living at home, and an increasing concern for the quality of the environment led, over time, to the holiday aspirations of Western Europeans becoming more sophisticated. By the end of the 1980s, newspaper reports of polluted seas, poisoned water, and dirty beaches in Spain were increasingly common in those countries traditionally sending the greatest numbers of tourists there. At the same time, Spain's reputation as a cheap destination was also beginning to go against it, as tourists increasingly returned home with stories of 'lager louts' and hooliganism.

Environmental improvements

Dealing with its environmental problems is now a matter of priority for the Spanish tourist industry. To encourage refurbishment, the government is offering low-interest loans to upgrade rooms and improve facilities. Planning regulations and their enforcement are now being

Fig 9.5 Foreign tourism in Spain − seasonal and regional distribution

Region	% by tourist areas
Balearic Islands	35.9
Canary Islands	19.6
Catalonia	16.9
Andalusia	12.5
Greater Valencia	9.0
Other areas	6.1

Quarter	% by season
January–March	14.3
April–June	22.2
July–September	44.7
October–December	18.8

Source: Tourism in Europe, *Trends 1989, Eurostat*

Balearics are going green

If all goes to plan, Spain's Balearic Islands – especially the biggest, Majorca – hope to offer tourists a cleaner, greener, quieter, more comfortable, and more luxurious environment in the years ahead.

Setting a trend now being followed in the rest of Spain too, the Balearics are currently in the middle of a prodigious investment of around Ptas 20,000 million in improving their entire infrastructure. The moves affect everything from accommodation to beaches, from pavements to policing, and information services to traffic control.

Some Ptas 12,000 million are going on amenities such as waste disposal, street lighting, road repairs and beach and leisure park maintenance. The aim, says Eduardo Gamero, promotions director for the Balearic Islands Tourist Council, is a better quality of holiday for visitors and life for residents.

The project involves an astonishing rise in the public budget – no less than 373 per cent up in 1990 and perhaps 500 per cent again in 1991.

In a series of local improvement projects in various districts, the Balearic Islands Council is funding 60 per cent of all work against 40 per cent by individual municipalities.

Mr Gamero said: "We want to set an example to encourage private enterprises to invest in their own businesses, leading to a complete renovation of the sector."

Perhaps most important for the long term is a plan to ensure that all holiday accommodation throughout the islands is surrounded by greenery and meets certain quality levels.

This means the eventual closure of many older hotels and a further tightening of the rules for new development, first introduced in 1984. Until then the apparently ceaseless growth in demand for hotel and self-catering accommodation meant little regard for the environment as developers simply kept on building wherever possible.

For the past six years it has been illegal to build without a strict minimum of exterior garden space per room. The figure started at 30 square metres, then it was doubled, then doubled again and the regulations now insist on 130 square metres. That means a hotel of 200 rooms must have at least 26,000 square metres of surrounding gardens.

At the same time, loans are no longer available for building anything below the four or five-star categories, inevitably pushing up the infrastructure quality further in the long term.

Mr Gamero said: "We need to lose around 50,000 beds in the region to meet our target and several older hotels have already been shut down, mostly in the urban centres. Some are being converted into offices or private apartments. We think many three-star hotels in particular should become residences for the elderly or hospitals. Hotels over 20 years old will have to be converted or renovated.

"And there are some interesting stories. The old five-star Hotel Mediterranea, for example, was turned into apartments but the owner, who started as an assistant waiter there 30 years ago, has turned the lobby into a luxury restaurant identical to when he first worked there – complete with furniture and lamps of the period and a similar quality of service."

At the last count in 1989, there were 777 hotels in all, 622 bed and breakfast hostels, and 29,000 tourist apartments. Majorca has around 250,000 beds, 70 per cent of them in hotels. Ibiza's 100,000 beds are split evenly between hotels and self-catering, while only some 35 per cent of the 70,000 or so beds in Menorca are in hotels. Formentera has around 15,000 beds.

Fig 9.6 (*Source:* TTG Europa, *25 April 1991*)

taken seriously: in 1989, for example, a new law was passed – a fuller version of an earlier 1969 Law of Coastal Areas – banning any new building nearer than 100 metres from the shore. In 1990, the Balearic Government itself announced a series of measures, costing 12 billion pesetas, to improve the environment for tourists. Details of the measures are given in the article shown in Fig 9.6. The resort of Benidorm alone has pledged almost 60 billion pesetas over five years, to be spent on the creation of golf courses and parks, beach cleanliness and safety, and a clampdown on litter and noise.

Diversification and the move towards quality tourism

The Spanish tourist industry's other strategy in the face of its difficult times is to cut down on its low-yield mass tourism and to diversify the product, spreading its visitors around the whole of the country; introducing them to the cities, the quieter beaches and, above all, the countryside of Spain's interior. In doing so, they hope to follow the example of Italy's transformation during the 80s, from a collection of cheap mass tourist coastal resorts to a predominantly up-market destination which people now visit for its art and culture and expensive holidays in the countryside.

The idea is not entirely new. Moves to encourage inland travel date back to the construction of Spain's **paradores** (state-owned hotels) in the 1920s. In the 1960s, the parador policy was intensified, and new ski resorts were also built by regional governments in Andalusia, the Sierra Nevada and Catalonia, providing facilities which complemented those on the coast.

The difference is that efforts to encourage tourists to spend their holidays in rural areas are now at the centre of the official tourism policies of Spain's national and regional governments. Following the example of Spain's northern regions with their attractive rural resorts in areas such as Asturias and Cantabria, other regional governments have begun to emphasise the promotion of 'green' tourism, by creating and widening their networks of parks and nature reserves, while marketing new products such as excursions on foot, on horseback, boating, etc.

Typical of the new tourist products now on offer is the Balearics farmhouse accommodation scheme, as described in Fig 9.7. This policy has received the full financial backing of the EC, which sees social benefits as well as tourism opportunities in encouraging country-dwellers to stay on the land and in their villages. Figure 9.8 outlines the social problems of certain Spanish rural areas.

However, the policy of promoting the natural resources of Spain's interior at the expense of its coastal resorts has not met with universal approval, for various reasons. First, questions have been raised as to whether Spain's natural resources can cope with the impact which increased tourism will create. The travel writer, Alison Rice, is among those who feel that tourism has already damaged enough of Spain, and should not be further encouraged in new, fragile regions. Her views are given in Fig 9.9. Second, the official policy is deeply resented by those operating tourism businesses around Spain's coast, whose feelings of having been betrayed by their government are described in the article in Fig 9.10.

analyse and use at own ideas ie by criticising the idea / statement.

Fig 9.7 (*Source:* TTG Europa, *25 April 1991*)

New plan for farm stays

A farmhouse accommodation scheme has been launched by the Balearic Islands government aimed at involving local farms in the tourism industry.

Agrotourism, as it is called, is designed to give tourists a real taste of the Balearics' rural life, providing an alternative to tourists' usual perception of the region as being all sun, sand and sea.

Eduardo Gamero, director of promotions for the Balearic Islands, said: "We realise that in recent years many holidaymakers have visited the Balearics without ever discovering the beautiful countryside that makes up the majority of the islands.

"Our new farmhouse accommodation scheme, however, will enable the growing number of travellers to our islands to enjoy a green holiday in an unspoilt environment and will also help our local farming community."

These farmhouses will be featured in European tour operators' brochures and the Balearic Islands government plans to attract a minimum of 7,000 new holidaymakers to the region as a result of the scheme.

All the participating farmhouses will contain a maximum of six bedrooms and will continue to operate as farms while tourists are staying there.

SPREAD OF GHOST VILLAGES
HAUNTS SPANISH REGIONS

Roy Wickman
ALICANTE

JUST a few kilometres from the crowded beaches and discos of Spain's Mediterranean coast, many once-thriving villages stand deserted and in ruins. In many others, only a few pensioners remain and the villages seem doomed.

But now the European Community has stepped in to halt the flight from the land by helping to fund an ambitious project in the mountain regions near Gerona, Lleida and Tarragona in Catalonia, in north-east Spain.

The Pts8,440 million ($77.4m) project aims to stop the progressive abandonment of these poor rural areas by offering incentives to stay, including proper salaries, good services and an attractive environment.

Most EC cash will be spent on agricultural output, conserving the landscape, diversifying economic activity and improving the infrastructure.

But the problem goes much deeper further down the coast, affecting Valencia and the mountain villages inland of the dazzling tourist resorts of the Costa Blanca. Young people now refuse to continue scratching a living from the parched landscape.

Here the villages are dying. A recent survey of eight villages near Alcoy in Alicante province shows that in seven years there were 125 births and 288 deaths. In the village of Alcolecha, there were 44 deaths and only eight births.

Only a few years ago, 300 people lived in the village of Famorca, half an hour's drive from the coast. Now there are barely 50 inhabitants, including a handful of children. Only one elderly couple lives in the main street. A little further up the mountain is Tollos, where only 13 people now live.

These villages are caught in a vicious circle. As the young people leave for the jobs and nightlife in cities or coastal tourist resorts, village shops close down and agricultural land falls into ruin. The death knell for these villages is often the closure of the local school. One Alicante village was so worried when most of its 15 remaining pupils were due to be sent to an upper school, that parents and local authorities refused to send them.

Rescue ideas are coming in, but tourism appears to be the only way of breathing life back into poor areas. Some villages are rushing to open their long-abandoned Roman and Moorish remains, and medieval castles and palaces. Other villages, backed by local mayors, are clubbing together to build luxury services such as swimming pools and sports centres.

A spokesman for the Catalonian government said: "The population of regional villages is disappearing as the people leave to work in the cities. Our projects encourage people to stay, not only to preserve agriculture, but also to save the natural environment."

Some villages strike gold if they suddenly become fashionable. One of these is Forna, hidden in a valley only a short drive from the Costa Blanca resort of Oliva. The Moors and Christians battled bloodily over Forna's castle, but the British have quietly moved into the valley below.

Forna's only school was shut 20 years ago and all but 25 indigenous inhabitants have deserted the village. Now more than 70 of Forna's 100 houses belong to British people.

The British have not only saved the village from extinction, but also keep its fiestas alive.

In Valencia, which has also been granted an EC subsidy, there are 155 municipal districts in danger of being abandoned, with three crisis zones in Castellon and one in Alicante province. A spokesman for the Valencian government said: "It is absolutely vital we stop the abandonment of these villages. Who will look after the environment if not local people?

"When there are very few people left in a village, and they are elderly, it is very difficult to reverse the decline. We must give them a decent standard of living and enough money to live in dignity."

The projects begun so far include better roads and water supplies, health and education services, sports facilities and cultural activities.

Fig 9.8 (*Source:* The European, *2–4 August 1991*)

CASE STUDY

FARM TOURISM IN THE AUSTRIAN TIROL

Austria and tourism

Situated at the heart of Europe and bordering six other countries, Austria has been on trade and tourist routes for many centuries. The landscapes and economies of its nine federal provinces vary considerably: 40 per cent of the country is at over 1100 metres, with the central and western areas being dominated by the Eastern Alps. Most of the population, along with the main industrial areas, is located on the eastern plains.

Austria's principal agricultural areas are to the north of the Alps and along the banks of the Danube, with production in both areas being dominated by grain, cattle and pigs, as well as

This policy makes some disturbing assumptions.

Surely in the established resorts, once the infrastructure is corrected to cope properly with the great numbers of holidaymakers, their transport and their sewage, little more harm can be done to the environment there? The habitat is no longer vulnerable. It is already ruined. What about the habitat of the interior and the undeveloped stretches of coastline? What happens to them if you develop them?

About 53 per cent of the species of mammals found in Spain are classified as under threat. The Cota Donana, Spain's premier national park and one of Europe's most important wild-life sanctuaries is in danger of drying up because water is being extracted first for irrigation and now for tourist developments. The World Wide Fund for Nature says the park is also being polluted by insectides, fertilisers and now by increased recreational activities.

The nature reserve near Barcelona and the national park in northern Spain are also under threat because of their increased popularity. Spain's main ecology group Adena believes that this tourist policy of spreading the load all over Spain is heading for the same pitfalls as the old one.

Fig 9.9 (*Source:* The Observer, 4 February 1990)

fruit growing and winemaking. In the medium range mountain regions, there is more cattle breeding and forestry, while the higher mountain regions to the west can only support extensive grazing and forestry, with farms being predominantly small, traditionally run stock-rearing units.

While farming methods have changed very little over the centuries, developments over recent decades in other sectors and growing mechanisation on farms have led to a marked drift of labour away from agriculture. In the 20 years following 1960, the number of workers in agriculture more than halved, and many of the farmers who remain are now working part-time in local industry, forestry or tourism. This case study is based on a report on farm tourism compiled by Gwen Pritchard for the British Travel Educational Trust.

Farmhouse accommodation in Austria helps farmers supplement their income, and encourages them to stay on the land. The accommodation provided is usually on a bed and breakfast basis: only in the case of a remote location, where there are no restaurant facilities within three kilometres, is a farmer allowed to provide extra meals without being subject to health regulations and tourist hotel taxes. These regulations are designed to protect Austria's small hotels and guesthouses, which would face fierce competition from farmhouses if the latter were authorised to provide meals at all times of the day. The number of guests allowed in a farmhouse is restricted to nine beds, and any farmer offering more accommodation is liable to the same rate of taxation as ordinary hotels.

In many of the main tourist regions where there are a large number of farmhouses offering accommodation, these have organised them-

Fig 9.10 (*Source:* TTG Europe, 25 April 1991)

No help for the Spanish Costas

Leading hotelier Pierre Turpault has launched a bitter attack on the Spanish government's failure to help the tourism industry.

Mr Turpault, president of the Confederation of National Hotel and Restaurant Associations in the EC and a hotelier on the Costa del Sol, slammed the official policy that alternative tourism should be fostered at the expense of the traditional beach holidays.

"It is absolute rubbish to say that 'sol y playa' tourism is dead", Mr Turpault told *TTG Europa.* "All our studies have shown that 85 per cent of visitors still want sun and beach.

"They may want other things too, but I don't believe people want something different – they just want more. They want a better quality product and that's why hoteliers have to get act now and renew their installations.

"It's fine to attract middle-class tourists, but there just aren't enough of them to fill the 600,000 beds on Spain's coasts."

Turpault pointed out that the industry was in crisis long before the Gulf war.

"For the past year we have tried in vain to get some kind of government help. Madrid has received funds from the EC, but does not want to pass it on."

Mr Turpault criticised Secretary of State for Tourism Ignacio Fuejo's emphasis on "what he calls tourism of the future", meaning conventions, rural tourism, culture etc., while forgetting the coasts.

He said: "Fuejo has said they are not in business to help failed hoteliers. In other words the crisis is all our fault, not because of the strong peseta or the filthy state of the sea.

"The authorities didn't say that in the 70s when we were bringing all the tourists to Spain.

"I agree that our hotels must be renewed and that our service should be improved but we have created wealth for Spain for 20 years. Shouldn't the government help us now?

"We're never going to be a cheap destination again. So we have to improve quality and that's not easy without help."

The Gulf conflict has sharpened Spain's tourism industry crisis. Tour operators' booking for summer packages are 50 per cent down.

Viajes Melia, one of the country's biggest travel agencies, is reported to be on the point of collapse and Iberia Airlines has lost £2.7 million a day since the year began.

This winter Costa del Sol hotel occupation is 20 per cent down on 1990. Twenty-four hotels, usually open all year, have closed for the winter.

"If the crisis carries on and there's no relief, quite a few people won't be able to carry on. It can't be good for the tourist image of Spain if half the trade goes broke," said Mr Turpault.

selves into **bauerlicher gastering**, (farmhouse circles) to promote farm tourism in their regions.

Tirol

In Tirol, the average size of a farm is between 12 and 20 hectares, the amount of available land for agriculture being severely limited due to the ever-present danger of avalanche and floods in many areas. Seventeen per cent of the land area in the province is kept as nature reserves and another 0.7 per cent for ski runs. The Tirolean provincial government's policy on agriculture is biased towards keeping the average size of farms relatively small, in order to maintain the level of the rural population, especially in areas where it is necessary to cultivate the land in order to maintain the slopes and forests and prevent landslides and avalanches.

Tourism is immensely important in Tirol, where the industry employs one in four of the local population. Three-quarters of visitors to the area are from outside Austria, spending about 120 million bednights in the province each year. As a consequence, most of the farmers who farm part-time are also involved in tourism activities, especially during the winter months, when they are employed by the cable car companies or the ski schools.

Of the 400 000 beds available in Tirol, 145 000 are in private accommodation, including small guesthouses, pensions and farmhouses. There are about 7000 farms in the province, most of which offer guest rooms. The majority are registered only with the local tourist office, being listed in the accommodation guide in the **privatzimmer** section, along with other small, private bed and breakfast accommodation.

Farmhouse booking service and classification scheme

Of all Austria's farmhouse circles, it is still only the Tirolean circle which has established a centralised booking office. In other regions, clients still have to book directly with the farms themselves. The Tirol booking service was established in 1980, on the initiative of the Tirol Chamber of Agriculture, mainly to help boost farm tourism in the Ostirol, a poor, relatively inaccessible area detached from the main part of the province, and which borders with Italy.

One objective of the service was to provide a central information point for clients to contact, thus easing the process of booking for the client and taking the administrative burden away from the individual farmer. The resultant reduction in the time taken to complete each booking transaction is a great advantage, especially for the many visitors from France and Italy and other non-German speaking visitors, who may experience communication problems with individual farmers.

In connection with the booking service, the Chamber of Agriculture also operates a farmhouse classification scheme. The four-category scheme ranges from the minimum standards category, which requires that a farm has good access, parking space, a telephone, separate dining room for guests and hot and cold running water (although not necessarily as part of en-suite facilities), to the top category which is reserved for self-catering farmhouse accommodation only, with full private facilities and a kitchenette.

Publicity and promotion

The Tirol farmhouse circle produces a brochure every three years, giving details of the farmhouse accommodation offered by those farmers who pay to be included in the brochure. Each farmer is, therefore, committed to membership of the scheme for a minimum of three years, paying an initial membership fee of 1000 schillings, plus 100 schillings, paid each year, for each bed space registered. 450 farms currently participate. An updated price list is inserted each year to accommodate a two to three per cent increase in tariffs.

The production of the brochure is in part financed by the Tirol Tourist Board, which is happy to help promote a product which it regards as aiming for quality rather than quantity. The Tourist Board also supports the Tirol farmhouse circle by representing its products at workshops and trade fairs, distributing its brochures free of charge both at home and abroad.

The farmhouse circle has also met with some success in attracting bookings from tour operators and travel agencies, with a confidential tariff being produced each year. Overwhelmingly, most of the interest is shown by the German retail travel trade, followed by the Austrians themselves, then Belgian travel agents and tour operators.

The tourist market

Traditionally, the main tourist market for the Tirol has been first and foremost Germany, followed by the Netherlands, Britain, the francophone countries and Scandinavia; but over the past few years, there has been a dramatic increase in the number of Italian visitors to the province. Regarding the long-haul markets, the USA is now the eighth most important market for Austria, particularly for the winter sports season, but concentrating on hotel accommodation. Australia, however, is a growing market which is showing great interest, especially in farmhouse accommodation, as a means of getting to know local people and experience the outdoor life. The Germans are mostly very independent, and, having no language problem, tend to book their accommodation directly, as do the Dutch. The French, on the other hand, usually require more assistance when booking, and 70 per cent of the centralised booking office's enquiries come from France.

Most Austrians have some knowledge of English, in particular the younger generations, who will have studied it at school from the age of ten. Until recently the direct promotion of farmhouse holidays in the English-speaking market was concentrated on the British Army in Germany, but a full promotional campaign, linked with Austrian Airlines publicity, was launched in Britain in 1988, with considerable success. The British clientele is largely composed of active older couples with high disposable incomes, who are keen on the outdoors as well as local culture and food.

Activity holidays

In common with much of Austria's farmhouse accommodation providers, the members of the Tirol farmhouse circle have been quick to respond to the rise in interest in activity holidays. A number of activity holiday packages are being developed and promoted, for the Tirol. Certain farms already offer accommodation with riding. Others have grouped together to participate in walking tours, in the Kobl and Pitztal areas, with packages including seven nights' half-board at different mountain farms,

a picnic lunch each day, the services of a guide, two farm tours, transportation of luggage, a welcome drink and a farewell evening. The cost of a week's package is around 3200 schillings. Similar cycling touring packages are also available.

There are also a number of special interest courses offered by farms, mainly based on traditional skills and crafts, such as wood carving and apple strudel baking.

Farmhouse produce

The slogan of the Tirol farmhouse circle is **natürlich gut**, (naturally good), and its promotion of farmhouse accommodation has emphasised the traditional food served to guests. Each guest making a booking at one of the circle's farms is offered a generous plate of *speck* (home-cured ham) and a glass of *schnapps* on arrival, as well as the guarantee of a copious farmhouse breakfast.

The preparation of cured meats, bread, pastries and dairy products is still very widespread on Austrian farms, and this feature is promoted in the Tirol farmhouse circle brochure. It also mentions the traditional farmers' markets held throughout the area, where home-made foods and crafts are on sale.

If a farmer chooses to sell some of his produce directly to the public, there is no income tax payable, if the goods are wholly home-produced. Once extra materials are included in their manufacture, tax has to be charged and paid by the farmer.

The future

Farm tourism has played a major part in attracting visitors to rural areas of Austria and in supplementing the income of the farming community. In the Tirol, farmhouse tourism has been instrumental in keeping the agricultural population from drifting into industrial employment in the towns and abandoning their traditional role of managing the woods and meadows of the Alpine landscape.

However, the pattern of tourism in Austria is changing, and farm tourism will be obliged to change too, in order to repeat the successes of past years.

Seasonal changes are taking place in Austria's tourism patterns. Winter sports have proved to be a great growth area for Austria – and for Tirol in particular – since the early 1970s, and the revenue for the winter season has been surpassing that of the summer season over the past few years. There is a distinct difference between the summer and winter visitor, however. The winter season attracts a more affluent international clientele, demanding high standards of accommodation and facilities, and, consequently, traditionally inclined towards using hotels which can offer a range of leisure facilities and a more sophisticated cuisine. The trends for booking holidays are also very different, bookings for the winter period being made well ahead, while summer visitors are more likely to book at the last minute, or find accommodation on spec.

As winter sports have continued to bring greater numbers of winter visitors to Austria, the summer season, on which farms depend, has recently become more difficult to promote, Austria and the Tirol increasingly having to compete with the attractions of the new long-haul destinations.

The activity holidays described above have been part of the farm tourism operators' response to the problem of a shrinking summer market. Another option for them may be to move towards developing a more year-round business, by convincing tourists, and tour operators, that farmhouse accommodation could be a good, budget alternative to the larger and more expensive hotels favoured by winter visitors.

CONCLUSION

Rural tourism is no longer regarded as a poor substitute, only intended for those who lack the means to spend their holidays by the sea. As Europe's coastlines become increasingly congested and concern mounts over environmental problems, the countryside is becoming the destination for a growing clientele in search of unspoilt surroundings and authenticity. The challenge for those living in the countryside is now to produce the right product at the high level of quality sought by this clientele, and to market it professionally.

This 'rediscovery' of Europe's rural areas is extremely timely, coming, as it does, at a time when rural life itself is under threat of extinction. The great interest in developing and promoting rural tourism currently being demonstrated by the EC testifies to the urgency of the situation. Tourism may have arrived just in time to save great expanses of European countryside from being finally abandoned by their inhabitants.

ASSIGNMENTS

1 Rural tourism symbols for Europe. The suggestion has been made that a logo should be designed for use as a 'seal of approval' to be used by all European rural tourism products achieving certain standards of quality.

It has also been proposed that rural tourism would benefit from a Europe-wide system of symbols or pictograms to represent the main elements of the rural tourism product: farmhouse accommodation, rural hotels, rural campsites, farm tours, bed and breakfast establishments in the countryside, etc.

Design a suitable 'European Rural Tourism' logo and a series of symbols or pictograms to represent the principal components of the rural tourism product.

The logo to represent rural tourism in Europe would be used on the publicity material of those operators achieving the standards of quality set for the logo, and could also be displayed on gateposts or walls of those establishments. It should therefore be simple, easily recognisable, and, as far as possible, self-explanatory.

The symbols should be clearly related, as a series, but sufficiently distinctive as to differentiate clearly between different rural tourism products. The international pictogram for youth hostels is a good example of a successful tourism symbol, and might serve as a model for a series of rural tourism symbols.

2 'Village Que J'Aime' competition. Euroter is a pan-European, non-governmental organisation, representing rural tourism. It is a round-table organisation for meetings, exchanges, dialogue and discussion between partners for the development of rural tourism in Europe; the partners

1 OBJECTIVES

EUROTER is organising the "Village que j'aime" European competition from January 1st 1990 to June 30th 1991.

This international competition is addressed at all those who, in European rural areas (from East to West and from North to South) are preparing themselves for an integrated development of tourism, respecting the environment, heritage and lodging.

Through the competition the best realizations and projects (near completion) to date will be publicized.

The files presented to the competition should especially testify to:
– feedbacks for local economy and employment,
– integration of amenities and tourist activities into the environment,
– active participation of the inhabitants in the development of tourism in their area and in receiving tourists,
– search for activities founded on rural cultural values,
– marketing of quality tourist products.

The competition is open to exemplary tourist operations:
– development for upgrading natural beauty spots,
– accommodation through restoration or building of new housing integrated into the environment,
– setting-up of cultural or nature activities through the use of the monument heritage and rural areas,
– collective organisation, on the local level, for the production and marketing of "green tourism" products.

The *Village que j'aime* competition covers countrysides, villages and small towns, coastal regions and the lower mountainside.

2 PARTICIPANTS

The "Village que j'aime" competition is open, in all the countries of the European Economic Community and Council of Europe:

– to local institutions (communes or commune groupings)
– to public or private rural associations and organisations

engaged in the global tourist development of a homogenous geographical, economic and cultural space.

Participation in the **"Village que j'aime"** competition is direct, on the European level, without regional or national heats.

3 MEANS OF PARTICIPATION

a) Registration request for the competition is to be sent to EUROTER before september 30th 1990, in the form of a simple letter together with a brief description of the operation presented (30 lines maximum),

b) If the project presented is in conformity with the competition rules, EUROTER will send the technical participation file to the competition (free participation) by return.
If not, EUROTER will specify the reasons for refusing the entry.

4 PARTICIPATION FILE

The technical file for participating in the competition should include:

a) the questionnaire duly filled in;

b) all the appropriate documents about the operation presented:
– detailed technical description,
– economic and financial documents,
– advertizing and marketing documents,
– photographs (black and white or colour), diagrams...
– possibly films (16/8 mm) - films will only be returned after the competition, on request.

The files may be presented in English, French or German.

The files should reach EUROTER before December 31st 1990.

5 JURY

The projects presented in the competition will be judged according to their orginality, their integration into the milieu, their economic contribution to the collectivity and the quality of local animation that they provide for the rural population.

An international jury, made up of representatives from:
– European institutions,
– Organizations lending their financial support to the implementation to the competition,
– consumers,
– media,
– and EUROTER and its members
will convene at the beginning of 1991 and will determine **the prizewinners who will be officially announced on June 30th 1991** at the latest.

The Jury's decision will be binding.

6 PRIZES

The "Village que j'aime" competition has prizes totalling 75,000 ECUS, i.e.:

1st prize - European Community prize	20,000 ECU
2nd prize - Council of Europe prize	15,000 ECU
3rd prize - French Postal Administration prize	15,000 ECU
from 4th to 9th prize	5,000 ECU

In addition, special mentions may be given to reward or publicize exemplary realizations with regard to providing facilities for handicapped people, senior citizen tourism, all-year-round tourism, interfrontier tourism, restoration of deserted villages...

The prizes will be given at a European ceremony organized during the 2nd quarter of 1991.

The amount of the prizes will be totally assigned by the prizewinners for the benefit of the prize-winning operations.

Each prize-winner will receive the "Village que j'aime" diploma - 1990 European competition - European Year of Tourism.

7 ADVERTISING

EUROTER will be responsible for advertizing the start of the competition and publishing its results by any appropriate means.

In addition, in order to raise the consciousness of the local population involved in the projects proposed to the competition and collectively mobilize them, EUROTER will make information material available to the applicants.

Participants in the **"Village que j'aime"** competition must accept the conditions of the present rules.

Fig 9.11 The *Village que j'aime* competition

being drawn from the private and public sectors, institutions, associations and professionals, on an international, national, regional and local level.

Within the framework of the European Year of Tourism, Euroter launched, as a campaign project, the '*Village Que J'Aime*' competition, the rules of which appear in Fig 9.11.

Prepare a participation file for the competition:

(*a*) Undertake the research necessary to identify an exemplary tourist operation, as defined under the objectives for the competition.

(*b*) Devise a questionnaire to elicit the responses which will testify to the operation's suitability for the competition – the feedbacks for the local economy and employment, etc, as specified under the objectives. Have the questionnaire completed by the tourist operation you have chosen.

(*c*) Obtain as many as possible of the documents specified under heading (*b*) of the participation file section of the competition rules.

OPEN FOR BUSINESS: TOURISM IN EASTERN EUROPE

The political changes which swept through Eastern Europe in 1989, and the largely peaceful revolutions which followed, have already had an immense impact on all aspects of life in those countries, not least in the realm of travel and tourism.

Just as relaxed rules on incoming visitors to Eastern Europe were leading to increasing numbers of Westerners travelling to that region, a new era of growth in East-West tourism has begun, as the citizens of those countries use their new freedom of movement to travel much more widely than ever before possible. Moreover, as the countries of Eastern Europe move towards democracy and free market economies, tourism itself has the potential to play an important part in the process of economic restructuring which lies ahead.

This chapter examines:
- Incoming tourism to Eastern Europe from the West
- Tourist trips made by East Europeans themselves
- Western investment in tourism facilities in the East

THE INCREASE IN TOURISM IN EASTERN EUROPE

Poland, Czechoslovakia, Hungary, Bulgaria, Romania, Yugoslavia, Albania and the former USSR – all of the phrases used in the past to describe all, or some, of this group of countries have suddenly become inaccurate and obsolete: the Soviet Bloc, the centrally planned economies, the Socialist countries . . . the monumental changes of the past few years mean that none of these terms now applies.

As these countries open their borders, tourism will be one of the first domains in which fundamental changes will be felt. These changes will mark the end of the pattern of tourism activity which has existed in Eastern Europe over the past 50 years or so, and herald new, radically different trends in travel for all purposes.

Thriving domestic tourism, a significant volume of international travel between the countries of Eastern Europe themselves, and an increasing, but relatively minor incoming tourist trade from the West, have been the characteristics of tourist activity in Eastern Europe for many decades. Each of these features, and expected changes to them, is examined below.

Incoming tourism from the West

Background

During the past few decades, many discouragements – deliberately placed or otherwise – were presented to those considering or undertaking a trip to an Eastern European country: first, the image of these countries, with their succession of military interventions and repression, their suspicion and secrecy, and their chronic shortages meant that they were not generally perceived as destinations for pleasure and relaxation; and second, for those who did make the trip, often because business reasons compelled them to do so, a series of obstacles lay in store, such as visa requirements, compulsory currency exchange, registration with the police and restrictions on movement within the country of destination.

Even although they badly needed the hard currency, regimes feared the disruptive effect on their own people of too many Westerners coming into their countries. In particular, they were concerned at the prospect of their own populations seeing too many foreigners who were obviously better off than they were.

Nevertheless, even before the events of 1989, receipts from incoming tourism from the West were growing steadily in Eastern Europe. The realisation that receipts from this form of tourism could help their struggling economies prompted many of these countries to take positive steps to open themselves up to incoming visitors.

However, the changes in official attitude towards tourism in recent years were prompted by various considerations:

• Contacts between East and West were no longer automatically considered as a source of corruption of pure socialist ideals by corrupt 'bourgeois' values

• The failure of heavy manufacturing industry alone to bring prosperity to the East made the services sector more attractive

• Those now in charge of directing the economies of the East were finally convinced that tourism was a worthwhile industry capable of bringing financial returns, just as investment in manufacturing plant is.

As a result, travel to the east by tourists orginating in the West has been growing rapidly over the past few years. The World Tourism Organisation puts the volume of West-East tourist traffic at around 10 million annually. This figure does not include traffic between the former East and West Germany or Yugoslavia's visitor numbers.

Different approaches to tourism from the West

In fact, although it is possible to detect overall tourism trends, the countries of Eastern Europe defy many attempts at generalisation in this field of activity. Although it is tempting to treat the countries of Eastern Europe as a homogeneous group, considerable political and economic differences have always existed between them. These can be detected in the wide range of different attitudes and policies with which these countries have in the past approached incoming tourism from the West. Three contrasting examples follow:

Yugoslavia was the first to adopt a more open policy with respect to tourism. During the 1970s and 1980s, Yugoslavia developed a major tourist industry, with a destination image and facilities similar to those of the Mediterranean West European countries, largely based on beach resorts. Between the beginning and the end of the 1980s, tourist arrivals in Yugoslavia rose from around six million a year to over nine million, a growth rate closely comparable to that of Greece during the same period.

By way of contrast, **Albania**, at the other end of the spectrum, remained at a stage of very tentative experimentation with tourism until very recently. It allowed no more than a few thousand tourists a year to enter its territory (estimates range from about 2500 to 10 000 annually), and then only as part of an organised tour group. There were severe restrictions on currency exchange and movement (for example, tourists were not allowed on public transport). But even Albania, with so much to offer in the way of natural resources – beautiful inland lakes, mountains, forests and attractive sandy beaches – has now joined the ranks of those countries willing to attract tourists from the West, as shown in the article in Fig 10.1.

The Eastern European country regarded as the most westernised is **Hungary**. With its long tradition of political stability, Hungary is Eastern Europe's foremost attraction for the West, for both business and leisure tourism. Its scenic countryside, Roman ruins, its Austro-Hungarian heritage, and good tourism infrastructure combine to place Hungary in the world's top 10 international tourist destinations. During the summer of 1989, every hotel room in the capital, Budapest, was taken, as well as every room in the hotels on the banks of Lake Balaton.

Stalin's outpost falls to lure of capitalism

THE once forbidden Stalinist land of Albania has a new, glittering ambition – to become *the* exclusive capitalist sun-spot of the 1990s. Forgetting its proletarian past, this poorest and most backward country in Europe has decided that the big bucks of the world's richest sun-lovers are the answer to its desperate economic straits.

A string of breathtakingly beautiful, white-sand beaches – known as the Albanian Riviera – are already enticing such up-market Western hoteliers as the French chains, Ibis and Mercure, as well as several Italian and Swiss companies.

Models of holiday villages and hotels, none less than four-star, already sit like a shimmering vision of the future in the office of Jeton Hajdaraj, head of Albania's state tourist organisation, Albturist. "We have signed contracts for 10,000 hotel beds with seven or eight companies," he says. At least half would be on the coast. This is ambitious, for at present Albania has only 1,600 tourist beds in the whole country.

Hajdaraj has

Albania pins its hopes on tourism to end its isolation and poverty, writes **Dusko Doder**

a few hard-nosed business ideas about how to make up-market tourism succeed. "First, we don't want any Albanian management," he says. "Foreigners must manage the hotels and own at least 50 per cent. If an Albanian managed the hotel, soon his cousins and friends would come and expect special treatment."

Indeed, though Hajdaraj has plans for the first hotels to open in 1993, the gap between the plans and the present reality could hardly be greater.

The drive from the capital Tirana to the coast takes eight gruelling and bumpy hours. On the narrow, pot-holed mountain roads, cars must swerve to avoid sheep, goats, horses and cattle. It may seem charming, but it's not quite what company presidents, show business personalities and rich play-boys expect from an exclusive resort.

All those beautiful beaches were meant to be admired from a distance. Albania's Orwellian leaders kept their people isolated from the outside world for the past four decades by virtually blocking access to the coast. Few roads lead right down to the beaches. And in the few "fishing" villages there are no boats. Former dictator Enver Hoxha did not want to take any chances that his people would escape across the narrow stretch of water that separates the Albanian Riviera from Corfu, shimmering tantalisingly just over six kilometres away.

Hajdaraj is testing the tourism waters by allowing a daily boat from Corfu to bring 200 tourists into the port of Sarandë, which boasts the only hotel on the coast. It may be a trickle by Mediterranean standards, but it is a huge leap forward for such an isolated country.

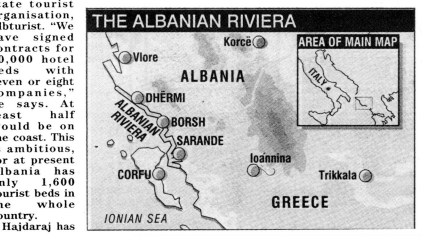

Fig 10.1 (*Source*: The European, *14–16 June 1991*)

ATTRACTIONS OF EASTERN EUROPE

What are the overall attractions of the Eastern European countries, and what are the assets which they will be able to use in the future to promote themselves as international tourist destinations?

In the short term, with the momentous events taking place in that region making headline news almost daily, the sheer curiosity of Westerners to see Eastern Europe for themselves will motivate many of them to visit that part of the world, especially now that restrictions on visitor numbers and visitors' freedoms are being lifted. Berlin, for example, continues to attract vast numbers of tourists, curious to see for themselves the site of the former Berlin Wall.

Otherwise, in the longer term, the attractions of Eastern European countries are as rich and varied as those of their Western counterparts. **Cultural tourism** has a very promising future, with the existence of numerous great cities of art such as Prague, Moscow, and Budapest, with their museums, art galleries and fine architecture.

Nor is Eastern Europe lacking in attractive **natural resources**, ranging from 'sea and sand' destinations such as Bulgaria, Romania, and Yugoslavia, to countries rich in lakes and mountains scenery, including Czechoslovakia, Hungary, Poland, and the former USSR. The Hungarians, with an entrepreneurial eye, have already made moves to attract more Western hunters into their immense forests.

Tourism for the purpose of **medical treatment** offers excellent prospects, too, with the ancient spa towns of the Austro-Hungarian empire, such as Karlovy Vary (formerly Karlsbad), for example. In this connection the Scandinavian Social Security system already refunds the cost of trips to the spa towns of the East taken for medical purposes. In Moscow, the hotel company Pullman is building a 250-bed 'medical-hotel', to capitalise on the expected influx of Westerners for operations for myopic disorders, in the treatment of which the Russians have made great advances.

Eastern Europe, therefore, abounds in destinations for a whole range of tourist activities. Even Siberia, for so long a by-word for the bleakest of environments and most sinister forms of repression, now offers tourist possibilities. The French tour operator, Terres d'Aventure, now offers trekking holidays in the Pamir mountains of Siberia, as well as in the Kizil-Koum desert, south of the Aral Sea.

Internal tourism flows within Eastern Europe

As is the case in Western Europe, tourism in most countries in the East is dominated by domestic tourist movements. As shown in Fig 10.2, Hungary is the only country where the tourists nights spent in registered tourist accommodation by its own nationals are outnumbered by those spent by visitors from other countries. (However, a vast proportion of domestic tourists in all Eastern European countries are lodged, not in registered tourist accommodation, but by friends and relatives. Taking this into account tilts the balance even further in favour of the dominance of domestic tourism.)

In the past, domestic tourism was the only type of tourism tolerated by most of the regimes of the East, for their own citizens, and enormous difficulties were faced by anyone attempting to obtain permission to travel abroad, particularly to the West.

Domestic tourism served two important purposes: not only did it ensure that the spending power of these countries' citizens was exercised at home instead of abroad (thus, preventing the 'leaking' of financial resources out of the country), but it also had the virtue of preventing these same citizens from being exposed to alternative, capitalist systems, which might have led them to question more the prevailing ideology of their own countries.

Fig 10.2 International and domestic nights in registered tourist accommodation (thousands)

Countries	1987 International	Domestic
Bulgaria	19134	24256
Czechoslovakia	10969	27832
Hungary	17516	12830
Poland	3319*	6999*
Yugoslavia	52299	57684

(*1985 figures, January–September only)
Source: World Tourism Organisation

In addition to this, domestic tourism was, and to a decreasing extent, still is, used by regimes in various ways, to further their own policies. The most widespread example of this is the use of 'incentive' travel, especially to health and rest resorts, in order to reward workers in key industrial sectors. This is widely viewed as an important practical means of stimulating the output and economic performance of those sectors involved.

As well as serving the above economic functions, domestic tourism is used to serve social ends as well. Much of the tourism available to the citizens of Eastern European countries is social tourism of the kind described in Chapter 7. Reflecting the prevailing ideology of the times, it had, at least until recently, a largely organised, group character, emphasising group solidarity at the expense of the individual. Youth tourism, in particular, was regarded as an important way of inculcating 'socialist education' upon the minds of young citizens. A large proportion of the existing accommodation stock of some Eastern European countries is still reserved for this kind of social tourism. In a recent study of Bulgarian tourism, the tourism researcher and lecturer, Michael Pearlman, estimated that at least 50 per cent of that country's accommodation base is reserved for social tourism for the Bulgarians themselves. A certain amount of this accommodation offers potential for being converted to standards suitable for incoming tourists from the West.

Regarding international tourism by East Europeans, this is largely characterised by internal flows within that region itself. Figure 10.3 gives the principal sources of incoming visitors for a selection of Eastern European countries.

Except in the case of Bulgaria, (whose arrivals figures are distorted by the presence of so many Turkish guest-workers *en route* to Germany) the majority of incoming tourists for these countries originate in other Eastern European countries.

During the 1970s, the need for those living in the East to obtain passports and visas in order to travel to another Eastern European country was abolished, and citizens were able to use their ordinary identity cards as travel documents, increasing the incidence of cross-border trips in the region.

OUTBOUND TOURISM FROM EASTERN EUROPE

While the vast majority of East Europeans' trips abroad are still made to other countries in the East, an increasing number are using their new-found freedom to travel to the West. Demand for this has grown in recent years, with the improvement in standards of living among certain classes of manual worker, and with the gradual opening up of borders in the East.

There is clearly a great pent-up demand in the East to travel to those countries which have been inaccessible for so long, and tourism promotion organisations in the West are already making moves to capture a part of this massive new market which has recently become available. Figure 10.4 describes the German National Tourist Board's (DZT) plans to attract Eastern European tourists.

However, many East Europeans making the trip to the West for the first time have been taken by surprise by the cost of hotels, restaurant meals and the goods for sale in the shops. The relative weakness of their own currencies means that, for the majority of ordinary East European visitors, their spending power falls far short of their being able to make such purchases. They have, therefore, been forced to improvise during their trips, and this has not always been to the satisfaction of

Fig 10.3 Principal generators of visitor arrivals in Eastern European countries, 1987

Destination	First 3 countries of origin (%)		
Bulgaria	Turkey 39	Yugoslavia 19	Poland 10
Czechoslovakia	East Germany 43	Poland 23	Hungary 19
Hungary	Czechoslovakia 27	Poland 20	East Germany 12
Poland	USSR 24	Czechoslovakia 27	East Germany 19
Romania	Yugoslavia 20	Hungary 18	Poland 14

Source: World Tourism Organisation

East Europe is top target

The German National Tourist Board is preparing for a battle with Austria over the holiday-makers of eastern Europe.

The DZT is a link up with the German Chamber of Trade, the Deutsche Handelskammer to lure Hungarians, Czechoslovaks and Poles to Germany.

The deputy market research manager of DZT Joachim Scholz said: "We hope to have some sort of representation in these countries by the end of the year.

Pamphlets about Germany have been prepared in several different languages. The Hungarian ones have already been printed and others in Czech, Slovak and Polish are almost ready."

He said this would give Germany a chance to compete with the Austrian national board, Österreich Werbung, which has already begun opening offices in eastern Europe.

Mr Scholz said the DZT had only fully appreciated the importance of the east Europe market after receiving European Monitor figures for tourism in Germany of the ITB Berlin in March.

This showed that 6.3 million holidaymakers to Germany in 1990 were from east Europe including two million Czechs and 1.8 million Poles.

"These figures match some western European countries.

"At the moment the spending power of these people is not as great, but that will change.

"Until now our Vienna office has been handling east Europe but it is really too much work. We will have some sort of representation in Prague, Budapest and Warsaw by the end of the year. DZT will be taking a stall at trade fairs in Czechoslovakia shortly.

"Our competitors Österreich Werbung have already been very active in these lands. We will have tough competition."

More than 30 million people visited Germany in 1990 including 1.7 from the US (up five per cent), 400,000 from Japan and 19 million from western Europe.

Mr Scholz blamed the fall on the opening of east Europe meaning that tourists were spending less time in Germany.

"They were hurrying through Germany to explore the east", he said.

"This is really the first time tourists have had such an opportunity. In a few years things may well even out again.

"The number of overnight stays are falling throughout Europe as people are abandoning the habit of spending three to four weeks in one place in preference for shorter breaks.

"However, the overall number of visitors to Germany as a whole was up three per cent, which is very pleasing."

"The main nationality of tourists to West Germany remained the Dutch followed by the Swedes, British and French.

Although Swedes and Danes visited the former East Germany encouraged by easy access, one third of overnight stays were made by east Europeans.

Fig 10.4 (*Source:* TTG Europa, *23 May 1991*)

operators in tourism businesses, as suggested by the article in Fig 10.5.

The group of Eastern Europeans for whom the cost of living in the West will least matter is the vast number of those who will be travelling there to visit friends and relatives. Throughout this century, many millions of Eastern Europeans have left their own countries, often for political reasons, to settle in the West. As travel out of Eastern Europe becomes easier, major tourist flows will be generated by this presence in the West of so many East Europeans and their descendants.

CASE STUDY
BUSINESS TOURISM INFRASTRUCTURE IN HUNGARY

The development of leisure tourism in Hungary during the late 1960s was accompanied by the

FRANCE is experiencing a tourist invasion from the east, as tens of thousands of Czechoslovaks, Poles and Hungarians enjoy their newly-acquired freedom to travel. Many of them head for the Cote d'Azur in dilapidated coaches which – to the irritation of local hoteliers and restaurant owners – serve as mobile dormitories for the impecunious visitors, who also bring all their own food with them.

St Tropez is packed with these threadbare tourists who gawp at sights they have long only heard about – especially the topless bathers on the beaches. But whether the visitors come from Moscow, Prague or Warsaw, the French regard them as little more than refugees on the expensive Riviera coast.

And an informal survey of east Europeans passing through the tourist office on the Champs Elysees revealed that each had an average of five francs – just under a dollar – to last the weekend.

There is however one exception. Paul Khomeriki, a Soviet company director whose 22-metre motor yacht, the Tair, spent last weekend berthed at a marina near Nice, is travelling in a style that most of his countrymen can only dream about.

The challenge for most citizens of the former Soviet bloc in their first real year of freedom is to see as much of France as cheaply as possible. But the welcome is not exactly heartening. While newspapers in the south complain of the penny-pinching habits of the new tourists, the mayor of Paris, Jacques Chirac, has ordered police to clear the city's parks and public gardens of the

Anne-Elisabeth Moutet
PARIS
and Martin Delgado

thousands of tourists, many of them east Europeans, who are camping illegally.

Vanloads of blue-shirted police officers have been doing the rounds of Paris's unofficial camp sites, advising the intruders to leave. A police spokesman said: "If they don't go, we'll have to be a bit more forceful about it, but we'll try to avoid any violence or unpleasantness. After all, these people came here because they like Paris."

There is only one official camping site in Paris, off the Bois de Vincennes, and its 500 spaces are unable to accommodate the huge numbers of visitors. In a city where a night in a cheap hotel can cost the equivalent of a week's wages in Poland, the only alternative is to improvise.

Motor-homes are parked all along the Place de la Concorde near the Tuileries wall. The Champ de Mars beneath the Eiffel Tower and the Trocadero Gardens are covered in tents.

Even the Champs Elysees gardens are not free of sleeping bodies, though the proximity of the Elysee Palace means that the police enforce the no-camping rule more strictly. Last year, Parisians welcomed the newly-liberated tourists with open arms. They were encouraged by heart-warming speeches from President Mitterrand and Culture Minister Jack Lang.

But this summer, it looks as if

France's honeymoon with eastern Europe is already over. The Paris tourist authorities, who had been rejoicing at the influx, now realise that many of the tourists contribute little to the economy.

Jacques Marti, who runs the souvenir kiosk outside Notre Dame, said: "Three quarters of the visitors here have been Czechs and Poles, and I reckon that all they can afford is to light a candle in the church.

"These people are not exactly good for my business. They don't buy less than other tourists; they simply don't buy at all."

Illegal parking by tourist coaches is one of the worst problems.

One tourism official said: "Lots of the coaches are ancient and in a terrible condition. They cause pollution, break down and cause traffic jams. And the drivers tend to get lost as they've never been to Paris before. Of course we're happy for these people to be able to visit Paris, but we'd be blind not to realise that they are causing problems for Parisians and other tourists."

At the camping site near the Bois de Vincennes, a Polish economist touring France for a month in a caravan with her family, said: "This is our first visit to the West. Even though things may be two or three times more expensive than Poland, we are not going to let that spoil our holiday. And anyway, we've stocked up with plenty of food from home."

A group of middle-aged doctors and teachers from Czechoslovakia were disappointed that they could not afford to go to a "real French restau-rant", but said "anything is better than nothing".

Fig 10.5 (*Source:* The European, *9–11 August 1991*)

Fig 10.6 Budapest's Convention Centre

rapid growth of business tourism in that country. Hungary's notable contributions to the sciences and the arts, as well as the development of its international economic and political activities, helped promote its image as a conference destination. Hungary is also a member of over 900 different governmental and non-governmental international organisations, giving it a considerable advantage when bidding to be the venue for these organisations' conferences.

Hungary is now the venue for several hundred international conferences, corporate and other professional meetings every year. Some of the most important recent conferences have been:

- The World Congress of UICC (World Organisation of Cancer Researchers) in 1985, with 6000 participants
- The European Cultural Forum in 1985, with 1000 participants
- The 36th Annual Meeting of the European Association for Animal Protection in 1986, with 1000 participants
- The second World Congress on Neuroscience in 1987, with 3500 participants
- The World Congress on Rheumatology in 1991, with 4000 participants
- The tenth Congress on Catalysis in 1992, with 1000 participants.

With the growth of business tourism in Hungary, the country's infrastructure for this activity has grown likewise.

Budapest is the jewel in the crown of Hungary's business tourism industry. The following extracts from Hungary's business tourism promotional material describe the facilities and services available.

Purpose-built conference facilities with accommodation

Some of the world's most famous hotel chains are represented in Budapest, including the Hilton, InterContinental, Forum, Hyatt, Ramada, Novotel and Penta. These four- and five-star hotels all have their own conference rooms as well as leisure facilities, so that delegates can find everything they need under one roof. The facilities at the Hotel Duna InterContinental (five-star) are described in Fig 10.7.

One of the largest, purpose-built conference centres of Budapest is the **Budapest Convention Centre**. This building of almost 11 000 square metres was opened in 1985 close to the city centre business district. This modern convention centre prides itself on the flexibility of its facilities, which enables it to host meetings of different sizes, from the 1750 people capacity of the large Pátria hall, to the smaller halls for 30 to 300 people.

On the technical side, the main halls are equipped with simultaneous interpreting systems for eight languages. The technical installations of the Pátria Hall make it suitable for television and radio broadcasts, while closed circuit TV and video systems can operate in the whole building, with monitors in the corridors. Conferences and meetings have at their disposal a modern technical studio with complete sound-recording, U-matic and VHS video-recording systems. Also available are the convention centre's 8 mm, 16 mm, and 35 mm film projectors and large video displays, together with

Fig 10.7 The facilities at Hotel Duna International

Description

One of Budapest's big conference hotels in the main business and shopping area of the city. All rooms offer a spectacular view of the Danube and Buda Castle.

Location

In Budapest city centre, beside the Danube.

Technical facilities

Booths for simultaneous translation in 6 languages in the Ballroom and 3 more portable booths for the other rooms; sound amplification, video system, TV, overhead, and slide projectors, screens, flip charts.

Accommodation

There are 340 rooms in the hotel, and about 970 rooms in several more hotels within walking distance.

Conference capacity

Function rooms	n	Theatre style	U-shaped table	Stand-up reception	Banquet
Ballroom	200	600	264	600	450
Ballroom + Foyer	–	–	–	800	550
Budavár	60	110	54	100	60
Diana	50	80	50	80	40
Starlight	–	–	–	80	80

Catering and entertainment

Csárda Restaurant—Hungarian dishes with local wines; Bellevue Supper Club—Rooftop dining with a spectacular view of the city; Rendez-Vous Restaurant international cuisine, Cocktail Bar and Coffee-shop.

Special attractions

Fitness centre with swimming pool, sauna, solarium, squash-court.

slide projectors, overhead projectors and electronic information displays, photocopiers and flip-charts. The telephone, telex and telefax services keep delegates in touch with the world beyond the conference centre.

The Budapest Convention Centre is owned by Pannonia, a chain of 48 hotels and 250 restaurants. It is connected by an indoor corridor to the 324-room Novotel Budapest Centrum (four-star), which is also owned by Pannonia, with a franchise contract to the French Accor group.

Converted conference facilities

As well as its luxury conference hotels and purpose-built convention centres, Budapest, with its 2000 year-old heritage has many attractive historic buildings of character which are also used for meetings, large and small. For example, overlooking the River Danube is the elegant Pesti Vigadó Concert Hall. Completed in 1833, the concert hall is remarkable both for its architectural beauty and as an important showpiece for Budapest's cultural history – Liszt, Wagner, Brahms, Debussy, Mahler and Bartók all performed there. Now, the Pesti Vigadó Concert Hall is a prestigious venue for conferences, social events, balls and banquets. The main hall can accommodate up to 600 seated delegates, and it is equipped with the same range of technical facilities found in the modern, purpose-built venues. Elsewhere in the city, many university buildings, are equipped to host conventions of many hundreds of delegates, while other historic venues include the neo-Renaissance Pest Town Hall, and even the Arts Centre of the Hungarian Army, which is housed in a 19th century mansion.

Opportunities for excursions

Whatever the immediate surroundings for a conference, delegates normally want to tour the city before or after the conference, or during a break in the conference proceedings. A sample of the kind of tours offered to business visitors is given in Fig 10.8.

Professional congress organisers

Those choosing Budapest as the venue for their conference have at their disposal a number of professional congress organisers, specialising in bringing together all of the above elements, to make the event successful.

The Budapest Convention Centre, for example, has its own professional congress organisers department which specialises in the complete organisaton and management of congresses and incentives. It tenders for congresses, works out

Fig 10.8 Some of the tours offered to business visitors to Hungary

Budapest sightseeing tour by bus or by boat

A half-day programme introducing the city's most attractive monuments, including a stop for refreshment in a cake shop café.

Budapest museums

Visit to the National Museum where the coronation regalia are preserved; visit to the National Gallery and the Budapest Historical Museum in Buda Castle.

Budapest medicinal baths

Visit to an ancient Turkish baths to the beautiful art-noveau Gellért baths and finally the Thermal Hotel on Margaret Island to take the waters and be refreshed.

Religious treasures of Budapest

Visit to the coronation church's treasury, to St. Stephen's Basilica, to the largest synagogue in Central Europe and the Jewish Religious and Historical Collection, the Calvinist Church in Kálvin square and to the National Lutheran Church.

Visit to Szentendre

Szentendre is a colourful artists' colony with cobbled streets and medieval architecture. Visit to museums, galleries and boutiques.

Cooking course

The chef of a top restaurant will demonstrate how to prepare some famous Hungarian dishes, including Gulyás. Those attending will receive a certificate.

Excursion to Lake Balaton

Full-day programme visiting the largest fresh-water lake in Central Europe, stops at Festetics Castle in Keszthely, at the famous wine-producing region of Badacsony, at the nature preservation area of Tihany Peninsula, and in the spa town of Balatonfüred.

the budget and performs various tasks such as:

• printing congress materials

• corresponding with congress participants

• maintaining records of those applying to a congress on its computer system

• managing the participation fees

• booking hotels of different categories according to the participants' requirements

• organising tourist programmes, enabling delegates to explore the city of Budapest and beyond

• organising programmes for those accompanying the participants.

However, many independent tour operators and travel companies have their own congress organisers, often specialising in a particular field. For example, **IPV-Intercongress**, whose main activity is tourist promotion and public relations, established a separate department for congress organisation in 1988. The experience of the staff lies mainly in the field of medical conferences, although their activity extends beyond this. IPV-Intercongress provides comprehensive services, including multi-lingual correspondence in connection with scientific events, brochures, printing and video services. The **Cooptourist Congress Bureau** was established in 1982, and has particular experience in the organisation of scientific events. They organise between 15 and 20 major events each year in Hungary, including exhibitions and incentive programmes as well as congresses. Finally, **Ibusz**, the oldest and largest Hungarian travel company, as well as organising conferences, has the largest incentive travel ground management team in Eastern Europe. Their achievements in this field include the event which they organised for the Young Presidents Association of the USA, which visited Budapest in 1989. 590 delegates were treated to an elaborate incentive package which included the following elements:

• speeches by eminent Hungarian figures

• a cocktail cruise to an island in the Danube where a giant 'circus' themed garden party was held, with nine tents, three stages, and 100 performers

• a special performance at the Opera House, hired exclusively for the evening

• a seated dinner in the Hungarian Parliament

• a companions' programme, including a fashion show, a cookery course, and a visit to the Hungarian mint.

This description of Hungary's assets as a business tourism destination is, however, far from typical of facilities and services offered by Eastern Europe as a whole, for business travellers. Facilities in other Eastern European countries are, by comparison, still very rudimentary indeed. Nevertheless, this example does show what can be achieved when a country makes a determined effort to attract this lucrative market.

FOREIGN INVESTMENT IN EASTERN EUROPE

One of the major difficulties which Eastern Europe is experiencing in expanding its incoming tourism from the West in particular is its poor infrastructure, especially its lack of good-quality hotels. Lacking the resources required to develop this infrastructure, Eastern European countries have had to look to the West for financial cooperation and the provision of expertise.

Since the 1980s' relaxation on foreign investment in Eastern Europe, many international hotel chains have become established there, often in joint venture schemes, whereby a hotel is partly owned by the Western developer and partly by the East European state. A very common arrangement is the franchise agreement, by which hotels in Eastern European countries are managed and marketed by Western companies. This arrangement offers the possibility of introducing into these hotels Western standards of hospitality and quality of service, which have traditionally been much higher than those prevalent in Eastern Europe.

Hungary is the country in which most of the major hotel companies are already present. In 1990, in Budapest, the East's most promising destination for business tourism several luxury hotels opened their doors: a five-star hotel built by the German company Kempinski, the four-star Helia hotel belonging to the Finnish group, together with the Austrian Corona Hotel and the Yugoslavian Liget Hotel, both three-star hotels.

Much activity is now focused on the former USSR, where Intourist, the state tourism agency, has given up its monopoly on hotel management and is now engaging in joint ventures. Moscow's shortage of quality hotels should be eased considerably over the next few years, as a result of the current hotel building programme. Sheraton plans to operate at least two hotels in Moscow, starting with a 450-room establishment opening in 1992. Hyatt, long-established in Budapest and operating in Belgrade since 1990, invited 16 Russian hotel managers to the USA that year, to train them up to international hotel management standards in preparation for the eventual opening of a hotel in Moscow. The German group's Moscow Olympic Penta Hotel opened in 1991, with 500 rooms in the heart of the city, to be followed in 1992 by the Prague Penta.

Accor has ambitious plans to expand in Eastern Europe, in which the company already has a presence. Their plans, as they stood in the summer of 1991, were as follows: to its six existing Novotels in Poland (all operating on a franchise basis), it intends adding three others, in Gdansk, Krakow, and Warsaw; in Hungary, the company has joined up with Pannonia, one of the two large domestic hotel chains, and plans to add an extension to the Budapest Novotel, as well as building the Aero Hotel, close to the capital's airport; in Czechoslovakia, the Prague Sofitel of 800 rooms will soon be joined by a Novotel, an Ibis and a luxury restaurant in the capital; in Bulgaria, Accor has two projects currently at the negotiations stage – a Sofitel and a Novotel in Sofia; in Yugoslavia Accor are studying the possibility of building a hotel on the coast, with water-cure facilities, together with another in the centre of Belgrade; finally, in Russia, two Novotels and a Sofitel are under construction. For the construction of their second Novotel in Moscow, sited close to Red Square itself, Accor collaborated with Lokomotif, the sports club of the Ministry of Railways. The managers of Lokomotif decided to invest in the tourism sector the profits they made when they sold some of their best footballers to Western clubs. Even with this expansion, Accor's hotels in the East will only account for four or five per cent of its worldwide hotel stock, which is close to a thousand units.

Most of the above examples of investment in the hotel stock of Eastern European countries are aimed at satisfying the urgent and growing need for accommodation for business travellers. Four- and five-star hotels throughout Eastern Europe currently charge notoriously high prices, beyond the reach of most leisure tourists.

Joint ventures with companies based in the West offer these countries the possibility of overcoming some of the bottlenecks and financial obstacles restricting their tourism development. However, for a successful and comprehensive tourism industry, these countries will also have to equip themselves with the supply of good two- and three-star hotels which form the bedrock of the leisure tourism industry of most destinations. For the moment, the priority in the construction of hotels appears to lie almost exclusively at the top end of the scale, because that is precisely where the maximum profits are perceived to be.

Eventually, however, as private enterprise becomes more established in their countries, East Europeans themselves will increasingly cater for tourists with more modest means than the average business traveller. In this way, tourism itself will have an impact on the process of economic reform, stimulating the growth of small and medium-sized privately owned businesses to serve the tourist trade.

Finally, there is one incoming tourist market for the East which will visit those countries regardless of the lack of hotels. East Europeans and their descendants now living in the West will take advantage of the new freedom of access to visit their friends and relatives in the East. This form of tourism offers a particular advantage to countries with an underdeveloped tourist infrastructure: the author Professor S Medlik recently made the point that, since many of those comprising the West-East flow will be visiting friends and relatives, they offer a prospect of tourism growth without the need for additional accommodation capacity.

CASE STUDY
TOURISM IN POLAND

Incoming tourism

The number of foreign tourists visiting Poland has varied considerably in recent years. In the 1970s, and particularly in their second half, Poland's cross-border tourist traffic noted a rapid increase, especially from other Eastern European countries, with which traffic became essentially easier after ordinary identity cards became reciprocally recognised as valid travel documents for crossing state borders.

However, foreign tourism came to a sudden halt in Poland during the years 1980–1982 as a result of the social and economic crisis in that country, particularly following the declaration of martial law in December 1981. During that period, the mutual facilitations in tourist traffic between Eastern European countries were suspended.

Research carried out by the **Instytut Turystyki**, the Polish Institute of Tourism, shows that the number of visiting foreigners began to rise again in 1983, to reach 8.2 million people in 1989, almost 80 per cent of the total 1978 figure and around 160 per cent of the 1978 level of visitors from the West. Figure 10.9 shows the progression during those years.

Figure 10.10 gives a breakdown of arrivals according to the purpose of the visit. It applies only to Western visitors, as those arriving in Poland from Eastern European countries are not required to state the purpose of their visit. The high percentage of trips to visit friends and relatives testifies to the large number of Poles living abroad.

Figure 10.11 gives a breakdown of Poland's incoming markets during the years 1976–1989, divided into Eastern and Western countries.

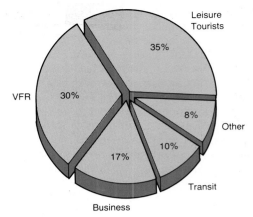

Fig 10.10 Structure of arrivals to Poland by purpose of visit in 1988

Tourism by Polish residents

Instytut Turystyki's research into holiday trips taken by the Polish people themselves in 1989 reveals some interesting trends and some useful contrasts with tourism in the West.

The general rate of holiday taking ranges between 30 and 40 per cent, except that a downward trend has been noted during the 1980s, caused by the economic crisis. In 1974 and 1977, 39 per cent and 36 per cent respectively of Poles took a holiday; in 1987 and 1989, the figures had fallen to 31 per cent and 33 per cent. Of this final figure, those going away more than once that year made up ten per cent. The number of those spending their holiday abroad has risen steadily, from only two per cent in 1979 to seven per cent ten years later.

Among the principal reasons usually given for not going on holiday was the impossibility of leaving the household, farm or family unattended. However, in 1989, financial obstacles to travelling moved up from the second to the first reason for not doing so. Generally, the younger the age, the higher the level of education and professional skills, and the better the material status of those polled by the *Instytut*, the higher their rate of participation in travel. For example, those with a secondary school education were 2.5 times more likely to travel than those with a primary education only, and those with a university degree made four times the number of trips, on average. Traditionally, farmers were the group least likely of all to take a holiday; they travelled, on

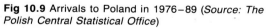

Fig 10.9 Arrivals to Poland in 1976–89 (*Source: The Polish Central Statistical Office*)

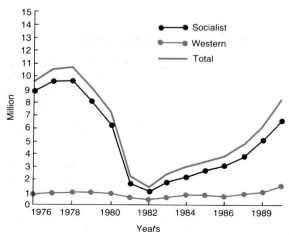

Fig 10.11 (a) Arrivals to Poland from abroad in 1976–1989 (in thousands)

Year	Socialist countries	Bulgaria	Czechoslovakia	GDR	Romania	Hungary	USSR	Yugoslavia
1976	8838.8	72.2	1735.8	5686.5	58.6	635.5	677.1	52.6
1977	9616.7	86.9	2177.9	5786.2	43.1	755.4	756.2	74.8
1978	9712.4	94.2	2171.5	5752.1	72.2	693.2	765.6	151.6
1979	8115.1	84.8	1763.7	4799.8	58.1	419.6	788.6	189.6
1980	6295.3	67.4	1549.6	3483.1	39.8	331.5	716.8	87.1
1981	1596.3	29.8	533.5	371.3	26.8	188.3	474.4	46.4
1982	1615.8	12.3	263.5	262.8	16.4	39.9	465.3	13.6
1983	1759.5	19.8	367.7	367.7	29.4	95.9	842.3	25.6
1984	2235.2	22.2	568.3	525.5	52.8	183.4	869.3	57.8
1985	2658.1	34.9	561.3	716.5	79.7	215.9	938.9	94.4
1986	3185.3	38.8	717.3	782.5	18.5	351.1	993.6	189.1
1987	3834.2	47.8	992.9	925.1	27.8	469.6	1166.3	186.6
1988	5692.1	51.7	1417.4	1681.4	21.7	567.8	1739.4	192.4

Fig 10.11 (b) Arrivals to Poland from abroad in 1976–1989 (in thousands)

Year	Western countries	Australia	Austria	Belgium	France	Nether-lands	Japan	Canada	USA	Germany W Berlin	UK	Italy	Scandi-navia
1976	784.4	9.3	35.0	15.2	80.0	24.3	6.9	11.3	50.8	283.9	43.2	26.9	117.4
1977	933.8	9.2	39.2	16.4	87.2	27.0	7.6	12.7	52.1	314.5	48.9	31.1	152.7
1978	982.8	8.2	43.2	16.8	84.0	27.7	7.8	12.8	55.2	327.5	51.1	34.0	168.9
1979	1016.4	8.3	44.7	16.8	85.0	28.9	9.3	11.9	59.5	327.0	52.4	42.0	163.8
1980	873.7	5.7	37.5	14.7	68.8	24.2	8.5	8.4	39.8	302.2	38.5	34.7	142.0
1981	575.3	4.1	24.2	9.3	41.9	17.2	4.9	5.0	23.8	193.0	23.0	19.5	91.1
1982	388.2	2.8	17.4	10.0	31.5	15.9	2.2	2.7	13.1	133.4	14.5	11.7	56.7
1983	642.6	4.4	26.9	12.7	44.9	24.7	3.5	6.2	27.8	245.8	23.3	19.0	88.2
1984	761.9	6.1	29.6	13.1	46.6	28.1	4.7	7.7	34.8	309.0	25.8	22.1	103.5
1985	786.1	7.0	29.6	13.6	44.2	30.1	5.7	8.7	43.6	321.3	26.2	24.4	105.1
1986	742.9	5.4	29.7	12.9	42.8	26.8	5.8	6.7	29.6	303.2	25.8	23.5	106.4
1987	942.2	7.3	37.9	16.5	54.2	38.3	8.3	10.3	50.8	380.4	33.4	34.6	102.2
1988	1103.5	8.5	53.1	19.1	56.2	45.8	9.5	11.8	57.9	451.9	34.2	40.4	144.9
1989	1587.8	11.8	75.5	23.7	74.8	51.6	13.1	18.4	96.3	649.6	46.6	59.7	227.0

average, ten times less frequently than salaried workers, and six times less than skilled manual workers. However, the research undertaken in 1989 showed an increase in participation in travel by Poland's farming population.

The most popular form of organised, collective travelling for Polish people are the various forms of institutionalised holidays sponsored by work establishments, associations, etc. Thirty-two per cent of holidays taken in 1989 were of this type. Other forms of organised travel, mainly to holiday camps, accounted for ten per cent, that year.

On the other hand, private, individually organised, travel was dominated by visits to friends and relatives – 34 per cent in 1989. The other forms of private travel, to hotels, camping sites, etc, accounted for the remaining 24 per cent.

Poland as a destination

Poland is not yet well developed as a destination, particularly for incoming visitors from the West, but it is widely regarded as having great potential for the future, for various reasons. Interest in visiting Poland is running high, partly due to the international celebrity status conferred upon it by personalities such as Lech Walesa of Solidarity and Pope John Paul II. Moreover, the country itself offers much in the way of attractions which will form the basis of a varied and extensive tourism trade.

Some of Poland's principal attractions as a

tourist destination are shown in the map in Fig 10.12.

The cities of Krakow, Gdansk and Poznan offer much in the way of mediaeval and Renaissance art treasures. In spite of enormous war damages, the monuments to Poland's past which abound in these, and other, cities have been painstakingly restored.

Poland was the second country to be assaulted by Nazi troops, thus starting the Second World War, and the country still bears many marks of the atrocities of war. These too now play a role as part of Poland's heritage. Many of the former concentration camps, such as Oswiecim (Auschwitz) have been turned into museums. Interest in the history of the Jewish people in Poland has prompted Polorbis, the state travel bureau to offer special Jewish tours of the country, visiting Oswiecim and Treblinka concentration camps, and synagogues and Jewish cemeteries in Warsaw and Krakow.

Poland's own population is the principal clientele for the **beach resorts** of the Amber coast, the name given to northeast Baltic coasts, and the Polish Riviera, centred on the seaside town of Kolobrzeg. **Rural attractions** include the Mazurian Lake District, a broad belt of forested lakelands stretching 300 kilometres across the northeast corner of the country, towards the Soviet-Lithuanian border. The region offers nature reserves, hunting, fishing and sailing opportunities. Finally, Poland's **winter resorts** are centred around the Beskid-Slaski Mountains.

Much remains to be done to provide Poland

Fig 10.12 Principal tourist destinations in Poland

with the infrastructure it needs to profit fully from its many attractions. The country is currently in the process of developing its tourist industry, mainly by means of joint ventures with Western companies. Hotel building and renovation is the priority, and recent projects include the 1100-bed Marriott, a Holiday Inn, and a Pullman hotel in Warsaw.

In the meantime, while improvements are already being made in every aspect of the country's tourism services, serious problems remain to be overcome.

PROBLEMS AND OPPORTUNITIES AHEAD

Problems to be overcome

The lack of good hotels represents only one aspect of the difficulties to be overcome on the way to establishing a suitable tourism infrastructure in the East. Problems highlighted by trips to Eastern Europe include the following, often-cited aspects:

● The poor state of many of the roads and the erratic availability of petrol

● Pollution. There has been scant regard placed in the past on the environmental impact of industrial processes in the East, and pollution and environmental degradation are rife

● The standards of service in many tourist facilities are often low. In the past, many tour operators have received complaints from their customers regarding the quality of the service in hotels. There is a great need for investment in staff training

● Poor marketing, tourist information, and tourism promotion is a further constraint. The quality of information supplied to tour operators and travel agents, and the general availability of tourism information within Eastern European countries urgently need to be improved

● Political attitudes. Many vestiges remain of the old 'Cold War' attitudes towards foreigners in the East, particularly among the officials with whom visitors are likely to come into contact. There is a need for a substantial reduction in bureaucracy as well as an extensive programme of staff training. In this way, Eastern Europe will create for itself an atmosphere in which tourism appears to be positively encouraged and not just tolerated.

Opportunities ahead

Side by side with these obstacles to be overcome, Eastern Europe presents many opportunities for the development of a successful tourism industry. Although starting from a low base, Eastern European countries, properly developed and marketed, have the potential to turn themselves into major tourist destinations. The rapid and extensive growth of tourism in Turkey, whose receipts rose from only US $370 million in 1982 to US $1668 million in 1987 shows what progress can be made in a short time, when a new tourism destination is well packaged and marketed. Eastern European countries have the added advantage of having been 'out-of-bounds' for many decades, adding to their appeal.

Incoming tourism offers countries in Eastern Europe an excellent opportunity to earn valuable foreign currency, to create employment, and to develop their domestic economies through the production of goods which tourists need. Investment in tourism will also lead to investment in the countries' wider infrastructure – communications, roads, water and electricity supplies, etc – benefits which will be shared by the host populations.

Finally, if properly approached, Eastern Europe's tourism industry has the potential to be developed *avoiding* some of the mistakes made in the West: overconcentration of facilities in certain areas, overdependence on one tourism market, and tourism which creates vast seasonal fluctuations, for example. It would be a lost opportunity and a great pity if, in the rush to develop their tourism industries, the countries of Eastern Europe were simply to recreate some of these mistakes, instead of using the opportunity to learn from them and to avoid them.

CONCLUSION

As escalating political changes in Eastern Europe lead to a new openness of attitude and to the growing readiness of these countries to integrate into the world economy, tourism has a major part to play, not only in breaking down East-West barriers, but in helping in the process of reconstructing the economies of the East.

Considerable problems remain to be overcome on the way to creating a fully-functioning, efficient tourism industry for Eastern Europe, but the natural and cultural riches of these countries, combined with the naturally hospitable nature of their ordinary inhabitants, form the foundation of an extremely promising tourism destination for the future.

ASSIGNMENTS

1 Bulgaria as a destination. Bulgaria is considered by many tourism professionals in the West to be the Eastern European country which offers the best opportunities for development for Western visitors.

As the Development Manager of a major tour operator, who has been given the task of researching Bulgaria's potential as a destination, write a report on what the country has to offer in tourism terms. Research the country as thoroughly as possible, and include the following in your report:

- Natural features of interest for tourism
- National specialities, such as food and wines
- Possible excursions which might be developed
- Any obstacles to tourism development
- Competitors already operating in Bulgaria.

Include at the end of your report a few suggestions for tourism products which your company might include in their brochure.

2 Promoting your country to Eastern Europe. As Marketing Manager of the National Tourism Organisation with responsibility for promoting tourism to your country from overseas, write a report describing:

(*a*) why you think that your country should promote itself in Eastern Europe

(*b*) the kind of specific tourism products you think should be promoted to East Europeans (e.g. those which might lessen the problem of seasonality or overconcentration in space)

(*c*) a brief marketing strategy for a promotional campaign in Eastern Europe.

INDEX

SERVICE BEFORE SELF

UCB
University College Birmingham

Library
Summer Row
Birmingham
B3 1JB
Tel: 0121 243 0055.
www.ucb.ac.uk